INTRODUCTION TO
CHRISTIAN
LITURGY

INTRODUCTION TO
CHRISTIAN
LITURGY

FRANK C. SENN

Wanda
May 2017

Fortress Press
Minneapolis

INTRODUCTION TO CHRISTIAN LITURGY

Cover image: © iStockphoto.com
Cover design: Alisha Lofgren
Book design and typesetting: Josh Messner

Library of Congress Cataloging-in-Publication Data
Senn, Frank C.
Introduction to Christian liturgy / Frank C. Senn.
        p. cm.
Includes bibliographical references and index.
ISBN 978-0-8006-9885-0 (pbk. : alk. paper)—ISBN 978-1-4514-2433-1 (ebook)
1. Liturgics. I. Title.
BV176.3.S46 2012
264—dc23   2012013114

Manufactured in the U.S.A.
16 15 14 13 2 3 4 5 6 7 8 9 10

In memory and honor of colleagues
who showed me how to preside in liturgy
in ways strong, loving, and wise.

Eugene L. Brand
Carl Dehne, s.j.
C. Marcus Engdahl
Robert W. Hovda †
Gordon W. Lathrop
Don E. Saliers
Ralph R. Van Loon †

Contents

Introduction
What Is Pastoral Liturgics?

This introduction to Christian liturgy is a pastoral liturgical handbook. I will define liturgy in the first chapter. But what does it mean to be pastoral? One dictionary defines pastoral as an adjective referring to the lifestyle of shepherds and other pastoralists such as cowboys as they move livestock around large areas of land according to seasons and availability of water and food. Since Christian leaders have been called "pastors" (shepherds), there is something in this definition that can help us understand what it means to be pastoral, especially in the liturgy.

Pastoral leaders (lay as well as ordained) have the responsibility of moving the assembly to the sources of nourishment—word and sacrament—and provide the kind of exercise—praise and prayer—that keeps the flock spiritually healthy. Providing what the flock truly needs sometimes involves moving it in directions in which it doesn't want to go, as real shepherds know from experience. The people need to hear sermons that challenge their assumptions as well as comfort them (in the biblical sense of strengthening). Pastoral leaders have sometimes striven to increase the frequency with which the people receive Holy Communion, which also means that for Protestants the sacrament needs to be celebrated more frequently. While this has sometimes been a source of contention, the ordained minister of the word and the sacraments is under orders to preach the word and administer the sacraments.

Pastoral liturgy is the study and application of liturgy in the actual life of the church. It explores the nature of worship as constitutive and expressive of the Christian faith and applies these insights and commitments in concrete worshiping communities. Pastoral liturgy grounds practice in the history of liturgy and the theology of worship while being sensitive to the needs and resources of the local community of faith. These needs may be related to the cultural background of the assembly. Resources may refer to the gifts of time, talent, and treasure that the assembly has at its disposal, which may be extensive or limited. Quite frankly, too many small parishes want to do the kind of liturgy that can only be performed in a cathedral church. It is a matter of pastoral leadership to discern what the local assembly is capable of doing with the personnel and finances it has and guide the assembly to doing its public work well.

Providing this guidance also requires pastoral leaders to be knowledgeable of the liturgical tradition. This introduction attempts to organize the knowledge of the tradition that pastoral leaders should have. But it is only an introduction. Worship leaders have to dig deeper. To that end I have appended to each chapter suggestions for further reading.

The field of liturgical studies is becoming more diverse as time passes, as can be seen in the array of seminar groups in the North American Academy of Liturgy. I will try to make this introduction as ecumenically broad as possible while also providing information on specific liturgical uses. The specifics assume that an ecumenical practice has developed, especially in the liturgical churches of the West, which is manifested in the orders and rubrics of various denominational worship books and liturgical manuals. I hope that this introduction will serve an ecumenical purpose, especially in those traditions based on the historic Western rite.

While I have been formed in this ecumenical liturgical tradition, I am aware that another ecumenical worship tradition has developed in Western Christianity that the late Methodist liturgist James White called "frontier worship." That tradition provides an order which is used in the evangelical revival tradition, in many African American churches, in seeker services, praise and worship services, and to some extent in Pentecostal worship. I will refer to it, but I admit up front that my experience of this tradition is limited.

Because I intend this handbook to be a practical manual, I have organized the information in this book under questions that any ordained pastor or layperson might ask. The questions are the subheadings of the chapters and are listed in the table of contents. The index will indicate where to find information on more discreet topics. I have also appended a chronology of events and documents in the history of Christian liturgy and a glossary of liturgical terms.

For further reading: Other introductions to Christian liturgy

Hatchett, Marion J. *Sanctifying Life, Time, and Space: An Introduction to Liturgical Study*. New York: Seabury, 1976.
Jones, Cheslyn, Geoffrey Wainwright, and Edward Yarnold, S.J. *The Study of Liturgy*, rev. ed. New York: Oxford University Press, 1992 (1978).
White, James F. *Introduction to Christian Worship*, rev. ed. Nashville: Abingdon, 1990 (1980).

1

Liturgy—A Practical Science

1. Why do we worship?
2. What is liturgy?
3. What does it mean to do liturgy "decently and in order"?
4. How do we discern meaning in liturgy?
5. How is the people's work the work of God?

1. Why do we worship?

We worship God because God our Creator desires his creatures to worship him. In Exodus 3 the voice from the burning bush commissions Moses to return to Egypt and bring the people of Israel out of Egypt so that they may serve (i.e., worship) God on his holy mountain rather than serve Pharaoh (3:12). In John 4 Jesus tells the Samaritan woman at the well that the true worship of the true God will take place neither on Mt. Gerizim in Samaria nor in Jerusalem but "in spirit and in truth," "for the Father seeks such as these to worship him" (4:23). In Revelation 4–5 the human creatures join the heavenly creatures in the eternal worship of God and the Lamb. The whole point of redemption is to glorify God. This eschatological goal of the human vocation is expressed in the opening question and answer of the Westminster Shorter Catechism (1647–48):

> What is the chief end of man?
> Man's chief end is to glorify God, and to enjoy him forever.

In Exodus 3:12 Israel's collective worship of their God is even the sign that it is Yahweh who sent Moses to deliver the people from slavery in Egypt. This seems like a strange sign since it is fulfilled only after the fact of Israel's deliverance. But we must understand that the reality of the gods in the world depends on having actual worshipers. Zeus is not a reality in our world today because Zeus has no worshipers. So, too, the God of Israel required worshipers to proclaim his reality in the world by glorifying him.

"Glory" (*kabod, doxa*) is a heavily charged word in the Bible. It has to do with God's character and reputation. It is the sign of God's actual presence in the world. God's glory descended into the tabernacle when God was present and so filled the tent that even Moses could not enter it (Exod. 40:34-35). Moses' own countenance was transfigured when he was in the presence of God and he had to put a veil over his face (Exod. 34:29-35). In the incarnation the eternal Word of God took on human flesh in Jesus and "we have beheld his glory, glory as of the only Son of the Father, full of grace and truth" (John 1:14). The apostle Paul held that believers are changed into God's likeness from one degree of glory to another as they enjoy God's presence and reflect his glory (2 Cor. 3:18). Three times in Ephesians 1:3-14 we are told that we are chosen and destined to "live to the praise of God's glory" (vv. 6, 12, 14).

Up until the Age of Enlightenment in the eighteenth century in the West, it was commonly held that worship is rendered *soli Deo gloria*—"to the glory of God alone." Since the Age of Enlightenment, it has been thought that the value of worship lies in the impact it has on worshipers. The concern is to effect the human response rather than to glorify God. But before worship can have an impact on worshipers, it must serve God. The English word *worship* literally means "worth-ship": giving worth to something. In its older sense in English of worthiness or respect (Anglo-Saxon, *worthscripe*), worship may on occasion refer to an attitude toward someone of immensely elevated social status, such as a lord or a monarch, or, more loosely, toward an individual, such as a hero or one's lover. Magistrates in England are still addressed "your worship." In the old *Book of Common Prayer*, at the exchange of rings in the marriage service the groom said to his bride, "with my body I thee worship." In this sense worship means "respect" or "serve."

The Greek New Testament word for worship is *latreia*, "to serve." Paul uses this word in Romans 9:4 to refer to the sacrificial rites instituted by God in the old covenant. Likewise, in Hebrews 9:1, 6, the term is applied to the official service of the priest in the temple.

But in Romans 12:1 *latreia* is expressed in the "living sacrifice" of their bodies with which Christians serve God. Thus Paul views the entire activity of Christians as service to God. In the vision of Revelation 7:15 and 22:3 the worship of God consists entirely of adoration (*proskynein*), in which the creatures fall down on their faces before God and the Lamb.

Worship cannot be done in the abstract; actual forms are needed to express our praise and adoration of God and by which we offer our prayer and thanksgiving. We can and must have a theology of worship so that we understand what, in faith, we are doing; but there must also be a practicable way of worshiping. In other words, the theory must have a corresponding praxis. Praxis is defined as a practical application of theory. Especially as applied to something that is done regularly, like worship, praxis is a habitual or established practice; it becomes a custom expressed by means of rites and ceremonies. The practice of worship in its communal and public mode, distinguished from purely personal and private expressions of worship, is called "liturgy."

2. What is liturgy?

Liturgy is the vehicle by which the public worship of God is performed. It may refer to an elaborate formal ritual such as the Eastern Orthodox Divine Liturgy and Roman Catholic Mass or a Protestant service, but it is not a term limited to Christian use. It can also refer to the daily Muslim *salat* (prayers) and the Jewish *seder* (order). As a religious phenomenon, liturgy is a communal ritual response to the sacred through activity reflecting praise, thanksgiving, supplication, or repentance.

Rituals may be associated with life events such as birth, coming of age, vocation, marriage, sickness, and death. These rituals are not just human interactions; they often have a sacred character and reference. The rituals serve as the means of establishing a relationship with a divine agency, as well as with other participants in the liturgy. Repetitive formal rites, in some ways similar to liturgies, are natural and common in all human activities such as organized sports and civic celebrations.

The word *liturgy* is not strictly religious in origin. It comes from the classical Greek word *leitourgia*, meaning "public work." In the Greek city-states, it had the sense of some public good that a wealthy citizen arranged at his own expense, either voluntarily or by law. A citizen might voluntarily build a road or erect a temple to a deity as his liturgy. At Athens, the citizen assembly (*ekklesia*) assigned liturgies to the wealthy, and there was a law by which any man who had been assigned a liturgy while a richer man had none could challenge him either to undertake the liturgy or to exchange property. Paul used the term *liturgy* in this way in 2 Corinthians 9:12 to designate his voluntary effort at gathering an offering from his congregations in Macedonia and Greece for the poor in Jerusalem. This was his public-works project. Since liturgy is a service rendered, the English word *service* can be an equivalent of "liturgy."

In the Greek Old Testament (Septuagint), the word *leitourgia* was used to translate the service rendered by the priests in the temple. This use is seen also in the New Testament in terms of the priestly service rendered by Zechariah, the father of John the Baptist (Luke 1:23), and also the high priestly ministry of Jesus the Christ in the heavenly sanctuary (Heb. 8:6). In Acts 13:2 it applies specifically to the worship of the church.

Liturgy can thus refer to a public and well-defined ritual. It is often translated as "ministry" or "worship" in English-language Bibles. But there is a difference between "liturgy" and "worship" in that worship suggests the honor and praise accorded God communally or individually, in the public assembly or in worldly activity, whereas liturgy suggests something that is done communally and publicly, or is at least communal and public in derivation even if it is a ministration extended to those absent from the assembly.

Another reason for preferring the term *liturgy* to *worship* as a comprehensive name for this public and communal event is that it is also "divine liturgy" or "divine service." That is, God works through these rites of word and sacrament, praise and prayer to make them means of grace. Liturgy is not only the assembly's public work or service to

God (worship proper); it is also God's public work or service to the assembly. This will be discussed in question 5.

I should note that throughout this book I prefer the term *assembly* (*ekklesia* = called-out gathering) to "congregation" or "parish," because it more comprehensively describes the group gathered to do liturgy. "Congregation" is often understood to mean a corporate entity with membership. "Parish" is often understood to mean the people of a particular geographic location. We note that *ekklesia* is not any assembly or gathering, but a "called-out" one—an assembly called out of the world. In a sense the citizen assemblies of ancient Greece were "called out" of the ordinary business of the city (as all legislatures are) in order to do the work of the city in a way divested of personal interest. The legislatures are supposed to look after the interests of the whole city. So, too, Christians, coming together as a liturgical assembly, are to "leave all earthly care behind" and do the work of the city to which they are called, the city of God, the heavenly Jerusalem. When "earthly cares" are brought into assembly (as in preaching and prayer), it is in order to gain a different perspective on them than one has in the ordinary affairs of worldly life.

We should note that in Christianity a distinction is sometimes made between "liturgical" and "nonliturgical" churches based on the elaborateness and/or antiquity of their public worship. But to the extent that a group follows a ritual, a pattern of activities or behavior, that group has a liturgy. Thus even the open or waiting worship of Quakers is liturgical, since the waiting itself until the Spirit moves individuals to speak is a prescribed form of Quaker worship, sometimes referred to as "the liturgy of silence." Typically in Christianity, however, the term *the liturgy* refers to a standardized order of a religious service, be it a service of word and sacrament or a service of public prayer. The term *free church* historically meant free of the prayer book, specifically the Anglican Prayer Book, not a free-for-all. Even Pentecostal worship has certain elements that will always be found in its practice, although Pentecostalism is the least slavish tradition when it comes to following an order.

In recent liturgical renewal, what is included in "the liturgy" is more comprehensive than just the script in the worship book. It includes the activities of gathering for worship (e.g., receiving worship materials in the narthex, pre-service music), the interactions that may not be prescribed in the worship book (e.g., announcements, special music), and the activities of exiting (e.g., ministers and worshipers greeting one another, post-service music). In other words, everything that the assembly does when it comes together to do its public work before God and the world is its liturgy. Since liturgy is done in the context of "coming together," the Greek word *synaxis* (the same root as in "synagogue") has been used to name the ritual being performed.

3. What does it mean to do liturgy "decently and in order"?

Many liturgical reformers want to go back to the worship of the early church, even the New Testament church. This is not to be recommended. On the basis of what we read in the New Testament, worship in early Christian communities was not always being done "decently and in order" (1 Cor. 14:40). The earliest written description of Christian worship, Paul's First Letter to the Corinthians, bespeaks an assembly whose public work lacked theological integrity and was spiritually chaotic. Their communion practices fractured instead of unifying the community (1 Corinthians 11) and their use of spiritual gifts failed to edify (1 Corinthians 14). The congregation wasn't presenting itself very well to the rest of the city either. Remember that a congregation of perhaps several dozen people gathered in someone's home in a crowded urban neighborhood was sure to attract the attention of the neighbors. What kind of a witness was this worshiping community making? Their gathering for the Lord's Supper had to be socially revolutionary, including slaves and masters, patrons and clients, at the same table eating and drinking the same fare, as befits their common baptism into the one body of Christ. Waiting for one another was a practical application of "celebrating the Lord's death," who put down his own prerogatives for us (Phil. 2:5ff.). Their speaking had to be intelligible: prophesying was preferred to speaking in tongues because it was a proclamation of a word of God intended for all rather than just the edification of the individual.

To do liturgy decently in the light of the concerns Paul expressed in 1 Corinthians means that liturgy must be theologically grounded and communally sensitive. Our public work before God and the world expresses meaning. Done in the name of God (Father, Son, and Holy Spirit), liturgy says something about the God who is the object of our worship. What are we communicating about God in the way we do our liturgy? Paul was saying that the Corinthians were not proclaiming Christ crucified in their meal practice and in their exercise of spiritual gifts. The tradition of the eucharistic institution text (1 Cor. 11:23-26) and the great hymn to love (1 Corinthians 13) were brought to bear as critical correctives of Corinthian practice. Note that the institution narrative certainly predated Paul's apostolic mission and the love hymn may also have predated Paul. In other words, the great tradition was brought to bear on local practice to correct abuses.

Paul did not tell the Corinthians to no longer gather for the Lord's Supper or to cease practicing the gifts (*charismata*) because these practices had been abused. Nor, in the sixteenth century, did Martin Luther throw out the Mass and start over with a new order of service. There was already theological integrity in the practices; the abuses simply had to give way to proper use. Liturgical practices, rightly used, communicate something right about God (orthodoxy comes from *orthodoxia*, "right praise"). Christ gives his body and blood, broken and shed for us for forgiveness of sins, life, and salvation. The Spirit gives gifts that build up the community. These correct beliefs are also communicated in the historic liturgy and all its local uses. The continuing proper use of this liturgy builds up a community of faith in Jesus Christ crucified and risen again. This is what is at stake in doing liturgy decently: doing liturgy with theologically integrity and with concern for building up the faith of the assembly.

To return to the situation in ancient Corinth addressed by Paul, there was also to be order in the assembly. In the cultural context of ancient Greek and Roman religious practice, women could prophesy in the assembly (see 1 Corinthians 9—women were oracles in ancient Greece and Rome), but they shouldn't disrupt the service with their questions

(1 Corinthians 14). The masters and patrons (the leisure class) had to wait for the slaves and clients (the working class) to get off work before beginning the meal; otherwise they would be eating their own supper, not the Lord's Supper (1 Cor. 11:17-22). If speaking in tongues ("glossolalia") was practiced, there should be interpretation so that others would be edified. Glossolalia should be restricted to two or three at most and only two or three prophets should speak—one at a time (1 Cor. 14:27). These admonitions from the apostle give some indication of how disorderly the assembly could be in Corinth.

Doing liturgy "in order" means at least two things; each point is equally important. First, "in order" means that *there is an order to be followed, a progression of activities that gives shape to the liturgy.* The Reformed tradition was correct to see elements of order in the New Testament. These are not laid out in such detail that we can get an order of service from the New Testament. But, for example, Acts 2 indicates that apologetic and evangelistic preaching leads to repentance and baptism; baptism brings the newly baptized into an assembly gathered for the apostles' teaching, the breaking of bread (Eucharist), fellowship, and the prayers; this assembly maintained a common chest to take care of the needs of its members. It is said that this description of the early church and its order in the book of Acts is an idealistic picture. For our purposes that is even better than an actual picture (if there was really a difference). It means that there is something normative about it for the subsequent life of the church. The church has an *ordo* (order) that it follows. The normative ordo seen in Acts 2 and as it developed in the next few centuries is:

- evangelical outreach (this developed later on into informational talks, such as Augustine's *On Christian Doctrine*)
- acts of repentance (this developed later into the catechumenate)
- baptism (washing with water and the gift of the Holy Spirit)
- apostolic teaching (regular Scripture reading and preaching in the assembly)
- the breaking of bread (celebration of the Eucharist)
- fellowship (this was expressed later in the love feast)
- the prayers (this developed later into common prayer offices)
- sharing in common (offerings for the poor, diaconal ministry to those in need)

When we read on in Acts, we see in chapter 6 that there was a charge of unequal distribution of goods and services to the Jewish and Hellenistic widows in the community. The apostles could not be distracted from preaching and prayer to look after the administration of social services. So they directed the community to elect seven men of good repute to take care of this ministry. (In a case of affirmative action men with Greek names were chosen who might look after the needs of the Hellenistic widows, who felt that they were being discriminated against.) Whether these seven men were deacons in the sense of the developed office, they were certainly exercising a diaconal ministry as they assisted the apostles in the apostolic oversight of the church. By the time of the *Didache*, a church manual written at the end of the first century, and the letters of Ignatius of Antioch early in the second century, the apostles and prophets no longer existed in the church, but bishops (overseers) and deacons (servants) were elected by the local community, to which Ignatius adds presbyters (elders) who provide counsel to the bishop.

So the other thing that "in order" means is that *ministers are chosen by the local assembly to exercise leadership roles*. To make a long and complicated story simplistically short, there emerged in the church orders of ministers who had liturgical functions. *Bishops* were the chief pastors of the local church who had primary responsibility for preaching, teaching, and administration of the sacraments and presided at the liturgy as they were able. *Presbyters* (later called priests, but this is misleading because *presbyteros* and *hiereus* are not the same) took charge of portions of the bishop's flock not able to gather around the bishop because they were geographically distant (the parishes). *Deacons* assisted in the bishop's liturgy by reading the Gospel, leading the intercessions, administering the cup in Holy Communion, and taking the sacrament to the absent. In the description of Sunday worship in Justin Martyr's *Apology* 67, there were also readers and the people (*laos*) constituted a baptized priesthood who always assented to the prayers with their "Amens." In the travel diary she kept on her pilgrimage to the Holy Land in the late fourth century, the Spanish nun Egeria noted that the deacons sang litanies and that the people responded "Kyrie eleison"—"Lord, have mercy."

Other ancient descriptions of liturgy indicate the development of cantors to lead the singing of psalms and hymns of praise sung by the people. The people also offered their gifts in procession for the needs of the community and its liturgy (e.g., bread and wine for the Eucharist, candles, olive oil). By the fourth century choirs were developed to sing psalms and hymns during processions, and acolytes were appointed to perform a variety of tasks. It is not a matter of good liturgical order for one minister to do everything. Liturgy done "in order" requires a variety of roles; this is what gives it a communal character. Liturgy done "in order" also requires that each role is respected. Pastors do not usurp the roles of other ministers; nor do other ministers usurp the pastor's role to preside. A division of roles in the assembly would be as follows:

- processions—acolytes carrying cross, tapers, banners, incense
- psalms, hymns, spiritual songs—the people led by cantors and choirs
- collects—the presiding minister
- readings—readers
- Gospel—a deacon or the preacher
- sermon—a bishop or presbyter (pastor)
- intercessions—deacon or assisting minister
- offering—gathered from the people by ushers
- Great Thanksgiving—presiding minister (bishop or pastor)
- Holy Communion—presiding minster assisted by deacon, assisting minister, and additional communion ministers as needed
- post-communion prayer—traditionally offered by the presiding minister; may be offered by a deacon, an assisting minister, or by the congregation
- blessing—the presiding minister; a bishop if present

4. How do we discern meaning in liturgy?

Liturgy is a symbolic activity. The word *symbol* comes from the Greek *sumballein*, "to throw together." In symbols, meanings are thrown together, and often accumulate. Religions are complex symbol systems, and Christianity is no exception. Symbols are complex because, unlike signs, symbols seldom mean only one thing; meanings accrue from sacred texts and historical experience. When people are confronted with symbols or symbolic activities, they usually don't get every meaning at once. In fact, it is questionable whether symbolic meanings can be exhausted, especially because meanings are interrelated in a symbolic system. The term *symbolic system* is preferred to the word *symbolism* in the fields of anthropology, sociology, and psychology when referring to a system of interconnected symbolic meanings. The term *symbolism* denotes the symbolic meaning of a single cultural phenomenon, as in the symbolism of the Advent wreath. Liturgy is a whole symbolic system.

Meanings of symbols and symbolic systems are best derived from the text, object, or activity itself rather than being imposed on them from something else. For all its richness, this is the danger of allegory. Allegory can assign meanings to an action, object, or text from outside the action, object, or text in a way that fails to take account of its historical context or literal meaning. On the other hand, allegorical interpretation is a time-honored approach to meaning and there is a kind of allegory that derives meaning from within the symbolic system. In this case the meaning assigned to certain actions, objects, and texts is not just a free-floating association of ideas. This can be seen in the allegorical interpretation of the church fathers of antiquity, especially those associated with the Alexandrian and Antiochean schools, which they applied to the Bible and also to the liturgy.

These fathers did not ignore the historical meaning of the Scriptures, but they believed that the Bible is not just historical; it also conveys a spiritual meaning. Classical exegesis of biblical texts divided meaning into four classifications:

- the literal-historical meaning—what the text says and what actual events it reports
- the allegorical meaning—how it refers to the mystery of Christ and the church
- the tropological or moral meaning—how the text is related to personal life
- the anagogical or eschatological meaning—how the text relates us to the kingdom of God yet to come

In other words, when the literal text or historical event is contemplated in faith, it relates us to Christ, it has application for the practical life of faith, and it is a sign that points us to the life of the world to come.

One of the best theological interpreters of the liturgy was Theodore of Mopsuestia (350–428). Since the allegorical interpretation of the Bible meant finding Christ in all of the Scriptures (both Old and New Testaments), he also looked for Christ in the liturgy. The aspect of Christ that Theodore thought most related to liturgy is his role as high priest. Christ exercises that role in the heavenly sanctuary, as the letter to the Hebrews proclaims. But he performs his priestly mediation on behalf of his brothers and sisters before the Father's throne because he accomplished our salvation as a human being in human family, as Hebrews also proclaims. So just as the liturgy images Christ's priestly offering and intercession in heaven, so it images Christ's redemptive activity on earth. In proclaiming Christ in the liturgy, Theodore synchronized the individual acts of the liturgy with the stages of Christ's life. Thus, in his mystagogical homilies (homilies on the mysteries or sacraments), Theodore suggested that the offertory procession images Christ being led to his passion; the spreading of the linen on the altar images the liturgical work of Joseph of Arimathea in preparing the body of Jesus for burial; the epiclesis, at which the celebrant steps back from the table and bows, images the resurrection of Christ. As Hans-Joachim Schulz points out, these theological interpretations of Theodore became standard explanations of the liturgy in the Byzantine tradition.[1]

A similar kind of allegorical interpretation developed in the expositions of the Mass in the medieval West, of which one of the earliest is from Amalarius of Metz (born at Metz, in the last quarter of the eighth century; d. c. 850). It is noteworthy that Amalarius, bishop of Trier, once served as an envoy to Constantinople. In the medieval Western commentaries the whole Mass was seen as a dramatic imaging of the passion of Christ, even to the point of embroidering large crosses on the chasubles worn by the celebrants who served *in personal Christi* (in the role of Christ). In fact, there was a great deal of interest in allegorical meanings of the various vestments the priest wore. Allegorical interpretation not only explained the meaning of what was going on in the liturgy, it also contributed to liturgical practice.

A tighter form of spiritual interpretation is typology. In the Bible itself types of God's actions in creation and redemption are replicated in later actions. Thus, Deutero-Isaiah proclaims the return of the exiles from Babylon as a type of the exodus. Jesus is presented in the Gospels variously as a new type of Moses or David or Elijah. Not surprisingly, the church fathers saw baptism as a type of salvation through water, as seen in the creation of the world from the formless water, the rescue of Noah and his family in the flood, the exodus of Israel through the Red Sea, the crossing over into the promised land under Joshua, and identification with the baptism of Jesus in the Jordan by John the Baptist.[2] As Robert Taft points out, the Antiochene fathers were more prone to employ a typological interpretation of the liturgy than the Alexandrians, since they employed it in their interpretation of Scripture. What was prefigured in the Old Testament has been fulfilled in Christ and has passed over into the sacraments in expectation of its personal and eschatological application.[3] Typology figures strongly in the development of lectionary readings (especially in relating Old Testament readings to the Gospel readings), but also in prayers of blessing such as those over the paschal candle at the Easter Vigil and over the water of the font at Holy Baptism.

After two centuries of rigorous historical-critical reading of the Bible and a century of historical-critical explanations of the liturgy, we do not retrieve spiritual exegesis very easily. Allegorical explanations have especially been harshly criticized and largely put aside by liturgical scholars. But what we see in the theological interpretation of the liturgy in the church fathers is an attempt to relate what is happening in the liturgy to the knowledge of God in Christ that has been revealed to us in the Scriptures. We may be uncertain about the application of the allegorical and typological methods today, but as we look at what actually happens in liturgy we need to ask what meanings are suggested on the basis of our knowledge and experience of the Christ event. Liturgy is not done decently if its theological dimension is ignored. I do not mean that liturgy should be controlled by a dogmatic system, but that the liturgy itself suggests meanings. Look at the following bits of liturgical data and consider the meanings these data suggest.

- The "fixed day" of Christian worship is Sunday, the first day of the week, to honor the resurrection of Christ. Church fathers even called Sunday "the eighth day," suggesting its eschatological character as the day beyond the weekly sabbath.[4]
- The principal Sunday liturgy has been the liturgy of word and meal, or the Eucharist. This suggests that there is a relationship between the Lord's Day and the Lord's Supper.
- Texts of the liturgy, such as the canticles or songs of praise, indicate that God the Holy Trinity is the object of worship.
- The terminations of prayers indicate that Christ is the mediator of prayer, since we pray "through Jesus Christ our Lord."
- Christ "the lamb of God who takes away the sin of the world" is also the subject of Christian worship. The high point of the liturgy of the word is the reading of the Gospel in which we hear of the words and deeds of Christ himself. The high point of the liturgy of the meal is receiving Holy Communion in the body and blood of Christ.
- There are two distinct parts of the principal liturgy: one that focuses on the word and the other that focuses on the meal. Traditionally, everyone is welcome to hear the reading of Scripture and preaching, and it has been called the liturgy of the catechumens. But only the baptized (and sometimes only a portion of the baptized) are welcome to receive the sacramental signs of the Eucharist. The liturgy of the sacrament has been called the liturgy of the faithful. The implication is that something is received in Holy Baptism that is needed in order to receive Holy Communion, that the gift of communion is a strengthening of the baptismal life.
- There is a diversity of roles in the liturgical assembly, so that one person isn't doing everything. The church as the body of Christ is a community with a diversity of gifts of the Holy Spirit. The church is created by the Spirit in the image of the Holy Trinity who is a community of persons.
- There are other gatherings during the week, especially for prayer, that sanctify the times of the world in which we live. But the Sunday gathering for word and sacrament remains the principal one, which reflects the priority of the paschal mystery for Christian liturgy: "Christ has died. Christ is risen. Christ will come again."

Deriving meaning from this kind of data is what liturgical theology purports to do. It does not ask, What is the meaning of liturgy or of worship? It asks, rather, What meanings are conveyed in the texts and actions, and even the ordo, of the liturgy?[5]

There has been much discussion in liturgical theology about the relationship between what the church fathers called the *lex orandi* (the law of prayer) and the *lex credendi* (the law of belief). Prosper of Aquitaine, a disciple of Augustine, wrote in the heat of the Semi-Pelagian controversy, "let the law of prayer [*lex supplicandi*] establish [*statuat*] the law of belief [*lex credendi*]" (he was appealing to prayers that show we are totally dependent on God's grace). The discussion of the relationship between worship and belief has sometimes devolved into a debate between the priority of liturgy on theology or of theology on liturgy in terms of which has influenced which. This is an important discussion, but I decline to engage in it in this book because it belongs more to theory than to practice. It is enough to take seriously the axiom that "praying shapes believing," that those who pray routinely in a certain way will be formed in faith.[6] Precisely because liturgy is a symbolic activity people apprehend meanings in it. Aidan Kavanagh suggests that because people experience God in liturgical acts it is an act of primary theology which provides grist for the secondary theology that reflects on this experience of encounter.[7] Precisely because it is an experience of encounter with God in Christ through the Holy Spirit, it has theological meanings—meanings about God. Liturgy is not only the people's work; God is at work in, with, and through the liturgy.

5. How is the people's work the work of God?

Liturgy is essentially a service that is rendered for the public good. We saw that both individuals and groups may undertake a service project for the good of their community. Using this basic definition, liturgy is also a service that God undertakes for the good of his creation, especially his human creatures.

In the Old Testament God gave to his people both the word for their instruction (*torah*) and the sacrificial cult by means of which the people would have access to God. "Torah" can mean specifically the Ten Commandments or the whole five books of Moses that lead up to and explicate this set of divine instructions. The divine instruction also includes the sacrificial cult. The animal offerings were required because "without the shedding of blood there is no forgiveness" (Heb. 9:22). When Adam and Eve sinned against God and each other, animals were killed by God to provide clothing for them (Gen. 3:21). Cain and Abel brought sacrifices to the Lord. Cain's was unacceptable because he brought fruit, while Abel's was acceptable because it was the "firstborn of his flock" (Gen. 4:4-5). After the flood receded, Noah sacrificed animals to God (Gen. 8:20-21). God commanded the nation of Israel to perform numerous sacrifices according to certain procedures God had prescribed. First, the animal had to be spotless. Second, the person offering the sacrifice had to identify with the animal. Third, the person offering the animal had to inflict death upon it. When done in faith, this sacrifice provided forgiveness of sins. Another sacrifice called for on the Day of Atonement, described in Leviticus 16, demonstrates forgiveness and the removal of sin. The high priest was to take two male goats for a sin offering. One of the goats was sacrificed as a sin offering for the people of Israel (Lev. 16:15), while the other goat was released into the wilderness (Lev. 16:20-22). The sin offering provided forgiveness, while the other goat provided the removal of sin. It undoubtedly seems strange to us that animals were the sacrificial victims, because they did no wrong. But that is the point. Since the animals were sinless, they died in place of the sinner performing the sacrifice. Thus animal sacrifices were commanded by God so that the individual and the nation could receive the gift of forgiveness of sin and so that individuals and the nation could offer a sacrifice of thanksgiving for the gifts God gave.

John the Baptist recognized this when he saw Jesus coming to be baptized and said, "Look, the lamb of God who takes away the sin of the world!" (John 1:29). The apostolic proclamation (*kerygma*) is that Jesus Christ who rendered perfect obedience to the Father, and therefore was without sin, willingly gave himself to die for the sins of humankind (1 Tim. 2:6). As 2 Corinthians 5:21 says, "For our sake God made him [Jesus] to be sin who knew no sin, so that in him we might become the righteousness of God." We are justified by faith (trust) in the sacrifice of Jesus Christ, by which we are reconciled with God and receive the gift of forgiveness. The sacrifice of Christ fulfills and thus replaces the sacrificial cult of Israel. But it is impossible to understand the theology of the sacrifice of Christ without reference to the Old Testament cult.[8]

As in the Old Testament, so under the New Testament there must be means, a ministry, by which reconciliation with God is accomplished and forgiveness of sins experienced. As in the Old Testament there is a divine instruction, so in the New Testament there is the gospel (*evangelion*) or good news, which is the proclamation of this reconciliation and forgiveness on account of the sacrifice of Christ. As in the Old Testament the *torah* was expanded into Scripture, so the *evangelion* is heard in Scripture. As in emerging Judaism the Scripture was read and commented on in the synagogue, so in the church the Scripture is read and preached. As in the synagogue the Torah reading received pride of place, so in the Christian assembly the Gospel reading receives pride of place. As in the synagogue other readings of Scripture (*Haftorah*) supported the Torah reading, so in the Christian assembly other readings (Old Testament, New Testament epistles) support the Gospel reading. As in the synagogue preaching was an explication and application of the readings (as we see in Jesus' response to the reading of Isaiah in his hometown synagogue in Luke 4), so in the Christian assembly preaching grows out of the words of Scripture that have been gratefully heard and received by the faithful as the word of God.

This gospel word of forgiveness and reconciliation is also applied in words of absolution and blessing. The word of forgiveness pronounced to the individual or the assembly by the minister who stands in the role of Christ (*in persona Christi*) is the word of God himself to sinners who have sincerely repented and confessed their sins. Benedictions or blessings are also words of God proclaiming his favor on his people. The Scriptures show that the Lord alone is to be blessed since God alone is the source of every blessing (Luke 1:68; Rom. 1:25; 9:5; 2 Cor. 11:31; Eph. 1:3; 1 Pet. 1:3). All blessings come from God; they are conveyed by God's words that create, protect, and foster life. The word of God is effective and conveys the gift that it proclaims. The paradigmatic benediction is the one proclaimed by Aaron the priest in Numbers 6:24-26): "The Lord bless you and keep you…" This was the blessing God authorized the priests to place on the people who assembled in his presence (Num. 5:23). Martin Luther may have been the first exegete to emphasize this. In his commentary on Genesis he compares the speaking of blessings to the declaration of an absolution and describes blessing as "God's works through our ministry."[9]

There are not only spoken words of God in the liturgy; there are also the "visible words" of the sacraments. *Sacramentum* in Roman usage referred to sacred signs, such as the standards carried by the legions. Augustine of Hippo defined sacrament as a visible sign of an invisible grace. The term *sacrament* came to be applied to what the Greek church called the saving "mysteries" of Christ: Holy Baptism and Holy Communion. The term *grace* comes from the Greek *charis*, which means "gift." These sacramental rites instituted by Christ (Matt. 28:18-20—go and baptize in the name of the Father and of the Son and of the Holy Spirit; 1 Cor. 11:23-26—do this meal for the remembrance of me) are accomplished by earthly signs (water, and also oil; bread, and also wine). By doing the rites we receive the gifts they convey—forgiveness of sins, new life, and eternal salvation. The phenomenon of "gift" is crucial to understanding the character of the sacraments. It is the central reality that unites sacramental activity both to God's triune life and to the corporate identity of the assembly as the people of God and body of Christ.[10]

While human beings perform the rites, the sacraments are actually God's acts administered by those ministers who are have been aside by the Holy Spirit to serve *in persona Christi* and whom the church recognizes through ordination and call as holding the office of the ministry of the word and the sacraments. God intends his people to receive his gracious gifts and ministers are appointed to ensure that God's gifts are received.

It is because God acts in his word and in the sacraments of Christ to reconcile humanity with himself that the chief liturgy of the church is also called the Divine Liturgy.

For further reading

Brunner, Peter. *Worship in the Name of Jesus*, trans. M. H. Bertram. St. Louis: Concordia, 1968. Brunner explains the difference between the sacramental and sacrificial elements of worship as God's service to the congregation and the congregation's service before God.

Fagerberg, David W. *What Is Liturgical Theology? A Study in Methodology*. Collegeville: Liturgical, 1992. Fagerberg distinguishes between a theology of worship, a theology from worship, and liturgical theology. He analyzes the liturgical theological methods of Germanus of Constantinople and the Russian Orthodox theologian Alexander Schmemann.

Irwin, Kevin W. *Context and Text: Method in Liturgical Theology*. Collegeville: Liturgical, 1994. Irwin argues that liturgy is a full ritual activity that has to be observed from the perspective of the participants and described on the basis of their perceptions of that event. But the texts have also shaped the context of the participants.

Kavanagh, Aidan. *On Liturgical Theology*. New York: Pueblo, 1984. Kavanagh argues that "primary theology" is the encounter between God and the community of faith in prayer and rite and "secondary theology" is reflection on this encounter, including academic liturgical theology.

Lathrop, Gordon W. *Holy Things: A Liturgical Theology*. Minneapolis: Fortress Press, 1993. Lathrop expands the concept of ordo, developed by Alexander Schmemann (see below), to include the large categories of rite, time, and space, and probes the meanings implied in the juxtapositions of, say, teaching (catechesis) and bath, word and meal, Sunday and other days, Eucharist and daily prayer, and so forth.

Power, David N. *Unsearchable Riches: The Symbolic Nature of Liturgy*. New York: Pueblo, 1984. Power explores the meaning of symbol and ritual and argues that ritual and symbolic language is the core language of religious reality and faith.

Schmemann, Alexander. *Introduction to Liturgical Theology*. New York: St. Vladimir's Seminary Press, 1986. Schmemann was the first to propose that the ordo should be the source of theological reflection. But the ordo is more than rubrics (rules and regulations) and has to be interpreted on the basis of its underlying principles.

Wainwright, Geoffrey. *Doxology: The Praise of God in Worship, Doctrine, and Life; A Systematic Theology*. New York: Oxford University Press, 1980. Wainwright has a thorough discussion of the relationship between the *lex orandi* and the *lex credendi*. But see the refinement of this relationship in Kavanagh, *On Liturgical Theology*, 73ff. (see above).

2
History and Culture

1. What are the main periods of liturgical history?
2. What characterizes liturgy in each of these periods?
3. How does liturgy relate to culture in each of these periods?
4. What are the strategies of relating liturgy to culture?
5. How does inculturation work?

1. What are the main periods of liturgical history?

The periods of liturgical history coincide with general church and cultural history.

Early Church

The documentation for this period is sketchy but not insignificant. It includes references to practices and the citation of hymns, as identified by form critics, in the New Testament writings that were written between the 50s CE and the end of the first century. At about the end of the first century there is the church manual called the *Didache* (or "Teaching of the Twelve"), which includes a catechism ("the way of life and the way of death") and instruction on baptism, fasting, prayer, the Eucharist, hospitality, reconciliation, ministry, and discipline.[1] There is a full description of a baptismal Eucharist and a Sunday liturgy of word and meal in Justin Martyr's *Apology* (c. 150). Important information is conveyed by the lay North African Latin writer Tertullian (c. 300) in his treatises *On Baptism, On Prayer, On Penance,* and *On Purity*. A full church order called the *Apostolic Tradition* has been attributed to the Roman presbyter Hippolytus (c. 215); however, this treatise is only pieced together from later church orders, and there is no extant copy of the Greek version in which this church order would have been written.[2] Other early period writings with references to liturgical practice are the Letter of the Roman governor Pliny the Younger (c. 110), the Letters of Ignatius of Antioch (c. 110–115), and the treatise *On the Pasch* by Melito of Sardis (c. 160).

Late Antiquity

The fourth century, the time of the church's public emergence after the Edict of Milan (312), proved to be a liturgical watershed. The liturgical assembly moved from private houses into public halls (basilicas). Much more information is available for the liturgy of late antiquity from church orders such as the *Didascalia Apostolorum*, the *Apostolic Constitutions*, and the *Testamentum Domini*; the catechetical sermons of the bishops addressed to catechumens and the newly baptized; the prayer book of Sarapion of Thmuis in Egypt; and the diary of a Spanish pilgrim to the Holy Land named Egeria.

The fourth through the sixth centuries are regarded as late antiquity in the West (up through the pontificate of Pope Gregory the Great, 590–604); in the East late antiquity extends at least through the ninth century. In the period of late antiquity we see increasing unification and standardization of rites in federations of local churches gathered under patriarchal seats (Antioch, Alexandria, Rome, Constantinople, Jerusalem), and also growing differences between these families of rites.

For those churches in the East that came under Islamic domination, liturgical life was quite different than in Byzantine and Roman Christendom, although no living organism like an actual liturgical assembly remains stagnant. It responds also to the situation of cultural suppression. Christianity existed in countries east and south of the Byzantine Empire from Georgia to Ethiopia and east from Mesopotamia to Kerela in India and western China. These churches developed liturgical rites in the Syriac, Armenian, Georgian, Coptic, and Ethiopian languages.

Byzantium

Byzantine history has been divided into three major periods: the period of development between Constantine the Great (d. 337) through the iconoclastic controversy (711–802); the apogee of Byzantine culture from the time of the restoration of the icons (856) through the succession problems after Emperor Constantine VIII (1025–1055); and the long period of decline and fall (1081–1453), hastened by the tragedy of the Fourth Crusade, which witnessed the sacking of Constantinople by Frankish crusaders in 1204 (regarded as Byzantium's darkest hour, even darker than its final fall to the Ottoman Turks).[3]

Historical and theological events influenced the development of the West Syrian liturgies of St. Basil and St. John Chrysostom used in the Byzantine tradition. Doxological formularies were especially influenced by the trinitarian and christological controversies of the fourth and fifth centuries. Also, in response to Nestorius's attack on giving the title of *Theotokos* to the Virgin Mary, the Byzantines increased the use of the term in the liturgy, and now almost every string of hymns ends with one in her honor, called a *Theotokion*. These liturgies reached their full development by 800 (*Codex Barberini*, Gr. 336), and in the ninth century were translated into Slavonic by the Greek missionary brothers Cyril and Methodius. Even in the period of decline, however, new hymns were composed and new prayers written as the needs arose.

In the period after 800, further development was especially influenced by the monasteries. In fact, the liturgical books presently used by the Orthodox churches originated either in monasteries or have been greatly influenced by monastic practices. The principal liturgical book used in Constantinople after 800 was the Typicon of the Monastery of the Studion. The typicon is the most important liturgical book in the Eastern Orthodox tradition. Literally meaning "following the order," the typicon is a book of directives and rubrics that establishes the order of divine services for each day of the year. It assumes the existence of other liturgical books that contain the fixed and variable parts of these services. In monastic usage, the *typikon* of the monastery includes both the rule of life of the community and the rule of prayer.

After Constantinople fell to the Latin crusaders in 1204, a Palestinian monastic version of the Divine Office replaced that of the Great Church of Hagia Sophia.[4] This was the Typicon of the Holy Lavra of St. Savas of Jerusalem. To meet the needs of the Slavic world, which was evangelized by the Byzantines beginning with the mission of Cyril and Methodius in the ninth century, Slavic translations of the typicon as well as the Bible began as soon as missions to the Slavic world began. Thus, more than in the West, Eastern liturgy remained in the language of the people and that always offered the possibility of popular participation in the songs and ceremonies of the rites.

The Middle Ages in the West

The Western Middle Ages are usually divided into early (600s–1000s), middle (1100s–1200s), and late (1300s–1400s). The early period was marked by the settlement of the barbarian tribes that had moved into the Western Roman Empire and the evangelization of Europe north of the Alps. Liturgically, it was a time of the importation of Roman liturgy into the Carolingian Empire and the blending of Roman with Gallican material in the prayer books (sacramentaries), antiphonaries (choir books), and ordos (ritual manuals).[5] Two lines of sacramentaries were imported into Gaul: the Gelasian, which represent masses celebrated by a presbyter; and the Gregorian, which provided propers for papal masses. These books did not have all of the material needed for the church year in the Gallican church. A sacramentary sent from Pope Hadrian I was supplemented (by either Alcuin of York or Benedict of Aniane). The supplement begins with the word *Hucusque*—"up to here." "Up to here" there is pure Roman material; from here on there is local material.

The middle or high period was a time of crusades to recapture the Holy Land from the Muslims and the importation of ancient Greek learning and philosophy acquired from interaction with Arab scholars. The emergence of mendicant (traveling) religious orders (e.g., Dominicans, Franciscans, Carmelites) saw the invention of missals and breviaries, in which all material needed for the celebration of Mass and the Divine Office was gathered into one book,[6] and the further standardization of Franco-Roman liturgy through the unified uses of the religious orders. A way of engaging the laity in the Latin liturgy was through processions on major days in the church year and to mark special occasions. Books called processionals emerged from the eleventh century on that contained chants (litanies, psalms, and antiphons) sung in procession.[7]

The late period saw the devastations of plagues and death across Europe and, perhaps as a consequence, the emergence of popular paraliturgical devotions (e.g. the rosary, the Way of the Cross) to feed the people spiritually whose religious needs were not met by official Latin liturgy with its increasing calendar complications. The official liturgies themselves became more complicated in the fourteenth and fifteenth centuries because of the complications of calendars and the addition of prayer offices to the breviaries. Books called ceremonials provided precise instruction on the performance of the rites.[8]

Reformation

The Reformation of the sixteenth century was, in part, a reaction to the religious insecurity of the Christian people and the increasing legalism of liturgical life. But the variety of reform proposals and the intransigence of the papacy resulted in a splintering of Christianity into Protestant and Roman Catholic churches characterized by their respective confessions of faith. Protestant confessional communities include Lutheran, Reformed, Anabaptist, and Anglican.

All of the major Reformers—Martin Luther, Ulrich Zwingli, Martin Bucer, Jean Calvin, Thomas Cranmer, Olavus Petri—produced liturgical orders, sometimes two or more in which a development can be seen in their theological commitments and pastoral concerns. In the case of Martin Luther, he was not of a mind to discard his Latin Mass (1523) when his German Mass was published (1526); they were intended for different social settings: city and village. In the case of the two or more orders produced by Zwingli (1523, 1525), Bucer (several in the 1530s), Calvin (1539 in Strasbourg, 1542 in Geneva), and Cranmer (1548–49, 1552), a theological development can be discerned. Alongside the so-called magisterial Reformation there was a radical Reformation comprising reformers and sects often grouped under the category "Anabaptist." Liturgical evidence for Anabaptist practice is provided by Balthasar Hubmaier, but only for his community.

Western Catholicism became Roman after the Council of Trent in the implementation of the conciliar decree that all local churches in communion with the bishop of Rome should use the Roman rite—that is, the rite of the diocese and province of Rome. Reform of the Mass (1570) and the breviary (1568) was entrusted to the Roman Curia and a Congregation of Rites was established to deal with rubrical matters that might arise from time to time.[9]

Post-Reformation Period

The post-Reformation period saw a legalistic standardization of liturgy in the various confessional traditions. Uniformity was actually first legally enacted in England by successive Acts of Uniformity (1549, 1552, 1559) passed by Parliament that required exclusive use of the *Book of Common Prayer*. Uniformity was made possible by the new technology of printing and the mass production of liturgical books.

Enforced uniformity produced a reaction in all of these traditions: Puritan-ism, Pietism, Jansenism. Reformed confessions in different countries produced vari-ous Reformed churches: Swiss and German Reformed, French Huguenots, Dutch Reformed, Scots Presbyterianism. The failure to secure an enduring Puritan Common-wealth in England (1644–1660) resulted in denominational splintering in England into Anglican, Presbyterian, Congregationalist, and Baptist churches.

Pious practices existed alongside official liturgy in both the Roman Catholic and Lutheran traditions: a resurgence of popular devotions among Roman Catholics and the pietistic conventicles among Lutherans. However, liturgy was far from sterile in either Roman Catholicism or Lutheranism. In both of these traditions there was an architectural and music enrichment of liturgical celebration.

The post-Reformation period was also a time of extensive Roman Catholic mis-sions to parts of the world newly discovered or experienced by Europeans. Francis-can friars accompanied the Spanish conquistadors to Mexico and the regions in the Western Hemisphere that became Spanish colonies to engage in evangelism among the Native Americans. The Catholic Church also acquired a beachhead in the Philippines and through the Jesuits began mission work in Japan and China. These mission fields all provided opportunities for cultural adaptation, some of which, in the case of the Chinese rites, became controversial.[10]

Age of Enlightenment

The Age of Enlightenment had an impact on the Western European churches and even, to some extent, on Russian Orthodoxy during the reign of Czar Peter the Great (1694–1725). The eighteenth century was a time of great historical research. Ancient church orders, sacramentaries, and the *Ordines Romani* were discovered and published. These discoveries had no impact on Roman Catholic liturgical orders, but knowledge of the ancient church orders had some influence on the "wee bookies" and the 1764 Communion Service of the Scottish Episcopal Church; the nonjuring Scottish Episcopal Church was not bound by the standardization of the Prayer Book of the Church of England. Due to the Scottish consecration of Bishop Samuel Seabury of Connecticut, the Scottish Communion Service had an influence on the *Book of Common Prayer* of the Protestant Episcopal Church in the U.S.A.[11]

Church orders in the Lutheran countries were regulated by law, but permission was granted to pastors in the Lutheran Consistory of Hannover to make "alterations and improvements" in "consultation with the more cultured members of their congrega-tions."[12] The result of this liberty is evident in an 1808 Agenda, which is marked by texts of the Words of Institution and the Lord's Prayer rewritten to express humanistic interests. Enlightenment influences may also be seen in the 1811 order of Mass and the Manual of the Church of Sweden. Antitrinitarian schism in New England Congrega-tionalism produced Unitarianism. The rationalist religion of the Age of Enlightenment profoundly affected preaching and hymnody.

Revivalism

There was bound to be a reaction to rationalist religion. This first took the form of revivalism. Revivals occurred in the mid-eighteenth century in Britain under John and Charles Wesley—leading to the emergence of Methodism—and in British North America in the 1740s. The Anglican preacher George Whitefield brought revival to the British North American colonies and became the first real celebrity in the colonies. It had a major impact in reshaping the Congregational, Presbyterian, Dutch Reformed, and German Reformed denominations, and strengthened the small Baptist and Methodist denominations, but had little impact on Anglicans and Quakers. As among the Pietists in Germany, people began to study the Bible at home, which effectively decentralized the means of informing the public on religious manners and fostered the individualistic trends already present in the Enlightenment.

Beginning at Cane Ridge, Kentucky, in 1801, there was a Second Great Awakening that swept the American frontier. It was originally organized as a typical Scottish Presbyterian communion gathering. In the 1790s Presbyterians in Kentucky, southern Ohio, and northern Tennessee traveled to each other's sacramental communion services, which typically began on Friday or Saturday and continued through Monday. Joining them in increasing numbers after a meeting at Red River in Logan County in June 1801 were Methodists and Baptists as well as the unchurched. The revival of August 1801 at Cane Ridge, organized by Presbyterian minister Barton Stone, was the climactic event of the Western Great Revival. It was estimated that some twenty to thirty thousand persons of all ages, representing various economic levels, both white and black, freemen and slaves, traveled on foot and on horseback, many bringing wagons with tents and camping provisions. Because of the numbers of people attending and the length of the meeting, Cane Ridge has become the metaphor of the Great Revival.

The camp meetings spread up and down the western side of the mountains from New York to Georgia. Rev. Charles Finney (1792–1875) was a key leader of the evangelical revival movement in America. From 1821 onward he conducted revival meetings across many northeastern states and carried the revival even into New York City, where for a time he pastored at the Broadway Tabernacle before going to Oberlin, Ohio, where he served as a pastor, college professor, and college president and became a leader in the abolitionist movement. Before leaving New York, however, he systematized the revival technique for use in any setting and coined the term "new measures" in his famous essay *Lectures on Revivals of Religion* (1835). Finney held that no order of worship was set down in the New Testament. We are free to use whatever measures will save souls.

Romanticism

Against the rationalist view that worship exists primarily to edify the worshiper, romanticism tried to recover worship as an activity intended to give glory to God alone (*soli Deo gloria*). This was expressed especially in the effort to recover historic forms of the liturgy, especially in Lutheran and Reformed traditions. Recovery began in France with the renewal of Benedictine monasticism at the Abbey of Solesmes under the leadership of Dom Prosper Guéranger after the devastations of Catholic church life in the French Revolution.

Comparable liturgical restoration movements flourished in Germany (e.g., Wilhelm Löhe, Theodor Kliefoth) and England (i.e., the Oxford Tractarian Movement and the Cambridge Ecclesiological Movement), which resulted respectively in evangelical catholic movements in Lutheran and Reformed Churches and Anglo-Catholicism. Löhe's *Agende* (1845) was brought to the American Midwest by immigrants and it contributed to the retrieval of historic Lutheran liturgy in the English-language Common Service of 1888.

Anglo-Catholics found the *Book of Common Prayer* lacking in fuller liturgical provisions, especially for the Eucharist. The English Missal published by W. Knott & Son Limited in 1912 was used by some Anglo-Catholic parish churches. It combined the order of Mass of Pope Pius V (as edited by Pope Pius X) with the lessons for all the Sundays of the year and certain feast days taken from the *Book of Common Prayer*. The lessons in the Roman Missal for the days not included in the calendar of the *Book of Common Prayer* were confined to an appendix.

Modernity

These two nineteenth-century movements of revivalism and romanticism had corollaries in two twentieth-century movements that have had profound impact on the history of worship and liturgy: Pentecostalism and the Liturgical Movement. Pentecostalism emerged from the Azusa Street Revival in Los Angeles in 1906 and the Liturgical Movement began in the Liturgical Week sponsored by the Maria Laach Abbey in the German Rhineland in 1914. As both revivalism and romanticism were reactions to rationalism, so Pentecostalism and the Liturgical Movement, seemingly so different in outward expression (free form vs. historic form), are spiritual reactions to the modern industrial and urban revolutions. Both are renewalist movements within global Christianity. Pentecostalism, in fact, has grown in hundreds of millions of adherents in Latin America and Africa. Both movements transcended denominational borders, appealed to worship patterns found in the early church, championed an explicit rather than an implicit faith, promoted the active participation of the people in worship, and proposed ecclesiologies that made room for an expression of a diversity of gifts (*charismata*). The Liturgical Movement in particular recovered an understanding of liturgy as "the public work of the people" and placed a new emphasis on the priesthood of all believers. It promoted this new emphasis by proposing a diversity of ministerial roles in the liturgical assembly.[13] The aims of the liturgical movement of the early twentieth century found expression in the Constitution on the Sacred Liturgy of the Second Vatican Council (*Sacrosanctam Concilium*).

2. What characterizes liturgy in each of these periods?

Early Liturgy

Early on a pattern emerged of Christians gathering in one another's homes to share the Eucharist. The earliest Eucharist thus had a domestic setting and followed the format of a Greco-Roman symposium. In fact, John 13–17 is in the form of a symposium with eating and drinking, a dramatic action (Jesus washing his disciples' feet), a discussion of this action that becomes Jesus' farewell address to his disciples, and Jesus' high priestly prayer.[14] This was an evening gathering during the first century, but early in the second century the time of the gathering was moved to morning in response to an imperial ban on supper clubs. When the ban was lifted, Christians continued to meet in the morning for prayer and Eucharist (the sacramental elements now removed from the context of an actual meal).

Second-century evidence shows that Christians met on the first day of the week (Sunday), which they called the Lord's Day, to read the prophets (Old Testament) and "memoirs of the apostles" (New Testament), hear the presiding minister's commentary on these readings (preaching), pray for one another and for the world, offer bread and wine, over which the presiding minister gave thanks "to the best of his ability," share the bread and cup, and distribute the elements to the absent by the deacons. There was also a collection for the poor and needy.

By the third century processes of confession, penance, and reconciliation developed to deal with grave sin and lapse from the faith under persecution. Property confiscated by the Roman government during persecution shows that the church was also acquiring the title to houses and houses for assembly were becoming houses of the church. Such a house church has been excavated at Dura-Europas on the Roman-Persian border in Syria.

Late Antique Liturgy

The most significant change in Christian liturgy during the fourth century was that the liturgical assemblies moved into public halls (basilicas) given to the church by the emperor. Larger crowds in bigger spaces required more attention to choreography. This was especially the case with processions at the entrance of the bishop, at the offertory when the people presented their gifts, and at the time of communion when the people went to stations to receive the consecrated bread and wine. The basilica with its aisles accommodated these processions. Psalms also accompanied the offertory and communion processions. The singing of psalms and hymns necessitated trained choirs, which in Rome became the Schola Cantorum. The school of singers was also an actual school in which boys learned to read and served as lectors.

Yet at the same time as liturgy moved into basilicas, it also moved out of doors. This accounts for the repetition of litanies at the beginning of the current Byzantine liturgy, that is, the *enarxis* with its triple litanies and antiphons concluding with the thrice-holy hymn (Trisagion). It became the practice in urban churches such as Rome, Constantinople, and Jerusalem with its pilgrimage sites to conduct liturgies at "stations," which required processions from place to place. The litany developed as a processional prayer.

Early Medieval Liturgy

The Carolingian Frankish rulers, especially Pippin III (the Short) and Charles the Great (Charlemagne), desired to bring order into their unruly realm by importing and imposing Roman law and Roman liturgical books. This was more complicated than they had thought, because liturgical books are living documents that undergo continual emendation. Every time a new book was brought north from Rome it had differences from the previous book. Moreover, there were days in the Frankish church calendar for which the Roman books provided no propers, such as Sundays in Advent. The form and essential components of the medieval Mass were assembled and stabilized through the blending of Roman and Gallican material during the Carolingian era, thanks largely to the organizing zeal of Charlemagne and the efforts of monastic liturgists like Alcuin and Benedict of Aniane.

A further complication is that in the early medieval liturgy each of the main participants had a separate book that contained only the texts proper to his office. Thus there is not one book for the early medieval Mass but several: the sacramentary for the celebrant, the epistolary (epistles) and evangelary (Gospels) for the subdeacon and deacon, and the antiphonary and graduale for the choir. A master of ceremonies for a pontifical Mass (celebrated by a bishop) would need an ordo, which provided the order of service and ceremonial directions. Not until the tenth century is there evidence of a tendency to assemble the disparate components in a single book, the missal, which a priest could use to celebrate Mass without assisting ministers.

High Medieval Liturgy

Liturgy in the high Middle Ages demonstrated both an interiorizing of piety and an outward accumulation of drama. On the one hand, private prayers said while vesting (allegorizing the meaning of each vestment) and prayers of confession of sins said in the sacristy or at the foot of the altar were added for the celebrant and his servers before the beginning of Mass. Private prayers for the celebrant were also added during the preparation of the gifts at the offertory and before and after receiving communion. On the other hand, there were musical developments in the composition of sequences and tropes as well as the development of liturgical dramas.

The sequence, also called the prose to distinguish it from the versified hymns sung in the prayer offices, was an extended nonbiblical song inserted after the Alleluia. The popularity of the sequence is attested by the many collections circulating in the Middle Ages, and the fact that in some areas a proper sequence was sung on every Sunday and major feast. The execution was entrusted to two choirs (usually of men and boys, respectively), the strophe being sung by one and the antistrophe by the other to the same melody.

A similar type of liturgical evolution was the addition of phrases of music or text, or both, to the existing chants; these additions are collectively referred to as "tropes" (from *tropare*, "to sing"). Tropes were found in almost every type of Mass chant and some office chants. Often tropes acted as introductions to the existing chant, but many were a series of reflective additions or commentaries inserted between each phrase of the original text. Some Mass settings acquired their name because of the trope, such as *Missa orbis factor* from the Kyrie—"Lord, omnipotent Father, God, Creator of all, have mercy." Like the sequence, tropes were most frequently used on Sundays and important feasts. Both tend to be local; only a few acquired universal status, such as the sequences *Victimae paschali laudes* for Easter, *Veni, sancte Spiritus* for Pentecost, and *Lauda Sion salvatorem* for Corpus Christi.

Liturgical drama also developed from the practice of troping texts. On solemn feasts such as Easter and Christmas, the prayer office was interrupted, and the priests represented, in the presence of those assisting, the biblical event that was being celebrated. At first the text of this liturgical drama was very brief, and was taken solely from the Gospel or the office of the day. It was in Latin prose. But versification crept in. The earliest of such dramatic "tropes" of the Easter service are from England and date from the tenth century. Soon verse pervaded the entire drama, prose became the exception, and the vernacular appeared beside Latin. Once the vernacular had completely supplanted the Latin, however, and individual inventiveness had at the same time asserted itself, the drama left the precincts of the church and ceased to be liturgical without, however, losing its religious character. The most famous of these liturgical dramas were for Easter (*Quem queritis in sepulchro, O Christicole?*—"Whom do you seek at the sepulchre, O followers of Christ?") and for Christmas (*Quem queritis in presepe, pastores*—"Whom do you seek at the manger, O shepherds?").

Late Medieval Liturgy

By the late Middle Ages, the texts and rubrics of the Mass and Divine Office had become very complicated. The liturgical rites were still in Latin, but vernacular elements were seen in the addition of carols or chorales to sequences in Germany (e.g., *Christ ist erstanden* to *Victimae paschali laudes*, using the same tune as the sequence) and in the development of a pulpit office known as Prone. Included in this office were catechetical items, bids and intercessions in the vernacular language, and a prayer of confession of sins. Prone influenced later Reformation orders (e.g., Apostles' Creed, sermon, announcements, intercessions, confession of sins, and declaration of grace). Whole communities were also drawn into processions at Candlemas, on Palm Sunday, at Rogationtide (the three days before the Ascension)—with processions through the fields marking the parish boundaries—and on the new medieval feast of Corpus Christi, which involved all the trade guilds of the town. The emphasis in lay participation was on seeing. Nowhere was this more the case than in seeing the elevation of the host at the words of consecration in the Mass. But most people received communion only once a year.

Reformation Liturgy

The Protestant Reformation's emphasis on the Bible as the ultimate authority in all matters of faith and practice led to a new focus on the sermon, which should be a literal (i.e., grammatical-historical) exposition of the biblical text with an application to faith and life. Since "faith comes from what is heard" rather than from what is seen, the word tended to supplant ceremonies. The word also attacked superstitious abuse, and some popular customs such as candles on Candlemas, ashes on Ash Wednesday, and palms on Palm Sunday were abolished. The word also needed to be understood, so liturgies were put into vernacular languages. Since so much Christian liturgy is based on the Bible, good biblical translations were needed for the liturgies—for liturgical texts as well as readings.

Lutheran worship especially featured congregational singing of vernacular hymns to catechize the people. The Reformed eschewed nonbiblical hymns but provided vernacular metrical psalms for congregation song. Holy Communion was celebrated less frequently than the Roman Mass had been, but a new emphasis was placed on the reception of communion by the whole congregation. Thus, even though celebrations were reduced to three or four times a year, the faithful received communion more frequently than had been the case before the Reformation. Martin Luther, Martin Bucer, and Jean Calvin preferred celebrations of Holy Communion every Sunday and festival. Calvin was not able to convince the city council of Geneva to move beyond the quarterly communion schedule. As long as there were communicants, weekly communion occurred among Lutherans. However, a practice that discouraged frequent reception of communion was examining the announced communicants on their knowledge of the catechism and their moral lives. Confession of sins and catechization served to "fence the table."

Post-Reformation Liturgy

Liturgy in the post-Reformation period reflects a hardening of confessional positions. Liturgies and ceremonial practices became symbols of confessional identity. So, for example, Roman Catholics practiced Solemn Benediction of the Blessed Sacrament, especially after Sunday Vespers. The Reformed broke the bread and distributed it to the communicants. Against Reformed influence, Lutherans elevated the bread and cup and proclaimed verbally the true body and blood of Christ along with this act of ostention. Eucharistic doctrine was thus differentiated by ritual gesture.

There was little development of liturgical forms in the post-Reformation period, except in the Free Church tradition. But especially among Roman Catholics and Lutherans, there was a flourishing of the music and arts of worship (to be discussed in the next section) that greatly enriched liturgy. New church buildings in the Baroque style also enriched the ambience of Catholic and Lutheran worship.

Similar development in the Anglican tradition was interrupted during the middle of the seventeenth century with the establishment of the Puritan Commonwealth, the suppression of the Prayer Book, the dissolution of cathedral and collegiate choirs, and the destruction of organs. The Prayer Book was restored in 1662 in the restored monarchy, along with cathedral and college choirs, related musical development typified by Henry Purcell, and a new style of Anglican architecture promoted by Sir Christopher Wren, who rebuilt St. Paul's Cathedral and many of the parish churches of London after the disastrous fire of 1666. With the restoration of choirs and organs, Anglican cathedral and collegiate worship was enriched with new musical settings and anthems. However, village churches in England were served by west-gallery amateur bands.

Rationalist Liturgy

A major change occurred in thinking about worship in the Age of Enlightenment. Enlightenment thinkers believed that worship should exist primarily for the edification of the people. This meant, especially in the view of Roman Catholic rationalists, that ritual should be simplified and textual redundancy eliminated. An attempt at liturgical reform was launched by Pope Benedict XV in 1741, but after six years of work he rejected the work of his liturgical commission. Another significant attempt at liturgical reform occurred in Tuscany in 1786 under Duke Leopold II and Scipio de Ricci, Bishop of Pistoia. A synod held in Pistoia called for a return to the liturgy of the early church and the independence of each diocese in matters of liturgy and worship (a desire also of French dioceses, and so the proposal was called "Gallicanism"). The synod also called for the active participation of the laity in the Mass, the use of the vernacular, the elimination of masses being celebrated simultaneously in the same place, reception of communion at Mass, rigorous preparation of parents and godparents for the baptism of their children, and curtailment of processions and popular devotions. There was popular resistance to these measures, and De Ricci was deposed as bishop when Duke Leopold became Holy Roman Emperor in 1790. In 1794 Pope Pius VI condemned eighty-five propositions of the Synod of Pistoia.

The Enlightenment had more of an impact on Protestant liturgy than Catholic. In Lutheran churches word and sacrament fell out of balance. Holy Communion ceased to be celebrated as the principal service every Sunday and festival and was either appended to the service for those who wished to remain after the rest of the assembly had been dismissed, or was celebrated four times a year as in the Reformed practice. The concern was that communion would "lose its meaning" if celebrated too frequently. Preparing to receive Holy Communion became a major spiritual effort that included announcing one's intention to receive and being examined by the pastor. First communion was usually delayed until after the rite of confirmation, which was being restored in Lutheran churches at the end of the eighteenth century as a cultural rite of passage.

Revival Liturgy

The American frontier camp meetings, first organized by Presbyterians as communion gatherings, produced a new ecumenical form of worship that followed a three-part structure: (1) warm-up songs ("preliminaries"), (2) reading of Scripture and preaching, and (3) altar call (originally to the Lord's Supper but later to the "anxious bench" for prayer). James F. White has called this order the "frontier tradition."[15]

This form of worship became pervasive in Protestant churches and replaced or altered traditional denominational orders. Thus preliminaries included songs of gathering and praise, testimonies, the offering, and the pastoral prayer. Both the offering and the intercessions lost their connection with the word and the meal. The high point of the service was the sermon. Under the influence of camp-meeting practices, pulpits were reduced in size and often became podiums on which the Bible and the preacher's notes could be placed. But sermons were no longer read; they were delivered *ex tempore* so that the preacher could freely move about the stage and more effectively engage the hearers. Seating was arranged around the pulpit, which might be placed in the corner of a square room (the "Akron" plan), and, like an auditorium or theater, the floor was slanted to provide for better sight lines. As revival preachers had song leaders and made use of singing, so organs and choirs that had been abolished in Reformed churches were brought back into Reformed worship because the music could make an impact on the assembly. The choir and organ was typically placed behind and above the preacher. Three chairs became obligatory on the platform: one for the pastor, one for the song leader, and one for the guest preacher. The "altar call" typically was reserved for Sunday evening rather than Sunday morning services and was no longer an invitation to Holy Communion.

Little attention was paid to the church year in the revival tradition, other than Christmas and Easter. This did not preclude the development of other types of festivals and commemorations such as Memorial Day, Mother's Day, Father's Day, Children's Day, Independence Day, and the National Day of Thanksgiving. In other words, the civil calendar was effectively the liturgical calendar. New Year's Eve Watch Night services were a feature of Methodism but became popular in black churches, probably because of the gatherings on New Year's Eve in 1862 to await Abraham Lincoln's Emancipation Proclamation taking effect on January 1, 1863.

We should note that revivalism and Pietism fostered a missionary fervor that led to the organization of foreign-mission societies and the sending of missionaries to other parts of the world. The missionaries usually took with them revivalistic patterns of worship or pietistic emphases that, because of a bias against ritualism, did little to promote liturgical inculturation in the mission fields of African, Asia, or Latin America.

Romantic Liturgy

Romanticism constitutes a reaction to the rationalism of the Enlightenment with its desire to return to models from the past, including liturgical models. The restoration of Benedictine monasteries in France under the influence of Dom Prosper Guéranger of Solesmes generated a need for the books necessary for the Divine Office. The chanting of psalms and canticles led to the revival of Gregorian chant at Solesmes, which Pope Pius X urged all to join in singing in his 1903 *motu proprio* on church music, *Tra le Sollecitudini* ("Among the cares of the pastoral office...").

If this seemed like a tall order, it should be noted that Lutheran liturgical restoration in Germany and America accomplished some measure of success in getting whole congregations to join in singing at least simple plainchant. But supporting the assembly's singing of chant required the use of the organ, and organ accompaniment of chant became lugubrious, as was hymn singing generally in the nineteenth and early twentieth centuries. In America especially, Protestant retrieval of chant and hymnody and of the church-year calendar and lectionary struggled against the revival songs and the promotion of the civil calendar in the churches.

Pentecostal Liturgy

From the beginning Pentecostal assemblies crossed economic, racial, and gender barriers. Recognition of gifts given to individuals to build up the whole body and spontaneous expression has been encouraged. Individuals can make their personal contribution to worship through the use of their gifts; in this way active participation is broadly inclusive. An order of service may be followed, but it can be altered easily to accommodate personal or communal need.

Prayer is an important part of Pentecostal worship. Thanksgivings and intercessions may be offered by any in the assembly and all join together in corporate yet individual prayer during times of speaking in tongues. Even during sermons persons in the assembly may spontaneously voice their agreement with or encouragement of the preacher. While the practice of interjecting comments and exclamations during the sermon is especially identified with black worship, it is in fact characteristic of much Pentecostal worship. Formulaic prayers are rare in Pentecostal worship, even in connection with the celebration of the sacraments. The frequency of celebration of Holy Communion varies from one Pentecostal assembly to another.[16]

Liturgical Renewal

Frequent celebration of Holy Communion among Protestants and frequent reception of communion by Roman Catholics has been a hallmark of liturgical renewal. Appealing to ancient practice and contemporary need, liturgical renewal sees the Eucharist as the summit of the liturgical life of the church and the source of Christian mission in the world. Liturgical renewal is a renewal of the liturgy itself as the public work of the people of God. The role of the people in offering praise and prayer was augmented. In architectural settings that gather people around the table, representatives of the people read from the Scriptures, offer prayer petitions, bring forward the gifts at the offertory, and assist with the distribution of communion. The liturgy expresses the corporate life and mission of the church and employs the gifts of its members.

3. How does liturgy relate to culture in each of these periods?

Cultural influences on the liturgy are many and various. In what follows I single out one or two major relationship between liturgy and culture in each historical period.

The Early Period: Jewish and Pagan Influences
Both Jewish and pagan influences are foundational to early Christian liturgy. Christianity inherited from the Jewish tradition the canon of sacred Scripture, the idea of gathering to read and expound on these writings, particularly on a weekly fixed day (Sabbath/Lord's Day), the celebration of annual festivals (Pesach/Pascha and Weeks/Pentecost), and patterns of prayer, especially those associated with meal (*berakah*, *todah*). Early Christianity was perceived by the Romans as a Jewish sect since its first adherents were mostly Jews.

But both Christianity and Judaism emerged in the Greco-Roman world of the first centuries of the common era and were influenced by the pervasive Hellenistic culture. We have already referred to the form of the symposium banquet that influenced both the Christian Eucharist and the Jewish Passover seder.[17] Christians assembled to celebrate the Lord's Supper in private homes or public inns where, to the Roman authorities, they were like other supper clubs. The suppression of supper clubs by the emperor Trajan c. 110 probably contributed to removing the Lord's Supper from the actual meal at night to an early-morning ritual meal consisting only of bread and wine. Roman bathing technology also influenced the practice of baptism as did the custom of laying on hands for the manumission of slaves.[18] Roman wedding and burial customs also influenced emerging Christian practice, including the need to exchange pagan sacrifices to the gods of the hearth and libations for the dead in the *refrigerium* for the celebration of the Eucharist in homes and cemeteries.

Late Antiquity: Imperial Court Influences
The church's public emergence in the Age of Constantine saw not only liturgy moved into public buildings called basilicas but also saw imperial favors bestowed on the bishops of the church. The bishop's court, at first held to effect reconciliation among Christians, was used to settle civic disputes as well. This put the bishops into the position of being magistrates, and in the highly developed ceremonial structure of Roman society, this resulted in bestowing on the bishops certain insignia and privileges, which in turn made their way into the liturgy.[19]

Since bishops were made equal to the *illustres* (the highest dignitaries in Roman society), they were granted the privilege of wearing the pallium (a kind of stole), the mappula (a ceremonial napkin), and the campagi (a special kind of footwear), and probably also a golden ring. They also had the privilege of sitting on a throne of a certain prescribed height, the right to be accompanied by lights and incense, and to be greeted with a kiss of the hand. The bishop of Rome was granted almost equal dignity with the emperor, which included being greeted on his arrival by a band of singers, having his portrait hung in public places, being waited on by attendants at his throne, and being greeted with a kiss of his foot. The honorific bestowal of crowns is attested in many inscriptions, and the custom of doffing crowns to higher rulers is reflected in the presbyters casting down their golden crowns before the throne of God and the Lamb in Revelation 4.[20] Crowns were awarded to wealthy patrons and military heroes. These crowns were originally fashioned of wood in the shape of laurel leaves and plated with gold. With the advent of oriental influence on the court in Constantinople, the Roman laurel-wreath crowns gave way to hats. These crowns (including the shape of the miter in the West) were given to bishops.

Thus the granting of imperial privileges to the bishop resulted in the ceremonial shaping of the entrance rite, as we see especially in *Ordo Romanus Primus*: the bishop greeted by the Schola Cantorum upon his arrival singing the Introit psalm, preceded in the entrance procession with lights and incense, and being attended at his throne by deacons and acolytes and surrounded by presbyters seated on benches around the throne (cathedra).

If pontifical liturgies in Rome and the West could become splendid events, they paled in comparison with the splendor of the liturgy in Constantinople when the emperor was present. We know exactly what happened in the Great Church of Hagia Sophia when the emperor was in attendance at the liturgy because it is meticulously described in *Book of Ceremonies of the Byzantine Court* compiled by the Emperor Constantine VII Porphyrogennetos (913–959).

Early Middle Ages: Royal Patronage of Liturgy in the Carolingian Empire

The Byzantine emperor exercised an actual role in the liturgy at Constantinople. But the Frankish kings and emperors became producers of liturgy. We have seen that Pippin III and Charlemagne had Roman liturgical books imported into their realm and caused them to be copied and used, thus promoting the merger of Roman and Gallican liturgical texts and practices. They recognized the power of the liturgy to unify their unruly realm and highly regarded *Romanitas* as an ideal.[21] But they also appointed the church officials, particularly the bishops and abbots, who would lead and direct these liturgies. In other words, the temporal rulers took on the normal function of bishops to establish liturgy and appoint its celebrants. Since bishops and abbots were themselves usually part of the secular governments, it was beneficial for a secular ruler to appoint (or sell the office to) someone who would be loyal. The well-established institution of proprietary churches, where the founder retained the right to appoint the clergy, blurred the boundaries between spiritual and temporal authority. In addition, the Holy Roman Emperor claimed and had exercised the special ability to appoint the pope, and the pope in turn would appoint and crown the next emperor. Thus a top-down cycle of secular investiture of church offices was perpetuated that led to the investiture controversy that came to a head in 1077 with the stand-off between Pope Gregory VII and Emperor

Henry IV at Canossa. In this Erastian system, the liturgical order was a matter of state law enforced by the civil authorities.

High Middle Ages: Gothic Height, Light, and Majesty

The high Middle Ages almost immediately evokes images of the Gothic buildings, especially the great cathedrals, that dominated the landscapes from the twelfth century on and housed Christian liturgy in spaces of great height, light, and majesty. The chief architectural characteristic of Gothic style is the pointed arch, which was a major architectural development (influenced by Arab arches). The pointed arch lends itself to a suggestion of height. This appearance is further enhanced by both the architectural features and the decoration of the building. On the exterior, the verticality is emphasized by the towers and spires and in a lesser way by strongly projecting vertical buttresses, by narrow half-columns called attached shafts that often pass through several stories of the building, by long narrow windows, and by vertical moldings around doors with their tall figurative sculpture.

Walls of Gothic buildings did not need to be as massive as the earlier Romanesque buildings. The load was borne by the flying buttress that arched externally from the springing of the vault across the roof of the aisle to a large buttress pier projecting well beyond the line of the external wall. These piers counteracted the outward thrust of the vault and buttress arch as well as stress from wind loading. The internal columns of the arcade with their attached shafts, the ribs of the vault across the rood, and the flying buttresses created a stone skeleton. Between these parts, the walls and the infill of the vaults could be of lighter construction. In fact, between the narrow buttresses the walls could be opened up into large windows. Throughout the Gothic period, due to the versatility of the pointed arch, the structure of Gothic windows developed from simple openings to immensely rich and decorative designs. The windows were very often filled with stained glass, which added a dimension of color to the light within the building as well as providing a medium for figurative and narrative art such as the windows at Chartres in France. The tall windows of the apse provided a semi-circle of light around the high altar that illuminated the focal point of the Mass, the elevation of the host.

The façade of a large church or cathedral, often referred to as the west front, is generally designed to create a powerful impression on the approaching worshiper, demonstrating both the might of God and the might of the institution that it represents. Among the best known and most typical of such façades are those of Notre Dame de Paris and Notre Dame de Reims. Central to the façade is the main portal, often flanked by additional doors. In the arch of the door, the tympanum, is often a significant piece of sculpture, most frequently Christ in majesty and judgment day. If there is a central door jamb or a tremeu, then it frequently bears a statue of the Madonna and Child. There may be much other carving, often of figures in niches set into the moldings around the portals, or in sculptural screens extending across the façade. In the center of the middle level of the façade there is a large window, which in countries other than England and Belgium is generally a rose window like those at Chartres or Reims cathedrals.[22]

The medieval church building not only achieved great height but also great length, since the series of arches could be extended indefinitely. A lady chapel was often extended from the apse, which provided another worship space behind the high altar. In fact, the building tended to be divided into compartments for different functions, most notably the nave, choir, and sanctuary, with partitions between each section. Side chapels, where private masses were celebrated, were set up off the side aisles and around the apse and often furnished by families or guilds.

Late Middle Ages: A Community of the Living and the Dead

One of the most important features of late medieval social life was the amount of attention devoted to the dead. Given the plagues that wiped out vast portions of the population, this attention was probably warranted. Confraternities forming burial societies provided decent funerals for their deceased members and arranged for masses to be said on the anniversaries of their deaths. The most frequently celebrated masses in the late Middle Ages were votive masses for the dead. Priests were ordained who did no pastoral work other than to offer votive masses. The wealthy endowed chantries in churches and monasteries to pray for their souls in purgatory. This tended to heap up the number of prayer offices for the dead to be said each day, which were added to the regular prayer offices recited by canons in cathedrals and monks in monasteries.

The Reformation: The Printed Word

It is hard to imagine how the Reformation could have spread without the invention of movable type and the printing press by Gutenberg c. 1450. The tracts and pamphlets of the Reformers were disseminated in thousands of copies in a matter of weeks. As concerns liturgy, it was possible with the technology of printing to make changes quickly that would be widespread almost immediately. In earlier times changes in liturgy were slow and well considered because producing books *in scriptoria* was a slow process. We see all the major Reformers producing two or more versions of reformed liturgies. Large Bibles for public reading and music books could still be expensive. But cheap copies of texts could be made available to the lay worshipers. Benches and pews were almost inevitable with the rise of the emphasis on the spoken and written word, not only to provide seats for hearers during long sermons but also to store the printed material needed for worship, such as hymnals and prayer books. The rise of the word was at the expense of the use of the body in worship. Benches and pews took up space that would previously have been available for the movement of people in processions or for kneeling in prayer. Worship became increasingly a rational exercise.

Post-Reformation Period: Baroque Architecture and Music

Baroque architecture was in part a response to the new need to hear as well as see. The new style was championed by the new Catholic religious orders, like the Theatines and the Jesuits, which aimed to improve popular piety and also promote doctrinal preaching. This new style was also embraced in seventeenth-century Lutheranism because the circular or oval forms of the Baroque building drew congregations around a pulpit to hear sermons and provided side and rear balconies as spaces for musical forces. Michelangelo's neoclassical Roman buildings, particularly St. Peter's Basilica, may be considered precursors of Baroque architecture. Michaelangelo's pupil Giacomo della Porta continued this work in Rome, particularly in the façade of the Jesuit church Il Gesu, which leads directly to the most important church façade of the early Baroque, Santa Susanna by Carlo Maderno.

In the seventeenth century, the Baroque style spread through Europe and Latin America, where it was particularly promoted by the Jesuits. Complex architectural-plan shapes, often based on the oval or the circle, such as the Frauenkirche in Dresden, and the dynamic opposition and interpenetration of spaces heightened the feeling of motion and engendered sensuality while also improving acoustics. With the lighting, curvaceousness, and often dizzying array of rich surface treatments in the buildings, architects unabashedly applied bright colors, gilded statuary, and illusory, vividly painted ceilings. The interior was often no more than a shell for painting and sculpture (especially in the late Baroque). Ceiling frescoes were especially popular. In the Bavarian, Czech, Polish, and Ukrainian Baroque, pear-shaped domes are ubiquitous. Some of these same features are seen in Lutheran Baroque churches in Germany and Scandinavia. Sir Christopher Wren's St. Paul's Cathedral in London is a slightly plainer Protestant version of the Baroque style.

Baroque music also used more elaborate ornamentation that reflected the opulent architecture of the period. Composers during the seventeenth and eighteenth centuries expanded the size, range, and complexity of instrumental performance and also established opera as a musical genre. Opera had an influence even on sacred and liturgical music, beginning with Claudio Monteverdi, who moved from opera to sacred music with his Vespers of 1610. Baroque music often strives for a greater level of emotional intensity than the preceding Renaissance musical style, and a Baroque piece often depicts a single particular emotion (exultation, grief, piety, and so forth) rather than several emotions within one piece. Like the architecture of the period, Baroque music employs a great deal of ornamentation, which was often improvised by the performer. Instruments came to play a greater part in Baroque music, and a cappella vocal music receded in importance. A high point of liturgical music was reached in the cantatas of Johann Sebastian Bach (1685–1750), based on readings and hymns for the day.

The Age of Enlightenment: Appeal to the Mind
Rationalism looked to the Bible for moral truth rather than scientific knowledge. Preachers were urged to inculcate practical virtues rather than dogmatic propositions. Worship should primarily edify the congregation. There was in both Roman Catholicism and Protestantism a concern for intelligibility and ritual simplicity. This was encouraged in Catholic Austria by Emperor Joseph II (1780–1790) and in Protestant

Prussia by King Frederick the Great (1740–1786). After Frederick's death, his philosopher, Immanuel Kant, wrote *Religious Within the Bounds of Reason Alone,* in which he emphasized the social dimensions of the sacraments as rites of initiation (baptism) and bonding (communion).

The Age of Enlightenment affected the spatial setting, art, and music of liturgy. The white New England meeting house with clear instead of stained-glass windows is the clearest example of unadorned Enlightenment architecture. Nothing would distract from focus on the spoken word. Sir Christopher Wren's new church buildings in London also reflected this ideal. They were "auditoriums" in that the main concern was to enable the congregation to hear the preacher.

By the end of the eighteenth century, there was a turn to the classical style in both architecture and music. The contrapuntal church music of J. S. Bach represented the end of the Baroque era in church music. The more homophonic music of his contemporary G. F. Handel was increasingly preferred and is exemplified in the classical style of J. C. Bach, Franz Josef Haydn, and Wolfgang Amadeus Mozart. The ideal of Enlightenment church music under Emperor Joseph II is seen especially in Mozart's masses and motets.

Revivalism: Appeal to the Heart

The wave of religious enthusiasm among Protestants that swept the American colonies in the 1730s and 1740s left a permanent impact on American religion. It resulted from powerful preaching that deeply affected listeners (already church members) with a profound sense of personal guilt and salvation by Christ. The Great Awakening and the later frontier camp meetings made religion intensely personal to the average person by creating a deep sense of spiritual guilt and redemption. The new style of sermons and the way people practiced their faith breathed new life into religion in America. People became emotionally involved in their religion rather than passively listening to an intellectual discourse in a detached manner. They joined enthusiastically in the singing of gospel songs and assenting to the sermon with their "amens."

The Age of Romanticism: The Quest for a Golden Age

Reason and revival, head and heart, were not as far apart as they might seem. Both approaches appealed to the individual. So, at first, did the intellectual movement known as romanticism. Romanticism was a complex artistic, literary, and intellectual movement that originated in the second half of the eighteenth century in western Europe, and gained strength in reaction to the Industrial Revolution. In part, it was a revolt against aristocratic social and political norms of the Age of Enlightenment and a reaction against the scientific rationalization of nature. An idealization of nature can be seen, heard, and read in romantic art, music, and poetry as evident in the paintings of John Constable, the music of Ludwig van Beethoven, and the poetry of William Wordsworth.

The movement validated strong emotion as an authentic source of aesthetic experience, placing new emphasis on such emotions as trepidation, horror, terror, and awe—

especially that which is experienced in confronting the sublimity of untamed nature and its picturesque qualities, both new aesthetic categories. It elevated folk art and ancient custom to something noble. Romanticism reached beyond the rational and classicist ideals to promote a revived medievalism and elements of art and narrative perceived to be authentically medieval, in an attempt to eschew the confines of population growth, urban sprawl, and industrialism.

Romanticism in liturgy engendered a search for ideal forms in the past, whether the Middle Ages or the sixteenth-century Reformation. There was an interest in retrieving and restoring these old forms and styles of celebration. These old forms had to be housed in the kind of spaces in which they originally flourished. The Gothic revival (also referred to as Victorian Gothic or Neo-Gothic) was an architectural movement that grew rapidly in the early nineteenth century, when increasingly serious and learned admirers of Neo-Gothic styles sought to revive medieval forms in contrast to the classical styles prevalent at the time.

In England, the Gothic revival was intertwined with a reawakening of "high-church" style or Anglo-Catholic belief. If revival liturgy, which flourished at the same time, can be characterized by a sense of the radical immanence of God, liturgical romanticism can be characterized by a sense of the transcendence of God. This sense of transcendence was facilitated by the revival of Gothic architecture, as promoted by the Cambridge Camden Ecclesiological Society (1839–1868), which followed the lead of the Roman Catholic architect A. W. N. Pugin (1812–1852). The long, dark Gothic nave gave the building an aura of mystery in which candles and vestments glittered amidst the pious gloom. The retrieval of the medieval Gothic church required a chancel separate from and between the nave and the sanctuary. In Anglican practice especially, the chancel was filled with lay choirs dressed in cassocks and surplices like pseudo-monks, which were relocated from the west gallery.

A Byzantine revival also emerged in 1840s in western Europe and peaked in the last quarter of the nineteenth century in the Russian Empire. It is seen in many churches and public buildings in the United Kingdom and the United States erected in the late nineteenth and early twentieth centuries. Its circle-within-a-square form lent itself to the auditorium plan favored by the revivalists, as in the Moody Church in Chicago.

Modernity: The Use of New Technologies

The desire to promote popular involvement in public life generally (e.g., political rallies, sporting events) had its counterpart in the movement to promote the participation of the people in their liturgy. This required providing material to assist the people. The improved technology of printing made cheap editions of books such as missals and hymnals and Bibles readily available. People could own their own copies. But churches also began to provide such books for worshipers. Then new and cheaper forms of printing also made it possible for local churches to duplicate their own materials. Perhaps the greatest revolution in the assembly's participation in the liturgy was the invention of the mimeograph machine. After that there was a succession of new technologies that have made an impact on our experience of worship: photo duplication, the Internet, PowerPoint projection, video screens, and so forth.

Television and the World Wide Web, as well as air travel, have fostered an awareness of the global church and led to a sharing of cultural-liturgical resources, even allowing local assemblies to acquire a more cross-cultural character. Local assemblies can sing songs from Christian communities in different parts of the world. Thus one encounters African American gospel songs being sung in Swedish churches and East or South African songs being sung in American congregations. Drumming and dancing, already a vital part of African worship, are now attempted in North America.

4. What are the strategies of relating liturgy to culture?

The relationship between liturgy and culture is a perennial pastoral concern. It is so on several levels. Culture is the way of life of a people by which they express their values and worldview. In complex modern societies people actually participate in several cultures simultaneously: a national culture, a regional culture, a local culture, an ethnic or racial culture, a family culture, and a religious culture. To which of these cultures should liturgy be relevant?

Certainly liturgy should be relevant to religious culture. Liturgy is itself an expression of the religious culture, which expresses faith values and a worldview that may challenge or support the values and worldviews of the other cultures in which the people participate. The cultures of the worlds inhabited by the worshiping people cannot be ignored in liturgy.

The strategic relationships of the gospel to the cultures of this world have been various and complex. H. Richard Niebuhr famously distinguished five such relationships: Christ against culture, Christ of culture, Christ above culture, Christ and culture in paradox, and Christ the transformer of culture.[23] All have been tried at different times in history; all have their advantages and disadvantages.[24]

Issues of how liturgy relates to culture loom large in a missionary situation. The Nairobi Report of the Lutheran World Federation Study of Worship and Culture identified four major ways in which liturgy relates to culture:[25]

1. Liturgy is transcultural—it includes orders and texts that witness to the church as a global communion.
2. Liturgy is contextual—it makes use of natural or cultural symbols that are indigenous to each locality.
3. Liturgy is countercultural—it always holds out a vision of an alternative worldview and lifestyle.
4. Liturgy is cross-cultural—it uses expressions from different cultures.

Liturgy that is catholic and evangelical should express all four of these cultural characteristics simultaneously. The historic liturgy includes texts that come out of many different times and places. Yet it also finds ways of incorporating contemporary expressions from its host culture (often expressions we don't think about because we take them for granted). But its eschatological perspective will always challenge the values of the world in which we live.

But mission strategy and pastoral need might result in one or another of these aspects being emphasized more than the others. In the mission field of North America, the desire to reach an increasing portion of the population that is unchurched has caused the contextual aspect of liturgy to receive special attention. The kind of seeker-oriented contemporary worship offered by the megachurches emerged at the same time as Donald McGavran (1897–1990) of Fuller Theological Seminary developed principles of "church growth" based on his experience in the mission fields of India. McGavran's work, which includes the seminal church-growth text, *Understanding Church Growth* (1970), substantially changed the methods by which missionaries identify and prioritize groups of persons for missionary work. It also stimulated the church-growth movement in the United States and around the world. Lead pastors of evangelical megachurches drew on his principles to reach the unchurched.

Three major principles of the church-growth movement are:

1. that God's will for every local congregation is numerical growth;
2. that the needs and sensibilities of the unchurched should determine the strategy of the church;
3. that the lack of adequate church growth worldwide proves the need for a new Reformation.

Pioneering megachurch pastors such as Robert Schuller, Bill Hybels, and Rick Warren embraced these principles and designed their outreach and worship to meeting people where they were. In the 1980s they and others developed seeker services that were high on entertainment value and didn't require a lot of knowledge in order to participate. The idea was to attract those who were alienated from the church from previous experiences or to those who had no experience of the church at all. Seekers would be drawn into the inner life of the church through small groups and midweek services where core Christian teachings would be communicated.

Ironically, the development of the Christian initiation of adults in Roman Catholic and other churches has not had a dissimilar objective. To be sure, seekers would encounter the core elements of the Christian faith in the Sunday liturgies. But the approach of the adult catechumenate is to take the seekers aside and explore with them these core elements to provide knowledge and understanding. For the liturgical churches the Sunday liturgy must be first and foremost relevant to the faith community whose public work it is, and it must be intact in order to form people in the faith. But even so, liturgical renewal is in agreement with the church-growth movement that liturgy must be rooted in the culture of the people.

5. How does inculturation work?

Sometimes it is necessary to intentionally bring elements of the local culture into the liturgy. This is called inculturation, and it works in different ways, as the Philippine Benedictine scholar Anscar Chapungco has demonstrated in his pioneering work. He identified at least three: creative assimilation, dynamic equivalence, and organic progression.[26]

1. *Creative assimilation* is the process of adding new cultural expressions to the received liturgical rite. The history of liturgy is full of examples since Christianity did not come into the world with a culture of its own. Its forms and content generated a culture, but along the way the historic liturgies assimilated elements of Semitic, Greek, Latin, and many other cultures as it moved from a base in the Mediterranean world east, south, west, and north. Almost everything in Christian liturgy is a cultural inheritance from some time and place. Liturgy is full of instances of cultural assimilation, especially in music and architectural assimilation, some of which have been identified in this chapter. It is a process that is still occurring.

2. *Dynamic equivalence* is the method of replacing one cultural expression with another that accomplishes the same thing for the sake of comprehending the meaning of the words or the ritual act. The terms *dynamic equivalence* and *formal equivalence* were first used by Eugene Nida to indicate contrasting approaches to translation, especially of the Bible. "Formal equivalence" attempts to render a word-for-word translation that is as faithful as possible to the original, even at the expense of natural expression in the target language. "Dynamic equivalence" attempts to convey the thought expressed in a source text in a natural way, even at the expense of literalness, word order, grammatical voice, and so forth, in the source text, if necessary.

The same issues come up in liturgical texts. For example, the Latin *Et cum spiritu tuo* has been translated "And also with you" rather than more literally "And with your Spirit." It has been argued that "And also with you" reflects the social greeting in the Semitic idiom that lies behind the Latin. Dynamic equivalence may also be sought for ritual acts such as the greeting (kiss) of peace. Since the greeting of peace is an act of reconciliation among the worshipers, one African ritual has the worshipers washing their hands in the same bowl, so as to say, "I have nothing against you."

3. *Organic progression* means developing new rites and prayers for situations that have not previously been encountered. For example, once upon a time the church had to come up with coronation rites. Current examples might be interfaith community services such as a communal response to a disaster (e.g., 9/11/01) or a national day of thanksgiving. Models from the past can be instructive for present and future pastoral needs.

For further reading

Bradshaw, Paul F. *The Search for the Origins of Christian Worship: Sources and Methods for the Study of Early Liturgy*, rev. ed. New York: Oxford University Press, 2006.

Chapungco, Ansgar J. *Cultural Adaptation of the Liturgy*. New York: Paulist, 1982.

Klauser, Theodor. *A Short History of the Western Liturgy*, 2d ed., trans. John Halliburton. New York: Oxford University Press, 1979.

Metzger, Marcel. *History of the Liturgy: The Major Stages*. Collegeville: Liturgical, 1997.

Palazzo, Eric. *A History of Liturgical Books from the Beginning to the Thirteenth Century*, trans. Madeleine Beaumont. Collegeville: Liturgical, 1998.

Ramshaw, Gail. *Christian Worship: 100,000 Sundays of Symbols and Rituals*. Minneapolis: Fortress, 2009.

Senn, Frank C. *Christian Liturgy: Catholic and Evangelical*. Minneapolis: Fortress Press, 1997.
———. *The People's Work: A Social History of the Liturgy*. Minneapolis: Fortress Press, 2006.

Stauffer, S. Anita, ed. "Nairobi Report." In *Christian Worship: Unity in Cultural Diversity*, Geneva: Lutheran World Federation, 1996.

Wegman, Herman. *Christian Worship in East and West: A Study Guide to Liturgical History*, trans. Gordon Lathrop. New York: Pueblo/Collegeville: Liturgical, 1985.

White, James F. *A Brief History of Christian Worship*. Nashville: Abingdon, 1993.
———. *Documents of Christian Worship: Descriptive and Interpretative Sources*. Louisville: Westminster John Knox, 1992.
———. *Protestant Worship: Traditions in Transition*. Louisville: Westminster John Knox, 1993.
———. *Roman Catholic Worship: Trent to Today*. New York: Paulist, 1995.

3
The Principal Order of Service

1. What are the names of the principal order of service?
2. How did this order develop throughout history?
3. What is the lectionary and how does it work?
4. What are the parts of a eucharistic prayer?
5. What is the difference between a "High Mass" and a "Low Mass"?

1. What are the names of the principal order of service?

The principal order of service has various names, most of which reflect the fact that it is centered in the meal known in 1 Corinthians 11 as "the Lord's Supper" and in the book of Acts as "the breaking of bread."

The term *Eucharist* was applied to this meal liturgy by Ignatius of Antioch and Justin Martyr. From the third century on, it was applied more to the eucharistic prayer than to the whole liturgy. But in the modern liturgical renewal movement, "Eucharist" has emerged as a preferred term for the meal liturgy. The *Book of Common Prayer* of the Episcopal Church in the U.S.A. designates this service as "The Holy Eucharist."

While the term *Eucharist* was also used in the Eastern churches, their term for the principal service is Divine Liturgy.

In the Roman Rite the term for the chief service is "Mass" (*Missa*). This term comes from the dismissal at the end of the service: *Ite missa est* (which is hard to translate; what is "It is sent"?). Martin Luther kept the term *Mass* in both Latin and German, although the term "Divine Service" (*Gottesdienst*) was also used.

The sixteenth-century Reformers also preferred the name "Lord's Supper" because of their partiality to the apostle Paul. The First Prayer Book of King Edward VI (1549) calls this service "The Supper of the Lorde and The Holy Communion Commonly Called the Masse." The Second Prayer Book (1552) designates it "The Order for the Administracion of the Lordes Supper or Holye Communion." In the Anglican tradition the service was usually called simply "Holy Communion." In the American Lutheran Common Service tradition, the names "The Service" and "The Communion" appeared on facing pages of hymnals. In *Lutheran Book of Worship* (1978), the name given is "the Service of Holy Communion."

Some Protestants might argue that for them the Service of the Word is the principal order of service because that is what is celebrated on most Sundays throughout the year. However, the very reason that the Protestant Reformers in the Lutheran, Reformed, and Anglican traditions used the ante-communion as their Service of the Word is because they thought it pointed toward the fullness of this order in the communion service.

2. How did this order develop throughout history?

Word and meal existed together in the principal Christian liturgy from the beginning, probably because the prevailing cultural form of the banquet that the early church used was the symposium, which included readings and discussion as well as eating and drinking.[1] In the previous chapter we traced the historical and cultural factors that contributed to the development of this form. Here I provide outlines of historical instances of the development of the principal service.

A. Sunday Liturgy in Justin Martyr's First Apology, c. 150
This is the first full description of a liturgy of word and meal, presumably as it was done in Rome since Justin is writing to the Roman Senate. The following outline combines the orders of service in chapters 65 (Baptism) and 67 (Sunday).

> Reading from the "memoirs of the apostles and the prophets" by lectors
> Preaching by the president
> Common prayer
> Greeting of peace
> Transfer of gifts of bread and wine mixed with water
> Eucharistic prayer by the president "to the best of his ability"
> The people assent saying "Amen."
> Breaking of bread
> Distribution
> Dismissal
> Collection for the poor left with the president
> Extended distribution of the consecrated elements to the absent by the deacons

B. The Jerusalem Liturgy, c. 385
This order of service is reconstructed on the basis of references in the *Mystagogical Catecheses* of Cyril of Jerusalem and the *Diary* of Egeria.

> The congregation assembles, men on one side, women on the other, clergy in the apse
> Lessons read by readers interspersed with psalms sung by a cantor with the assembly
>   responding to a refrain (antiphon)

The series of readings ends with the Gospel read by a deacon or a presbyter

Homilies given by the presbyters and finally by the bishop

Blessing and dismissal of the catechumens

Blessing and dismissal of the candidates for baptism (energumens or competentes)

Blessing and dismissal of the penitents

Prayers of the faithful in litany form led by the deacon, the people responding: Kyrie eleison; the bishop offers the concluding prayer

The kiss of peace exchanged by the clergy with each other and the people with each other

Loaves of bread and cups of wine brought to the altar

Apostolic greeting from the bishop and Sursum corda

Eucharistic prayer, including the Sanctus and institution narrative and concluding with intercessions and a doxology

The Lord's Prayer accompanied by another diaconal litany

"Holy things for the holy people" with the response "One alone is holy…"

Breaking of bread and communion administered by the bishop (bread) and a deacon (cup)

Psalm 33 sung during communion

Episcopal blessing and diaconal dismissal

C. The Byzantine Divine Liturgy in Codex Barberini, Gr. 336, c. 800

The Byzantine Divine Liturgy developed in the city of Constantinople (now Istanbul), which had earlier been called Byzantium. It is the second largest liturgical rite in Christendom after the Roman Rite. While this codex is from the early ninth century, it undoubtedly reflects the earlier development of the order of service. But it also shows that by the eighth century the Old Testament reading, the prayers over the penitents, and the prayer of blessing that concludes the liturgy of the word in the time of John Chrysostom have fallen away.[2] While there definitely was preaching, since we have examples of it, it is not specified in the order.

Prothesis (preparation of the bread and wine in the sacristy)

Blessing

Litany and prayer I

Antiphon I

Litany and prayer II

Antiphon II

Litany and prayer III

Antiphon III with added troparia (refrains), entrance procession, entrance prayer

Trisagion prayer and chant

Procession to the throne

Greeting: "Peace to all"

Epistle

Alleluia

Gospel
Prayers of the faithful
Cherubic hymn and prayer of the hymn
Great entrance with the gifts
Litany and prayer of the Proskomide
Kiss of peace
Nicene Creed
Eucharistic dialogue
Anaphora (either St. John Chrysostom or St. Basil)
Litany and prayer
Our Father
Prayer of inclination
Prayer of elevation
Elevation: "Holy things for the holy people."
Chant: "One is holy…"
Breaking of bread
Communion
Blessing with gifts: "O God, save your people and bless your inheritance"
Chant: "We have seen the true light…"
Gifts returned to the altar and incensed
Chant: "Amen. May our mouth be filled with your praise"
Gifts returned to the altar of preparation
Litany and prayer of thanksgiving
Dismissal
Prayer behind the ambo
Psalm 112:2, "Blessed be the name of the Lord…," thrice
Prayer in the Skeuophylakion (area to the right of the altar where vessels and
    vestments are stored)
Apolysis (dismissal prayer)

Note: Other Eastern liturgies (e.g., St. Mark, St. James) were influenced by the Byzantine Rite and generally follow it, except for their unique anaphoras. The Byzantine Rite is used currently in various languages by all the Eastern Orthodox churches and by the Greek Catholic churches (Eastern Rite churches that use the Byzantine Rite).

D. The Gallican Rite in the First Letter of Germanus of Paris (d. 576)

The term *Gallican Rite* refers in the first instance to the liturgy of ancient Gaul (France), and in the second to a family of non-Roman Western rites that flourished in western Europe until they were mostly displaced by the Roman Rite during the eighth century, but modifying the Roman rite in the process. Variants of this rite continued to exist in Milan (which was a gateway to Gaul) and Toledo (the Visigothic Rite). The following is the order of the liturgy described in the first letter of Germanus of Paris, published as

Expositio antiquae liturgiae gallicanae. The parts of the anaphora described by Germanus are similar to the parts described by Isidore, Bishop of Seville (d. 636), in his book *On Ecclesiastical Offices*. Propers for the Gallican liturgy are found in the *Missale Gothicum*.[3]

Preparation of the offerings
Praelegendum (entrance psalm)
Call for silence and greeting
Trisagion (in Greek and Latin)
Kyrie
Benedictus (Song of Zachariah)
Old Testament reading
Collect after the Old Testament reading
Responsory
Epistle
Benedicite opera omnia (Song of the Three Children from Daniel 3)
Thrice-Holy before the Gospel
Gospel
Sanctus after the Gospel
Homily
Preces
Collect after the Preces
Dismissal of the catechumens
Offertory
Preface to the faithful and collect
Reading of the diptychs and collect
Exchange of the peace and collect
Anaphora: variable *Contestatio/Immolatio* (introduction leading to Sanctus), variable *Vere Sanctus* ("Truly holy..."), institution narrative, variable *post mysterium* (prayer after the words of institution)
Breaking of the bread
Lord's Prayer
Episcopal blessing
Communion
Trecanum (post-communion hymn of thanksgiving to the Trinity)
Post-communion collect
Dismissal

E. The Roman Bishop's Mass in Ordo Romanus Primus, c. 700

The *Ordines Romani* are rubrical books. The first *Ordo* describes the ceremonies of a solemn Mass on Easter Day celebrated by the pope himself at St. Mary Major.[4] As in the Byzantine order of the same period the Old Testament reading has been dropped, but the Our Father has not yet been added; it was added by Gregory the Great. The

Nicene Creed was not added to the Roman Mass until the eleventh century. The *Ordo* gives directions for the Easter Day Mass, which allows for the communion of a large number of people.

A great entourage of civil and ecclesiastical dignitaries accompany the pope from the Lateran palace to St. Mary Major Church. Along the way a notary from that district informs the pope as to how many men and women were baptized the night before. All the books and vessels needed for the service at this station church are carried in the procession. At the church the pope is taken into the sacristy to vest and the gospel book is placed on the altar. When the pope is ready to enter the church, he is preceded by lights and incense.

Introit and Gloria Patri sung by the Schola Cantorum while the pope processes into
    the basilica, reverences and incenses the altar
Kyrie sung while the pope goes to his throne
Gloria in excelsis begun by the pope
Salutation (*Pax tecum*) and collect
Epistle read by a subdeacon
Alleluia sung by cantors
Gospel read by a deacon
Offertory psalm sung by the Schola while a deacon and acolyte prepare the altar
    and the pope receives the offerings of the notables, men and women separately. The
    bread offerings of the people are gathered into a linen sack held by the acolytes;
    the wine offerings are poured into a huge chalice called a scyphus. The archdeacon
    receives the bread and wine offerings of the pope and arranges them on the altar.
The pope goes to the altar and begins the canon
At the concluding doxology the chalice is elevated
Pax domini and greeting of peace
Fraction and commingling
Agnus Dei sung
The pope communes himself from the bread on the altar and receives the chalice
    from the archdeacon. He then returns to his throne. The archdeacon announces the
    place and time of the next station mass (for those who are leaving before commu-
    nion). There is a second commixture as bread from the pope's oblation is added to
    the bread in the sacks and wine from the pope's chalice is poured into the scyphus.
    (This may be regarded as consecration by contagion.)
The auxiliary bishops are communed by the bishop from his throne while the priests
    commune at the altar. The pope then goes down to commune the notables while the
    priests assist with the communion of the people. The people go to the communion
    stations to receive bread from the sack and drink wine from the scyphus with a
    straw (fistula).

During the communion the Schola sings the communion psalm. When the pope
gets to the women he signals the choir to stop the psalm and they go to the Gloria
Patri and antiphon.
The pope sits down and washes his hands and then goes to the altar for the final
prayer
Final prayer (*Oratio ad complendum*)
Dismissal: *Ite missa est*
Procession of all the ministers to the sacristy

Note: A special feature of Roman liturgy was the *fermentum*. Louis Duchesne explains:
"It was a matter of importance in the Roman Church that the ritual of Communion
should contain a clear and striking expression of ecclesiastical unity. Hence the custom
of the *fermentum*, that is, of sending consecrated bread from the bishop's Mass to the
priests at the *Tituli* [title churches]; hence also the significance of the rite of the *sancta*,
that is, of putting into the chalice at the *Pax domini* a fragment consecrated at the preceding Mass and brought forth at the beginning of the present one."[5]

F. Martin Luther's Formula Missae et Communionis, 1523

Martin Luther wrote: "It is not now nor ever has been our intention to abolish the liturgical service of God [*cultus Dei*] completely, but rather to purify the one that is now in
use from the wretched accretions which corrupt it and to point out an evangelical use."[6]
Luther's first revision of the Mass left the Mass entirely in Latin.

Sermon before the Mass (the place of medieval preaching missions) or
  after the Gospel
Introit for the day in the church year and Gloria Patri
Kyrie eleison (9 times)
Gloria in excelsis
Salutation and collect
Epistle
Gradual and/or Alleluia. No sequences or proses (except for Christmas and Pentecost)
Gospel with candles and incense
Nicene Creed sung while the altar is prepared
Preface leading to
Words of institution
Sanctus with elevation during the *Benedictus qui venit*
Lord's Prayer
Pax domini
Agnus Dei
Communion of the celebrant (private communion prayer of the priest retained,
  changing pronouns to plural)

Communion psalm sung during the communion of the people
Post-communion prayer (pronouns changed to plural)
Salutation and *Benedicamus Domino* (Let us bless the Lord. R/ Thanks be to God.)
Aaronic benediction or Psalm 67:6-7

Note: Communicants were to announce their intention to receive the sacrament on the day before, be examined and absolved, and move into the chancel during the creed as a witness to others.

G. Martin Luther's Deutsche Messe und Gottesdienst, 1526

Luther's German Mass and Order of Service was not intended to replace his Latin Mass but to be used in village churches lacking a professional choir. In this order Luther replaced some of the liturgical texts with chorale versifications. He expressed his opposition to liturgical legalism in the preface: "In the first place, I would kindly and for God's sake request all those who see this order of service or desire to follow it: Do not make it a rigid law to bind or entangle anyone's conscience, but use it in Christian liberty as long, when, where, and how you find it to be practical and useful."[7]

Introit psalm or German hymn
Kyrie eleison (3 times)
Salutation and collect
Epistle
German hymn
Gospel
Versification of the Nicene Creed (*Wir glauben all an einen Gott*) sung while the elements are prepared on the altar
Sermon
Paraphrase (catechesis) on the Lord's Prayer (from pulpit or altar)
Exhortation to the communicants (catechesis)
Words of institution sung over the bread
Distribution of the bread while the German Sanctus is sung
Words of institution over the cup
Distribution of the cup while the German Agnus Dei is sung
Post-communion prayer ("We give thanks to thee, almighty God...")
Aaronic benediction

H. The Order of Mass in the Brandenburg-Nuremberg Church Order, 1533

Of the numerous Reformation church orders in sixteenth-century Germany, this one was one of the most influential. It was drafted by Andreas Osiander, pastor of St. Sebaldus Church in Nuremberg, and Johann Brenz, pastor in Schwäbsich-Hall, at the request of Margrave George the Pious of Brandenburg and also used in Nuremberg, the first city to adopt the Reformation (in 1524).[8] The order of Mass is partly in Latin and partly in German, showing the influence of both of Luther's orders.

> Confiteor (prayer of confession said by the minister)
> Latin Introit or German psalm or hymn
> Kyrie eleison
> Gloria in excelsis
> Salutation and German collect
> Epistle in German (continuous reading)
> Latin gradual
> Gospel in German (continuous reading)
> Creed sung in Latin or German
> Sermon
> Exhortation to the communicants in German from the altar
> Words of institution sung in German
> Sanctus
> Lord's Prayer in Latin or German
> Pax domini
> Distribution of communion while the choir sings the Agnus Dei and a responsory in Latin or the congregation sings a German hymn
> Thanksgiving collect in German (fuller than Luther's)
> Aaronic benediction

Note: A Church Order for Brandenburg in 1540, under Elector Joachim II, expanded this order of service with Latin Proper Prefaces and Sanctus, four German prayers said silently by the celebrant during the singing of the Sanctus, and Latin verses sung by the choir during the offertory and communion.

I. Ulrich Zwingli's German Communion Service in Action oder Bruch des Nachtmals, 1525

Communion in Zurich was celebrated four times a year; therefore, this communion service was used only four times a year (although communion at Easter took up Maundy Thursday and Good Friday as well in order to commune everyone). The ordinary Sunday morning service at Zurich was a form of the late medieval pulpit office called Prone.[9] The communion service was as follows:

> Preparation of the elements
> Invocation
> Collect
> Epistle: 1 Corinthians 11:20-29. Response: "Praise be to God"
> Gloria in excelsis (said antiphonally between the men and the women)

Gospel: John 6:47-63. Response: "Praise be to God"
Apostles' Creed (said antiphonally between the men and the women)
Exhortation
Fencing of the table (forbidding the unworthy to approach)
The Lord's Prayer without doxology (kneeling)
Prayer of humble access (kneeling)
Words of institution
Breaking of bread
Ministers' communion
Communion of the people (the elements delivered to the people in their seats by the
   deacons)
Post-communion Psalm 113 (recited antiphonally between the men and the women)
Dismissal

J. Balthasar Hubmaier's "A Form of Christ's Supper" (1527): An Anabaptist Celebration of the Lord's Supper[10]

This is the only example of an early sixteenth-century Anabaptist liturgy. Hubmaier (c. 1480–1528), a former Catholic priest, was one of the few theologically trained Anabaptist leaders. He received a doctor's degree in 1512 from the University of Ingolstadt under Johannes Eck and became the university's vice-rector by 1515. After embracing Anabaptist tenets he was active in Switzerland and engaged in disputes with Zwingli. Twice imprisoned and tortured on the rack, he was burned at the stake at Vienna in 1528 (the year a number of Anabaptist leaders were executed by Catholic, Lutheran, and Reformed authorities); his wife was drowned in the Danube with a stone around her neck three days later. Hubmaier was considered especially dangerous because he believed that the ideal of a pure gathered church could be reconciled with the idea of a territorial church, and he experimented with this in the Austrian village of Waldshut. It was for this community that he provided *Ein Form des Nachtmals Christi*.

Confession of sins the week before the celebration
Reading and exposition of Scripture
Response by the congregation with the hymn, "Stay with us, O Christ"
Further teaching on the preaching text "from one to whom something is revealed"
Self-examination according to 1 Corinthians 11
Silence
Lord's Prayer
Pledge of love
Prayer of thanksgiving
Breaking and distribution of bread as the words of institution are spoken
Exclamation of thanks
Passing of the cup as the words of institution are spoken

Call to live the baptismal covenant
Blessing

K. Martin Bucer's German Communion Service in Psalter mit aller Kirchenübung, 1537–1539

The German service in Strassburg developed from the German Mass of Diebold Schwartz in 1524 through the various amendments under the superintendency of Martin Bucer after 1530.[11] When the Lord's Supper wasn't celebrated, the liturgy of the word (ante-communion) was used.

Confession of sins
Scriptural words of pardon (1 Timothy 1)
Absolution
Psalm or hymn or Kyrie and Gloria in excelsis
Collect for illumination
Matrical psalm
Gospel
Sermon
Collection of alms
Preparation of the elements while the Apostles' Creed is sung
Intercessions
Prayer of consecration
Lord's Prayer
Exhortation
Words of institution
Breaking of bread
Distribution of communion while a psalm or hymn is sung
Post-communion collect
Aaronic benediction
Dismissal

L. Jean Calvin's French Communion Service at Geneva in Form and Manner, 1542

Calvin served the French Protestant congregation in Strasbourg at Bucer's invitation from 1538 to 1541 and prepared a French service based on the Strassburg German service. When Calvin returned to Geneva, he prepared a service that made only a few changes his Strasbourg service.[12] Moving the words of institution from before the communion to before the exhortation and consecration prayer emphasized their role as a warrant for the celebration than as an act of consecration. Calvin was not able to persuade the Council of Geneva to celebrate Holy Communion more than four times a year. As in Strassburg, when the Lord's Supper wasn't celebrated the liturgy of the word (ante-communion) was used. This order influenced Reformed orders of service in Scotland (under John Knox) and The Netherlands.

Scripture sentence: Psalm 124:8
Confession of sins
Prayer for pardon
Metrical psalm
Collect for illumination
Reading
Sermon
Collection of alms
Intercessions
Lord's Prayer in a long paraphrase
Preparation of the elements while the Apostles' Creed is sung
Words of institution
Exhortation
Prayer of consecration
Breaking of bread
Communion while a psalm or other Scriptures are read
Post-communion collect
Aaronic benediction

M. The Holy Communion in the First Prayer Book of King Edward VI, 1549

The *Book of Common Prayer* was an entirely vernacular worship resource that included all offices needed in the parish church and cathedral.[13] It was largely the work of Thomas Cranmer, Archbishop of Canterbury. The Holy Communion was based on a number of sources, including the medieval Sarum (Salisbury) Use of the Roman Rite. The material from the invitation to communion through the comfortable words was an English translation of material from the Cologne Church Order (1543) authorized by Archbishop Hermann von Wied that was set into the Latin Mass in 1548 as the communion office. The form of the words of institution is from the Brandenburg-Nuremberg Church Order. Following Luther and Bucer, the Prayer Book invites the communicants to come into the choir (chancel) at the offertory. A full musical setting of this communion service was provided by John Merbecke in 1550.

Lord's Prayer (minister)
Collect for purity
Introite sung by clerkes (whole psalm)
"Lorde have mercy" sung three times by clerkes or said by priest
"Glory be to God" on high sung by clerkes or said by priest
Salutation and collect for the day

Collect for the king
Epistle
Gospel
Nicene Creed sung by clerkes or said by priest
Sermon or homily
Exhortation to communicants
Offertory sentences
Procession with gifts
Sursum corda
Preface (5 propers)
Sanctus and Benedictus
Eucharistic prayer including intercessions, commemorations, epiclesis, words of
   institution, memorial or oblationary prayer
The Lord's Prayer
Invitation to communion
Confession of sins
Absolution
Comfortable words
Prayer of humble access
"Lamb of God" sung by clerkes or said
Administration of Holy Communion
Post-communion verse
Prayer of thanksgiving
Blessing

Note: This order of service received renewed interest among the non-Jurors in the Scottish Episcopal Church in the eighteenth century, and from them it influenced the order in the *Book of Common Prayer* of the Protestant Episcopal Church in the United States in 1790.

N. The Holy Communion in the Second Prayer Book of King Edward VI, 1552

There was much criticism of the first Prayer Book. Cranmer solicited critiques from eminent reformers such as Martin Bucer before undertaking a revision. The communion service in the second Prayer Book is a drastic revision of the first, accomplished more through a relocation of various sections than by a thorough rewriting. The high altars had been demolished in 1550 and communion tables were set up lengthwise in the choir. There has been much debate on the theology of the Eucharist implied in the 1552 communion service, especially because of the formulas of administration. Communion was celebrated three or four times a year in most parishes. If Holy Communion was not celebrated, the ante-communion (liturgy of the word) was used, as in the Lutheran and Reformed practice.

Lord's Prayer said by minister
Collect for purity
Rehearsal of the Decalogue with response: "Lorde have mercy upon us, and encline
    our heartes to kepe thys law"
Collect for the day
Collect for the king
Epistle
Gospel
Nicene Creed said
Sermon or homily
Offertory sentences
Collection of gifts
Intercessions
Exhortation to communion
Invitation to communion
Confession of sins
Absolution
Comfortable words
Sursum corda
Preface (with five propers)
Sanctus (without Benedictus)
Prayer of humble access
Prayer of consecration
Words of institution
Administration of Holy Communion
The Lord's Prayer
Oblationary prayer or thanksgiving
"Glory be to God on high"
Blessing

Note: The Second Prayer Book was suppressed under Queen Mary I in 1553 but was restored under Queen Elizabeth I in 1559 with an Act of Uniformity passed in Parliament. The joining of the 1549 and 1552 communion distribution formulas in the 1559 Prayer Book made possible a more comprehensive understanding of the sacrament more congenial to the Elizabeth settlement. This order of service remained intact in the Church of England until the late twentieth century. It was also the communion service provided by John Wesley for the Methodists in America.

O. The Roman Mass in the Missale Romanum of Pope Pius V, 1570
The Council of Trent entrusted the reform of the Roman Mass to the Roman curia. The so-called Tridentine Mass is the Roman Missal of Pope Pius V, which is actually

the Liturgy of the Diocese of Rome, now imposed on all local churches in communion with the Bishop of Rome. It was the Roman Catholic Mass until the reforms after the Second Vatican Council. The last edition of this Mass was the 1962 Missal of Pope John XXIII.

Preparatory office of the celebrant and servers with mutual *Confiteor* ("I confess to almighty God...") and *Misereatur* ("May almighty God have mercy on you...")
Introit: Antiphon, psalm verse, Gloria Patri, antiphon
Kyrie, eleison (nine times)
Gloria in excelsis Deo (omitted when vestments are violet or black and votive masses)
Salutation and collect of the day or votive mass
Alleluia, gradual, and tract when appointed
Gospel with acclamations
Nicene Creed
Offertory verse during preparation of the elements
Offertory prayers
Lavabo (washing of hands)
Orate, fraters...
Secret prayer(s)
Preface dialogue (Sursum corda) and preface with proper, if appointed
Sanctus
Canon (including the words of institution)
Our Father with embolism, "Deliver us from all evil"
Pax Domini
Commixture
Agnus Dei and communion antiphon
Communion of the priest with private communion prayer and "Lord, I am not worthy"
If any of the faithful wish to commune the Confiteor is repeated by the deacon or server. The people say, "Lord, I am not worthy..." as they approach the altar.
Post-communion prayer
Salutation and *Benedicamus Domino*
Ite missa est
Trinitarian blessing
Last Gospel (John 1:1-14)

P. The Westminster Directory of Worship, 1644

The Puritan Parliament abolished the *Book of Common Prayer*, along with the monarchy and the episcopate. Since the Puritan party was composed of Presbyterians and Congregationalists the committee assigned to produce a new liturgy proposed instead a directory of worship. An order was provided with directions that could inform free prayer or be turned into prayer by the minister.[14]

Call to worship

Prayers of approach: adoration, supplications for worthiness and illumination

Old Testament reading (one chapter in course)

New Testament reading (one chapter in course)

Metrical psalms sung before or between the readings

Sermon

General prayer

Lord's Prayer

Offertory

Invitation exhortation and fencing of tables

Setting apart elements from all common uses

Words of institution

Exhortation

Prayer of consecration: include thanksgiving for creation and providence, for redemption, for the word and the sacraments, anamnesis, epiclesis

Breaking of bread

Distribution

Communion. The celebrant receives first and then the elements are passed to the
  communicants in their seats or around the communion table by deacons.

Exhortation to a worth life

Post-communion prayer

Metrical psalm of praise

Solemn blessing

Q. The Common Service of the Evangelical Lutheran Church, 1888

The order of service was prepared by a committee from several Lutheran church bodies
in America for use in English-speaking congregations. It was to be based on "the common consent of the pure Lutheran church orders of the sixteenth century, and when
there is not an entire agreement among them the consent of the largest number of
greatest weight."[15]

A Hymn of Invocation may be sung

The Invocation

The Confession of Sins

The Introit: Antiphon, Verse, Gloria Patri, Antiphon

The Kyrie (three times)

The Gloria in excelsis Deo

The Salutation and Collect of the Day

The Epistle

The Halleluia (omitted Septuagesima through Good Friday) or Sentence or Hymn

The Gospel

The Nicene Creed or The Apostles' Creed
The Hymn
The Sermon (ends with the Votum—"The peace of God which passeth all under-
    standing...)
The Offertory: "Create in me a clean heart, O God" sung by the congregation
The Offering of Gifts
The General Prayer
The Lord's Prayer
The Communion Hymn
The Preface Dialogue and Preface with Proper, if appointed
The Sanctus
The Lord's Prayer (said or sung by the minister)
The Words of Institution
The Pax
The Agnus Dei
The Distribution
The Nunc Dimittis
The Prayer of Thanksgiving (from Luther's German Mass)
The Salutation and Benedicamus
The Aaronic Benediction

Note: This order of service was adopted in various Lutheran hymnals for English language worship and served as the basis of the Common Liturgy in the Service Book and
Hymnal of 1958.

R. The Roman Mass in the Missal of Pope Paul VI, 1969

The reform of the Roman Mass after the Second Vatican Council is noteworthy for the
restructuring of the entrance rite to integrate the penitential rite into the order of Mass,
the restoration of an Old Testament reading with a responsorial psalm, the requirement
of preaching at Mass, litanized intercessions with responses for the people, four eucharistic prayers (the decision of Pope Paul VI), and use of vernacular. The International
Consultation on English Texts (ICEL) prepared texts for English-language use in the
Roman Rite in eleven countries and was adopted in the service books of several Protestant denominations that worship in English.

Entrance psalm
Invocation and greeting
Penitential rite with Kyrie and/or Gloria in excelsis Deo
Salutation and collect for the day
First lesson
Psalmody

Second lesson
Alleluia verse or Lenten verse
Gospel
Homily
Nicene Creed
Intercessions
Offering
Offertory song
Offertory prayers
Preface dialogue with proper preface
Sanctus
Eucharistic prayer (choice of four; later two eucharistic prayers for masses of recon-
  ciliation and three for masses with children were added)
Our Father with embolism
Peace of the Lord
Lamb of God
Communion with communion songs
Silent reflection
Post-communion prayer
Benediction and dismissal

S. *The Service of Holy Communion in* Lutheran Book of Worship *(1978)*

The *Lutheran Book of Worship* (LBW) was the product of eight years of work by the
Inter-Lutheran Commission on Worship representing four Lutheran church bodies.[16]
It drew together the fruit of the liturgical-renewal movement within the Lutheran tradition represented in the Common Service. LBW uses many texts that were prepared
for ecumenical use by the International Consultation on English Texts (ICEL). It also
distinguished roles in the liturgy for the presiding minister (ordained)—P, assisting
ministers (who may be a layperson)—A, and the congregation—C. The assisting minister roles correspond to traditional diaconal roles in the liturgy.

Brief Order for Confession and Forgiveness—P/C
Entrance Hymn—C
Apostolic Greeting—P/C
Kyrie (Byzantine Litany of Peace, first used in the Service Book and Hymnal)—A/C
Canticle of Praise: "Glory to God in the highest," "Worthy is Christ," or another
  hymn—C
Salutation and Prayer of the Day—P
First Lesson—A
Responsorial Psalm—C
Second Lesson—A

Alleluia or Lenten Verse sung by C or proper Verse sung by choir

Gospel—P with acclamations—C

Sermon—P

Silent reflection

Hymn of the Day (might be sung before the sermon)—C

Creed: Nicene or Apostles'—C

Intercessions—A/C

Greeting of peace—P/C

Gathering of gifts

Offertory: "Let the vineyards be fruitful" or "What shall I render to the Lord" sung by C or proper verse sung by choir

Offertory prayer (choice of two)—A/C

Preface dialogue and proper preface—P/C

Sanctus—C

Great Thanksgiving: choice of four eucharistic prayers including the institution narrative or a brief prayer leading to the Words of Institution or the Words of Institution alone—P with C interjections

Lord's Prayer (choice of ICEL text or *Book of Common Prayer* text)—C

Administration of Holy Communion while "Lamb of God" and other hymns are sung

Post-communion canticle: "Thank the Lord" or Nunc dimittis or another song—C

Post-communion prayer (choice of three)—A

Silent reflection

Benediction (choice of two)—P

Dismissal—A

Note: This order of service was included, with some changes in the Great Thanksgiving, in *Lutheran Worship* of the Lutheran Church–Missouri Synod (1982). It serves as the basis of the Holy Communion in *Evangelical Lutheran Worship* used in the Evangelical Lutheran Church in America (2006), and is still provided, again with changes in the Great Thanksgiving, in *Lutheran Service Book* of the Lutheran Church–Missouri Synod (2006).

T. The Holy Eucharist, Rite II, in The Book of Common Prayer of the Episcopal Church (1979)[17]

A penitential order may be used at the beginning of the liturgy

A hymn, psalm, or anthem may be sung

Blessing

Collect for purity

Glory to God in the highest or Kyrie or Trisagion

Collect for the day

One or two lessons
A psalm, hymn, or anthem may follow each reading
The Holy Gospel with acclamations
The sermon
The Nicene Creed
The prayers of the people
(Confession of sins, if not used before the liturgy)
The peace
Offertory sentence(s)
A hymn, psalm, or anthem may be sung during the offering
Preface dialogue and preface with proper
Great Thanksgiving continues (choice of four)
The Lord's Prayer
The breaking of the bread
Communion
During the ministration of communion, hymns, psalms, or anthems may be sung
Post-communion prayer (said by the people)
Dismissal

U. The Service of Word and Table in The United Methodist Book of Worship (1992)[18] and The Service for the Lord's Day in the Presbyterian Book of Common Worship (1993)[19]

The orders of service in these two books profited from the ecumenical liturgical work done throughout the 1970s and 1980s. The orders of service in both books are similar.

Gathering rite with hymns, songs, canticles
Prayer of illumination
Old Testament reading
Psalm
New Testament reading
Gospel
Sermon
Apostles' Creed or affirmation of faith
Prayers of the people
Sharing of the peace
Great Thanksgiving (multiple forms)
Lord's Prayer
Breaking of bread
Communion
Post-communion prayer
Hymn, song, canticle, or psalm
Charge and blessing

Note: One difference between the two orders is that the Methodist order places the invitation to the table with confession and pardon before the sharing of peace. The Presbyterian order places the confession and pardon in the entrance rite; the sharing of peace may follow the pardon or the prayers of the people.

V. Pentecostal Worship

Hundreds of millions of believers around the world participate in Pentecostal worship, but it is difficult to generalize about it.[20] Holy Communion may be celebrated four times a year, monthly, or weekly. Most baptize adults or older youth by immersion upon a profession of faith, but a few baptize infants by sprinkling. Preaching takes a variety of forms from biblical commentary to emotional appeals for the Holy Spirit's descent. There is congregational singing and there may be "special music" provided by choirs or soloists. The music varies from one Pentecostal assembly to another, including revival hymns, gospel songs, and contemporary Christian music. What is indispensable in Pentecostal worship is opportunity for the exercise of extraordinary gifts of the Spirit, such as speaking in tongues, prophesying, healing, and exorcism.

W. A Praise and Worship Order from the Vineyard Christian Fellowship

The Vineyard Christian Fellowship fits into the evangelical free-church tradition with some Pentecostal or charismatic characteristics. Vineyard services, like most contemporary services, depend heavily on an opening song medley selected by the song leader. A distinction is made between songs that praise God by speaking about God and songs that worship God by addressing God directly.

> Songs of invitation (gathering)
> Songs of engagement (drawing people in)
> Songs of exultation (praising God)
> Songs of adoration (worshiping God)
> (The administration of Holy Communion may occur here: words of institution are
>   spoken and communicants go to various stations to receive bread and wine)
> Songs of intimacy (feeling the presence of Jesus)
> Announcements
> Prayer
> Sermon
> Ministry time (may include prayer for individuals and charismatic activity such as healing)

X. An Emergent Church Order of Service from Jacob's Well in Kansas City

The "emerging church" is a postmodern phenomenon. Each little community (they tend to be small) agrees on the order and content and ambience of worship.[21] This order of service relates to the postmodern view that all perspectives are equally valid by engaging the congregation in discussion after the sermon/message and a sharing of insights. Like many other contemporary services, Jacob's Well employs a praise band and vocalists.

Music performed by the band as gathering songs

Announcements

Passing the peace

Quieter songs with more congregational singing

Pastor's sermon

Hearers write down comments on cards that may be shared later

Small-group discussions

Time of prayer

A brief quotation from Scripture serves as a preface to sharing the elements for communion

The band plays while people come forward to receive the bread and wine

A final song based on the day's message

A musical dismissal: "My friends, may you grow in grace"

Note: Some forms of emergent worship make more use of traditional elements than others; many write their own prayers. All emergent communities pay attention to the environment of worship, often making use of icons or slides placement of candles, as does the South Yarra Community Baptist Church in Melbourne, Australia. The pastor of this congregation, Nathan Nettleton, refers to its liturgy as "Bapto-Catholic"[22] His community follows the Revised Common Lectionary, celebrates Holy Communion every Sunday, and uses prepared proper prayers each week that are posted at www. laughingbird.com.

3. What is the lectionary and how does it work?

The principal service has two foci: the word and the meal. The liturgy of the word is centered on readings from Scripture with homiletical commentary, as we see in the example of Jesus in his hometown synagogue in Luke 4. A lectionary system developed in the church as it had in the synagogue. The lectionary is a system of readings from Scripture. Already in the second century we see in the witness of Justin Martyr that there were readings from what we call both the Old and the New Testaments: "the writings of the prophets" and "the memoirs of the apostles." Later evidence shows that books of the Bible were read continuously. Many biblical commentaries by church fathers are actually homilies delivered on the biblical books. However, with the emergence of special days of commemoration (e.g., Easter, Ascension, Pentecost, Christmas) and seasons of devotion (Lent, Advent), specific readings having to do with the events commemorated or the purpose of devotion were chosen. These are pericopes, or "cut-out" selections. We see this in Jerusalem in the fourth- and fifth-century pilgrimage rites. Naturally, as more festivals and commemorations and days of devotion filled the church-year calendar, a pericope system began to replace the continuous reading system. While a lectionary system also developed in the Jewish synagogue with a cycle of readings from the Law and the Prophets, it is unlikely that the synagogue lectionary influenced the church's lectionary, other than the general idea of reading from Scripture in some systematic way.

No complete lectionary systems exist before the seventh century, although there are references in the writings of the church fathers to certain readings being read on certain days. For example, we learn from Augustine's commentary on John that the book of Genesis was read during Lent, the books of Job and Jonah during Holy Week, the Gospel Passion narratives on Good Friday, the resurrection narratives on Easter, and the book of Acts during the Easter season. In fact, only with the development of a church-year calendar with specific days and seasons would a lectionary with pericopes even be needed; otherwise biblical books were read continuously. The earliest extant lectionaries are Bibles with marginal markings indicating the beginnings and endings of readings. While liturgies in the early centuries indicate readings from both testaments, by the eighth century in both the East and the West readings in the principal service were reduced to Epistle and Gospel. Books with just the Gospels (evangelaries) and just the Epistles (epistolaries), rather than the whole Bible, were written out for ease in transport and reading by the readers: the subdeacon (Epistle) and deacon (Gospel). Lists of pericope readings for the church year were appended to these books. By the eleventh and twelfth centuries, these books were supplanted by actual lectionaries that contained in sequence the Epistles and Gospels for the Mass.

A pericope system was established in the lectionary attributed to Jerome, the *Comes Hieronymi* ("Jerome" = "Jerusalem"), although it is probably several centuries later than that. This list of readings was included in the so-called Leonine or Verona Sacramentary and came into regular use in the Church of Rome in the Gelasian and Gregorian Sacramentaries. Other readings were chosen by the local bishop or pastor. As part of Charlemagne's project of standardizing liturgical practices in his domain, his ecclesiastical advisor Alcuin revised the *Comes Hieronymi* to include additional days observed in the Frankish Church and the whole season of Advent. He also eliminated Old Testament readings and shortened many of the Epistle and Gospel readings, undoubtedly to accommodate the stamina of the people. The next major change to the lectionary would not come until the thirteenth century when Trinity Sunday was established. The remaining Sundays in the church year came to be called Sundays after Pentecost in the Roman lectionary or Sundays after Trinity in the Lutheran and Anglican lectionaries.

The Reformation was at first drawn to the ancient practice of continuous reading (*lectio continua*) of biblical books with preaching through those books. This became a reality in the Reformed churches. But in the Lutheran churches as well as in the Church of England, there was a preference for the historic lectionary with its pericope system. Lutherans added propers for the twenty-fifth and twenty-sixth Sundays after Trinity, providing eschatological readings at the end of the church year. They also moved the commemoration of the transfiguration from the fixed date of August 6 to the last Sunday after the Epiphany, a fitting climax of the season that celebrates the manifestation of the glory and deity of Christ and a foreshadowing of the resurrection after the pre-Lenten and Lenten Sundays. The Roman Rite after the Council of Trent also retained this historic lectionary, so that there were many similarities in the propers for the church year in the Roman Catholic, Lutheran, and Anglican churches.

There was a concern in the modern liturgical movement that people should be exposed to a greater selection of Scripture, including the Old Testament. Certainly much of the Bible was read in the offices of the liturgy of the hours, but most people attended services only for Mass or Divine Service on Sundays, festivals, and days of devotion. The Constitution on the Sacred Liturgy of the Second Vatican Council called for "more reading from holy Scripture in sacred celebrations, and it is to be more varied and suitable" (35.1) and also for sermons that "draw [their] content from scriptural and liturgical sources" (35.2). In fulfilling this desire of the Council, the Concilium for the Implementation of the Constitution developed and published *Ordo Lectionum Missae* with the reformed Mass in 1969.

The Roman Lectionary presented a new three-year series of readings for the Mass that supplanted the historic one-year lectionary in the Roman Catholic Church. The next year the Episcopal Church in the United States, the Presbyterian Church, and the United Church of Christ adopted the *Ordo* as a basis for new lectionaries in their churches. In 1970 the Inter-Lutheran Commission on Worship (ILCW) also expressed its preference for a three-year series. In 1971 the ILCW published a revised one-year lectionary series, and two years later published their new three-year series, patterned after the Roman Lectionary for the Mass. Versions of the Roman three-year lectionary were included in the *Lutheran Book of Worship* (1979) as well as in the *Book of Common Prayer* of the Episcopal Church (1979). In adopting versions of this lectionary, Lutherans and Anglicans/Episcopalians in North America departed from their sister churches in Europe.

In this three-year lectionary, a Synoptic Gospel is assigned to each year. "Year A" focuses on the Gospel of Matthew, "Year B" on the Gospel of Mark, and "Year C" on the Gospel of Luke. The Gospel of John is used in all three during the Sundays after Easter and also serves to supplement Mark in Year B. In an effort to reintroduce the reading of the Old Testament, a first lesson, usually selected from the Old Testament, was assigned to each Sunday that was typologically related to the Gospel reading. The exception to this is the Sundays after Easter, on which selections are chosen from Acts. Epistles related to the Gospels for the Sundays within the festival seasons, but would be read *lectio continua* on the Sundays of the year after the Epiphany (Baptism of our Lord) and after Pentecost (Trinity). Thus on these Sundays no special effort was made to correlate the Epistle with the Gospel selection.

A number of churches were using versions of the Roman three-year lectionary, but there were discrepancies in the choice of readings and, especially in the season after Pentecost, the Sundays on which the readings were heard. The North American-based Consultation on Common Texts (CCT) worked with the international English Language Liturgical Consultation (ELLC) to put together a revision of the Roman Catholic three-year lectionary, which appeared in 1983 as the Common Lectionary.[23]

After a nine-year trial period, a Revised Common Lectionary was publicly released in 1992. The Common Lectionary was included in the worship books of the United Methodist and Presbyterian Churches (1989 and 1993 respectively). In 1994 the Evangelical Lutheran Church in America adopted the Revised Common Lectionary and included it in *Evangelical Lutheran Worship* (2006). The Revised Common Lectionary offered the churches a choice between two "tracks" in their use of the Old Testament in the season after Pentecost. "Track 1" adheres to the *lectio continua* principle, thus following week by week from a portion of a book, or, in the case of some books, the whole. "Track 2," on the other hand, designated the "Related Track," is intended to relate in some way to the Gospel for the day. Provision is made for the use of a responsorial psalm each Sunday after the first reading no matter which track is followed.

A different ecumenical lectionary was developed by the Joint Liturgical Group (JLG) for Anglican, Baptist, Methodist, and Reformed churches in Great Britain and Ireland. As revised in 1990, the proposed lectionary offers a four-year cycle of readings for Sundays, the three Synoptic Gospels over the course of three years and the Gospel of John in the fourth year. Unlike the Roman and Revised Common lectionaries, the JLG Lectionary offers no "controlling" reading; all three readings have equal value. The feature of this lectionary that most affects the calendar is the provision of a nine-week pre-Christmas season, combining the aspects of the older Kingdomtide and Advent seasons.[24]

Finally, we note that the German Lutheran Churches did not accept the three-year Roman Lectionary as a basis for their lectionary reform. Rather, they revised the historic one-year lectionary (that had previously been "ecumenical") and added to it a six-year series of preaching texts related to the Gospel. As in the other lectionaries, an Old Testament reading was added to the historic Epistle and Gospel.[25]

4. What are the parts of a eucharistic prayer?

The central text of the liturgy of the meal is the eucharistic prayer, sometimes now called the Great Thanksgiving. The narratives of the institution of the Lord's Supper in the New Testament, especially Matthew 26:26-27 and Mark 14:22-23, indicate that Jesus took bread and "blessed it" (*eulogysas*) and after supper took a cup of wine and "gave thanks" (*eucharistysas*) over it. This conforms with the Jewish meal-prayer tradition that we see in the *Berakoth* tractate in *The Mishnah*: the blessing of God for the bread before the meal and the thanksgiving over the cup at the end of the meal. This same division of prayers is seen in the *Didache* 9–10. The prayers before and after the meal would not be brought together into one unified eucharistic prayer or series of prayers until the actual meal fell away and thanksgiving was given over the bread and cup together. The earliest extant unified eucharistic prayers would be the third-century East Syrian Anaphora of Addai and Mari and the eucharistic prayer in the *Apostolic Tradition* attributed to Hippolytus of Rome.

The history of the eucharistic prayer is very complicated.[26] The Sanctus is included in the oldest manuscript of Addai and Mari but not in the *Apostolic Tradition*. Since the manuscript evidence for Addai and Mari is eleventh century, it is possible that it is a later addition in this tradition. We also notice that there is an institution narrative in the *Apostolic Tradition* but not in Addai and Mari. But the *Apostolic Tradition* is reconstructed from versions that appear later than the third century and not in the Greek in which the *Apostolic Tradition* was most likely written.

What is not debatable is that both the Sanctus and the words of institution have a place in fourth-century anaphoras. The form of the Sanctus and the institution narrative is less full in early Egyptian prayers and fuller in the Antiochene prayers. This might suggest that these texts first appeared in Egypt and migrated to Syria.

It is now well established that there was no single apostolic Eucharist from which everything evolved. It is more likely that different models developed in various local churches and that there was a tendency for churches to borrow from one another and then, at a later point in history, to accentuate differences as the local churches came under the hegemony of patriarchal churches (Antioch, Alexandria, Rome, Constantinople, and Jerusalem).

Two elements divide the East and the West: the epiclesis and the oblation. An invocation (epiclesis) of the Holy Spirit developed in the Eastern churches; the Holy Spirit is called down on the bread and wine to manifest or change them into the bread and the wine. The epiclesis is most highly developed in the West Syrian/Byzantine anaphoras of St. Basil and St. John Chrysostom. This is also the area in the church that was most engaged in the christological and trinitarian controversies of the fourth and fifth centuries. The West Syrian prayers develop a trinitarian scheme that has been most attractive to those working on worship books in the late twentieth century. The scheme is as follows:

Praise of God for God's work of creation leading to the Sanctus
Remembrance of the Son leading to the institution narrative
Offering of the gifts and invocation of the Holy Spirit leading to commemorations
    and intercessions
Concluding trinitarian doxology

Bridge phrases connect the different parts of the prayer. After the Sanctus there is: "Holy are you and all holy…," leading to a recital of salvation history. After the words of institution there is a summary of the remembrance (the anamnesis): "Remembering therefore the cross, tomb, resurrection on the third day, ascension, enthronement in heaven, second and glorious coming," leading to the offering—"We offer you your own from what is your own" (oblation)—leading to the epiclesis—"We implore you to send your Holy Spirit." The progression of thought is: remembering, we offer, and we implore. As theories of the eucharistic presence of Christ developed in the fourth century, it is not surprising that Eastern fathers (e.g., Theodore of Mopsuestia, John Chrysostom) pointed to the work of the Holy Spirit in bringing about the sacramental union of bread/body and wine/blood whereas Western fathers (e.g., Ambrose, Augustine) pointed to the efficacy of the words of Christ to make the sacrament.

There is an oblation or offering of the gifts in all the prayers because the eucharistic prayer said everything that needed to be said about the eucharistic rite, and separate offertory prayers are a later development. But the element of oblation became more highly developed in the Alexandrian and Roman prayers than in the Syrian, East or West. An early version of the Egyptian eucharistic tradition is the eucharistic prayer in the fourth-century Prayer Book (*Euchologion*) of Bishop Sarapion of Thmuis in lower Egypt. After an extensive trinitarian and cosmic introduction leading to the Sanctus, there is immediately an offering of the bread—"the likeness of the holy body"—leading to the words of Christ about the bread, followed by a quote from the *Didache* prayer about the bread scattered over the mountains gathered together to become one loaf as the church is gathered together out of every nation and becomes one, leading to an offering of the cup—"the likeness of the blood"—and the words of Christ over the cup, followed by an invocation of the Word (*Logos*)—not the Holy Spirit!—on the bread and cup that they may become the body of the Word and the blood of Truth. In the Anaphora of St. Mark, the introduction is expanded beyond all bounds and includes copious intercessions for the living and commemorations of the faithful departed and a petition to receive the thank-offerings of those who offered sacrifices as well as the cosmological references leading to the Sanctus. After the Sanctus, as in Sarapion, the words of institution are used as a warrant for the oblation. In other words, the element of oblation is the theological emphasis in the Alexandrian eucharistic tradition.

Egypt was the breadbasket of Rome and there was a lot of commerce between Rome and Alexandria. We have no extant Roman eucharistic prayer before the canon included in the *Codex Reginensis 316* (a Gelasian Saramentary) of the eighth century. There are only portions of a eucharistic prayer cited by Ambrose in *De Sacramentis* ("On the Sacraments"), but they are enough to show the influence of the Alexandrian eucharistic tradition.[27] It is not surprising, therefore, to find the elements of oblation, intercession, and commemoration so pervasive in the Roman canon, and the words of institution, from the standpoint of literary and theological analysis, serving as the warrant for the oblation (taking the bread and cup) rather than the climax of a narration of salvation history ("Do this for the remembrance of me"), as in the West Syrian prayers. The outline of the Roman canon is as follows:

Preface: praise of the Father with angelic beings through Christ who (proper)
Sanctus
We offer for the whole church (*Te igitur*)
For particular persons (*Memento*)
In union with the saints (*Communicantes*)

And for special needs (*Hanc igitur*)
Petition to accept the offering (*Quam oblationem*)
Because Christ commanded it (*Qui pridie* = Words of Institution)
Remembering Christ's saving work we offer these gifts (*Unde et memores*)
Accept our offerings as you did the offerings of Abel, Abraham, Melchizedek (*Supra quae*)
May your angel carry our gifts to your heavenly altar and may we receive it back as
  the body and blood of your Son (*Supplices te*)
Remember the faithful departed (*Memento etiam*)
And grant also a portion with all the saints, in spite of our sins (*Nobis quoque peccatoribus*)
Through Christ all good gifts come (*Per quem*)

The emphasis throughout the canon is on "our gifts," which are offered for the church and for particular needs. Martin Luther believed that this was the reverse of the purpose of the sacrament, which was that the faithful receive the gift of communion in Christ.[28] The heart of the sacrament is not gifts we offer but gifts we receive. The fact that the most common form of the Mass was the votive mass, the Mass offered for special intentions (paid for with a Mass stipend), Luther saw works righteousness and blasphemy in the heart of the Mass itself.[29] People were being taught to offer their gifts in expectation of benefits that Christ has already secured in his once-for-all atoning sacrifice on the cross. The liturgical consequence of this critique of the Mass, in Luther's view and action, was to delete all the prayers of the canon after the Sanctus and retain only the words of institution—sung aloud as a proclamation of the gospel, as we see in his German Mass. Other Reformers tried their hand at rewriting the eucharistic prayer in order to express more clearly the Reformation axis of justification by faith/atonement by the all-sufficient sacrifice of Christ. The most successful of these Reformation efforts at revising the eucharistic prayer along evangelical lines was probably that of Thomas Cranmer, Archbishop of Canterbury and primary author of the *Book of Common Prayer*.

In modern times there has been a tremendous amount of research on the eucharistic prayer. Late twentieth-century worship books have moved away from one canon and provided multiple options of Great Thanksgivings.[30] Eucharistic renewal has privileged the West Syrian anaphora structure because of its trinitarian structure and narrative elements. However, this has not been without its problems. Most of the new prayers have retained the Western tradition of a variable proper preface, which really limits the cosmological element in the introductory part of the prayer because the Western preface focuses on the specific work of Christ as celebrated in the seasons of the church year. The Roman Catholic prayers in particular have had difficulty with an epiclesis on the bread and wine *after* the words of institution, preferring such an epiclesis before the institution narrative (even in Prayer IV, based on the Anaphora of St. Basil). Thus, with allowances for particular denominational emphases, a common pattern of eucharistic prayer has emerged that contains these parts:

Preface with proper leading to
The Sanctus
Post-Sanctus narrative of salvation history leading to
The words of institution
Memorial acclamation
Anamnesis (Remembrance of the saving work of Christ)
Epiclesis (invocation of the Holy Spirit with petition for the benefits of communion)
Intercession and commemoration
Concluding trinitarian doxology

A study of the eucharistic tradition offers other models of eucharistic prayer that might serve as inspiration for new ways of observing the command of Christ to take bread and a cup of wine and give thanks. But certainly a concern in new eucharistic prayers would be to express the fullness of eucharistic faith. As the Swedish bishop and theologian Yngve Brilioth demonstrated, the Eucharist admits of multiple meanings and cannot be reduced to one or two. He highlighted thanksgiving, fellowship, memorial, and sacrifice, with the element of the mystery of the real presence of Christ pervading them all.[31] Geoffrey Wainwright has also recovered the early church's eschatological understanding of the Eucharist,[32] and eschatological elements such as the *Maranatha* acclamation ("Come, Lord Jesus") are found in current prayers.

There has been an explosion in writing eucharistic prayers since the 1960s. Many presiders prepare their eucharistic prayers. We recall the witness of Justin Martyr that "the president…sends up prayers and thanksgivings to the best of his ability" (*Apology* I, 67). But by the fifth century, councils were decreeing that priests who are unable to improvise their own prayers should follow the written prayers as approved. Later canons would require that the celebrants follow the written script. Even if the script is followed, it should be proclaimed to the best of the presider's ability, so as to engage the assembly in responding to this central prayer of the liturgy.

5. What is the difference between a "High Mass" and a "Low Mass"?

How shall the Eucharist be celebrated? The text is important, but there is more to the celebration than just words. There are different styles of celebration, usually appropriate to the significance of the day or occasion and the size of the assembly. In the Western Catholic tradition these different styles were signified by the terms "High Mass" and "Low Mass." These terms refer to the division of roles within the liturgy rather than the degree of solemnity invested in the celebration, such as the amount of music or ceremony employed. Strictly speaking, a High Mass requires a deacon and a subdeacon as well as a celebrant and other servers or acolytes. A Low Mass would have only a celebrant and at least a server, but sometimes even without a gathered congregation.[33]

A *missa cantata* or "sung Mass" may be a High Mass or a Low Mass, depending on whether there is a differentiation of leadership roles. In a sense, the simple Sunday service described by Justin Martyr was like a High Mass since it included a president, a deacon, and a reader. Conversely, the Mass in an Austrian church in which a Haydn or Mozart Mass is sung with choir and orchestra is a Low Mass if it involves only a celebrant.

The High Mass with multiple liturgical roles fully sung by the ministers and the people with the assistance of a choir is the ideal form of celebration. Low Mass originated in the early Middle Ages as a shortened or simplified form of the Solemn Mass. The practice had been that there was (at most) one Mass in a monastery or parish church each day. However, over time it became necessary to celebrate more than one on the same day, especially as the votive mass (a Mass of special intentions) became the most frequent form of Mass celebrated. It also became customary for monasteries to ordain most of their monks, though originally monks were almost all laymen. Saying a daily Mass became a matter of priestly devotion. For a while, concelebration, whereby several priests took a full priestly part in offering Mass, provided all priests with the possibility of celebrating Mass each day, but this custom died out. It was revived after the Second Vatican Council but has had the effect of emphasizing the Mass as a clerical event rather than a truly communal event.

Low Mass as a form of celebration falls short of the ideal because it does not reflect the communal character of liturgy. The celebrant took all of the liturgical roles while the single server took the part of the choir and congregation. Much of the ceremonials, such as the incensing and the kiss of peace, were omitted, and everything was recited in a low voice. Before the liturgical reforms in the Roman Catholic Church after Vatican II, this practice even had an impact on the High or Solemn Mass. The celebrant was expected to recite everything in a low voice, even what was sung by the deacon and the choir. This clearly fostered the idea that the priest was engaged in his own worship rather than leading the worship of the community.

However, the difference between a High Mass and a Low Mass reminds us that the liturgy on a nonfestival weekend might be scaled down in comparison with the full Sunday or festival celebration. It is not a matter of omitting nonessential items but of not omitting essential ones. The weekday Mass might have less music and omit hymns and sung responses but should never omit the readings, a homily, intercessory prayers, the peace, the Great Thanksgiving, the Lord's Prayer, the communion, post-communion prayer, and dismissal.

For further reading

Bouyer, Louis. *Eucharist: Theology and Spirituality of the Eucharistic Prayer*, trans. Charles Underhill Quinn. Notre Dame: University of Notre Dame Press, 1969. Bouyer sometimes claims too much on too little evidence, but this is the most thorough and ecumenical treatment of the eucharistic prayer through twenty centuries up to the eve of the reformed liturgical books.

Dix, Gregory. *The Shape of the Liturgy*, with Introduction by Simon Jones. London: Continuum, 2007 (1945). This is a classic book on the evolution of the liturgy, and many of Dix's hypotheses have been discredited. Simon Jones, in this edition, references many of Dix's critics, and also points out Dix's enduring value.

Jungmann, Joseph A. *The Mass of the Roman Rite: Its Origins and Development*, 2 vols., trans. Francis A. Brunner, C.S.S.R. Westminster: Christian Classics, 1986 (1948).

Mazza, Enrico. *The Celebration of the Eucharist: The Origin of the Rite and the Development of Its Interpretation*. Collegeville: Liturgical, 1999.

O'Connell, Matthew J., trans. *Roles in the Liturgical Assembly*. The Twenty-Third Liturgical Conference, Serge. New York: Pueblo, 1981.

Schultz, Hans-Joachim. *The Byzantine Liturgy*, trans. Matthew J. O'Connell. New York: Pueblo, 1980.

Thompson, Bard. *Liturgies of the Western Church*. Philadelphia: Fortress Press, 1980 (1961).

West, Fritz. *Scripture and Memory: The Ecumenical Hermeneutic of the Three-Year Lectionaries*. Collegeville: Liturgical, 1997.

4
The Liturgy of Time

1. *What does it mean to sanctify time?*
2. *Where did the liturgy of the hours come from?*
3. *What's the difference between cathedral and monastic prayer offices?*
4. *How did the liturgy of the hours develop throughout history?*
5. *How might daily prayer offices become daily once again?*

1. What does it mean to sanctify time?

We believe that the God who created all things also created time. The priestly account of creation in Genesis 1 relates God's purposeful activity on each "day" up to the seventh, which God declared to be a sabbath, a day of rest. Humankind, created in the image of God, is given not only the earth as home and the plants and animals as food, but also time. Because of humankind's expulsion from paradise a limit is placed on our time. We have only so much time in this world, only so many sunrises and sunsets, only so many days and weeks and months and years in which to live to the praise of God's glory and to minister to each other's needs. Time is a finite and therefore a precious commodity. Nevertheless, there is a sense that as we go about our daily work, at an ever more frenetic pace, we should periodically check in with our Creator, to ensure that what we are doing brings God glory and serves God's will.

There is a fundamental rhythm to life in this world that is marked out by the natural cycles of light and darkness and change of seasons by which we mark time. In spite of night shifts in the modern industrial world, and the 24/7 of modern global communication, we still possess an ancient sense that the workday begins at dawn and concludes with sunset and that when darkness descends it is time for rest and sleep. Of course, the night is never quiet. The night creatures are out and about, prowling for prey. Just so, night has been a threatening time for human beings. Those among us who work at night are often performing emergency services. In various parts of the earth the length of days and nights wax and wane, increasing our sense of security or threat. Darkness is often experienced as akin to the weight of gravity, pulling us down into the earth as twilight fades. Light is experienced as rising from above, drawing us out of chaos and into purposeful activity, just as God's light scattered the darkness of the precreated world. Our natural instinct is to ask God's protection at night and praise God in the morning.

Time is God's creation and God's gift to us. Since the times and seasons belong to God already, we cannot sanctify or make them holy. The times and seasons are holy because of the presence of the Holy God who relates to his people in specific ways at these particular times and seasons. We can only affirm the sanctification of time because of God's presence and the gifts of grace received at particular times, such as the gift of sabbath rest or the gift of joy in the resurrection on the Lord's Day or the gift of a new beginning in the morning and the gift of completion at night. We sense the holiness of the times and seasons and respond with our praise and prayer. In the words of Venantius Fortunatus's Easter hymn, "Welcome, Happy Morning," "Hours and passing moments praise thee in their flight." We experience Easter, "the queen of seasons," as the time of Christ's death and resurrection and this sense of death and resurrection is applied to all our sunsets and sunrises. In the light of this experience of death and resurrection time is no longer experienced merely as the hours passing and the years sliding by. The hours of the day and the seasons of the year are experienced as purposeful.

The faithful perceive the times and seasons as charged with God's purposes. This is why for Christians as for Jews the liturgical day begins in the evening, with Vespers, because the end of each unit of time reveals its meaning. The evening prayer of the church has an eschatological character. It was at the end of each day of creation that God saw that "it was good."[1]

2. Where did the liturgy of the hours come from?

Times of prayer are not just prayer breaks during the day. They are liturgical acts: acts in which the community of faith praises God for the grace-gift of the particular time on behalf of the creation, and prays for the needs of the world in which we live and move and have our being. The liturgy of the hours comes from the practice of setting aside certain times during the day for praise and prayer. Religious people pray at specific times during the day. This is true of Jews, Christians, and Muslims. Religious people have discerned morning and evening to be especially significant times for common prayer.

Among the sacrifices in the Jerusalem temple were the *tamid*, which were burnt on the altar every morning and afternoon and served as God's daily food (Num. 28:1-8). Undoubtedly prayer accompanied the sacrifices offered corporately and individually, as we see in the book of Psalms. And people did pray at the temple, as the New Testament indicates (Luke 1:10; Acts 3:1). The custom developed of Jews praying at the times of the daily sacrifices in the temple, perhaps in their homes or individually during the day and in the synagogues. Thus, when the Romans destroyed the temple in 70 CE, the daily prayers increased in importance for devout Jews, even as a substitute for the daily sacri-fices. Daily prayer came to be understood as spiritual sacrifices. The statutory elements of daily and sabbath synagogue worship specified in the *Mishnah* (*Tamid* 5:1) include:

Recitation of the Ten Commandments and the *Shema Israel* ("Hear, O Israel")
Praise of God (use of psalms)
Petitions to God (*Tefilliah* or Eighteen Benedictions)
Study of Scripture (especially Torah on the sabbath)

The New Testament contains a great deal of information about Christian prayer practices. Christians prayed daily (Acts 2:46), even "constantly" (1 Thess. 1:2). They prayed alone (Acts 10:9) and when they were together (Acts 2:46). They prayed in their homes (Acts 2:46), in the temple (Acts 2:46; 3:1), and in the synagogue (Acts 13:14-15). In their prayer they used "psalms and hymns and spiritual songs" (Col. 3:16-17; Eph. 5:18-20). They were to pray "for everyone, for kings and all who are in high positions, so that we may lead a quiet and peaceable life in all godliness and dignity" (1 Tim. 2:1-2). They were given a sample prayer by their Lord Jesus (Matt. 6:9-13; Luke 11:2-4). They prayed to God the Father in the name of Jesus (Matt. 18:19-20; John 14:13-14; 15:16; 16:23-26; 1 Cor. 1:2; Col. 3:17). As to the times, they were to "pray without ceasing" (1 Thess. 5:16-18; Col. 4:2; Eph. 6:18; Luke 18:1).

Nevertheless, specific times of prayer did develop among Christians. Did these times of prayer correspond to Jewish times of prayer? Robert Taft concludes that no straight line can be drawn from Jewish to Christian prayer because of uncertainty about the exact times of Jewish prayer in the New Testament era.[2] Also, Jewish prayer retained an improvisory character and formulas weren't written down until later times. And, in any event, the Christian prayer offices emerged in a Gentile context. Nevertheless, the *Didache*, which reflects practice in a Jewish Christian milieu at the end of the first century, exhorts Christians to pray the Lord's Prayer three times a day (*Didache* 8:3), although the exact times of recitation are not specified.

This lack of specific times is rectified a century later by Tertullian of Carthage (d. c. 220). In his treatise *On Prayer* 25, he attests that Christians pray at the third, sixth, and ninth hours (9 AM, noon, 3 PM) when the forum bell is rung, but he distinguishes these daytime prayers from "the legitimate prayers (*legitimis orationibus*), which, without any command, ought to be offered at first light and at dusk."

Clement of Alexandria (d. c. 215) insists that the Christian prays always, but noted the practice of praying at the third, sixth, and ninth hours (*Stromata* VII/7, 40:3). He also mentions prayer upon rising, before retiring, and during the night; also before, during, and after meals (*Stromata* VII/7, 49:3-4), although these may be given only as examples of "ceaseless prayer" rather than as specified times. For Clement Chris-tian prayer has an eschatological character. He mentions Christians facing east to pray, toward Christ the light coming into the world as the sun of justice. He also discusses the practice of Christians waking up during the night to have a prayer vigil, on the basis of Jesus' statement in Luke 12:35-37, "Blessed are those servants whom the master finds awake when he comes." "Therefore at night we ought to rise often and bless God" (*Pedagogue* 2:9).[3]

Later witnesses reinforce these early references and indicate an emerging tradition of Christian prayer in the morning upon arising, during the day at the third, sixth, and ninth hours, at night before retiring, during the night, and before and after meals. So far these are examples of household or individual prayer. Public and communal prayer would not arise until Christians were able to worship publicly in public spaces such as in the basilicas built for Christian assemblies, beginning in the fourth century. Before the availability of public places for assembly on a regular daily basis, there could only be domestic prayer, just as Christians gathered in one another's houses to celebrate the Lord's Supper. This means that when hermits and monks who went into wilderness places in deserts of Egypt, Palestine, and Syria to engage in "ceaseless prayer," they took with them the prayers of the household.

3. What's the difference between cathedral and monastic prayer offices?

The Christian hermits who moved into the deserts of Egypt, Palestine, and Syria in the third and early fourth centuries were looking for an alternative to martyrdom. Apart from the severe empire-wide state persecution of Christians under Diocletian c. 305, martyrdom was ceasing to be a way to witness to the faith. Asceticism, the living of a disciplined life of fasting and prayer, became a substitute for martyrdom. The aim of the ascetics was to cultivate a life of holiness by these ascetical means.

Anthony of Egypt (251–356) is the best known of these early hermits because of the biography written by Athanasius. But hermits also began living close to one another for mutual support, and this became the basis of the emergence of Christian monasticism. The first great organizer of coenobitic monasticism (hermits living together in a community) was Pachomius (c. 292–348). Pachomius had previously served in the Roman army and was a convert to Christianity. He had a gift for organizing communities (like military camps) and put it to use in the organization of the communal life of hermits. Eastern Orthodoxy looks to Basil of Caesarea as a founding monastic legislator, as well to as the example of the desert fathers. Shortly after 360 Martin of Tours first introduced monasticism to the West.

John Cassian, a Latin-speaking deacon attached to the service of John Chrysostom, patriarch of Constantinople, was sent to Rome to plead Chrysostom's cause before Pope Innocent I when the emperor forced the patriarch into exile from Constantinople in 404. While he was in Rome, Cassian accepted the invitation to found an Egyptian-style monastery in southern Gaul, near Marseille. In the process he wrote two books: *Confer-ences*, which is a series of interviews with Eastern hermits and monks about the spiritual life; and the *Institutes*, which concerns the daily life and prayer practices of the Egyptian monks. Books II and III of the *Institutes* concern, respectively, the canonical system of night prayers and psalms and the canonical system of daily prayers and psalms. The *Institutes* is the fullest description we have of Eastern monastic prayer.

The rise of monasticism at this time has been attributed to the immense changes in the church brought about by Emperor Constantine's legalization of Christianity in 313. As the world came into the church, the ascetics had to leave the church to leave the world. The earliest monks were laypeople who could engage in prayer on their own but had to come into the towns to receive communion at the bishop's church. They often carried the consecrated sacrament back to their cells for self-communion when they deemed themselves prepared. This was an extension of the practice of ordinary Christians taking the consecrated elements home with them during times of persecution or to commune themselves after a time of fasting. During the fourth century, bishops discouraged this practice. The solution for monks was to ordain some of their number as presbyters so they could serve the sacrament in the monastic communities.

Christianity was a legal religion in the Roman Empire after Constantine's edict in 313, but still had to contend with paganism. The subsequent transformation of Christianity into the established Roman religion under Emperor Theodosius after 379 ended the position of Christians as a small group that believed itself to be, at least ideally, the godly elite. In response to the new situation of the church in the world more advanced forms of commitment were developed for worldly (secular) Christians. One was the use of daily public worship in the basilicas.

Orders of daily prayer developed both in the monasteries and in the basilicas, some of which served as cathedral churches (seats of the bishop). Because these orders of prayer occurred at particular times during the day, they have come to be called the liturgy of the hours. Because, as liturgy, they became the official prayers of the church they have also been called the prayer offices, or, collectively, the Divine Office.

Since the hermits and monks took with them into the desert the forms of prayer they had known in their households, the hours of prayer in the monastery were the same as the hours of prayer we have already noted. The new situation in the monastery was the ability of monks to literally engage in "ceaseless prayer." The object of the monastic life was simply the cultivation of a life lived in total communion with God by immersion in the word of God. Hence, disciplines developed of praying through the entire book of Psalms in a given period of time (*recitation continua*) and reading through the entire Bible book by book (*lectio continua*). In Egypt this usually meant reading Scripture aloud followed by meditation communally or in the monk's cell. As formal rules of monastic life developed, it is not surprising that communities of monks gathered for prayer at the times Christians had been used to praying: evening, during the night, morning, and at intervals during the day.

All these times of gathering for common prayer would not be possible for Christians in "secular" life. The hours of prayer that seemed most feasible in the basilicas were morning and evening and occasional night vigils on the eves of the great festivals, of which Easter was the queen of vigils. Moreover, the prayer offices in the basilicas had to include ceremonies that would engage the attention of participants in these great spaces.

So the lamp lighting in the home at sunset became a great service of light ("lucernar-ium") at Vespers extolling Christ the light of the world. Church orders like the *Apostolic Tradition* and the *Apostolic Constitutions* provide a thanksgiving for light.

The Greek hymn, *Phos hilaron* ("Joyous Light of glory"), written in the late third or early fourth century is found in a collection of four songs to be sung in the morning, in the evening, before meals, and at candle lighting. *Phos hilaron* is to be sung at the light-ing of lamps in the evening and so is sometimes known as the "lamp-lighting hymn." Some of the words to the other three songs are from Scripture, so *Phos hilaron* is con-sidered to be the first actual nonbiblical hymn. Basil the Great (329?–379) spoke of the singing of the *Phos hilaron* as a cherished tradition of the church. The singing of hymns engaged the people in common prayer.

Egeria, the Spanish religious woman who made a pilgrimage to the Holy Land in the 380s and recorded what she experienced there in her travel diary, also reports the singing of the chanted response Kyrie eleison to a series of petitions sung by the deacon in Vespers celebrated in Jerusalem. There was also a solemn blessing of the people by the bishop at the end of the office. Thus the prayer offices in the basilicas were gatherings of the local church under the leadership of the bishop and deacons and with the assistance of cantors in the singing of psalms and hymns.

The so-called cathedral office is not known to us from actual liturgical books. It has to be reconstructed from eyewitness reports like that of Egeria or from references to practice in the sermons of great bishops such as John Chrysostom's commentary on Psalm 141, and from the survival of elements of cathedral practice in the offices of particular churches.

One element that was useful in the cathedral office was the development of anti-phons that could serve as repeated refrains sung by the people while the text of the psalm or canticle was sung by a cantor or choir. This is called responsorial singing. In the monastic communities the more typical way of singing psalms was antiphonal—two sides singing back and forth to each other. In the monasteries it was possible for whole communities to sing the psalms because the daily use of the psalter in large chunks made memorization possible.

The most noteworthy difference between monastic prayer and cathedral prayer would be the amount of psalmody and Scripture reading. Unlike the continuous recita-tion of psalms and reading of biblical books in the monastic prayer office, in the cathe-dral prayer office the psalms and readings would be selected for their relevance to the time of the day at which the office was celebrated. Thus standard daily morning psalms would be 51 or 63. Psalms 148–150 also constituted a cluster of psalms in morning prayer that is widely attested and later came to be called the Lauds psalms (because of their use in the developed office of morning praise or Lauds). The standard daily eve-ning psalm was 141. These psalms were accompanied by an incense offering, suggesting an allusion to the daily sacrifices of the Old Testament tabernacle and temple. Readings would be brief, if at all.[4]

A fateful development in the history of the liturgy of the hours was the monasticizing of the cathedral offices. There does not seem to be a simple explanation for this. Certainly the foundation of monasteries in urban centers, such as Constantinople and Rome, had some influence. Some ordinary Christians were drawn to monastic prayer, and it was easier to attend monasteries in the cities than in the deserts. Monastics were drawn upon for leadership roles in the church. Great bishops like John Chrysostom, Augustine of Hippo, and Gregory the Great held monasticism in high regard and might have preferred for themselves the contemplative life had they not been drawn into positions of responsibility in difficult times. These bishops drew upon the proximity of monasteries to staff daily prayer in the basilicas to relieve the clergy of this burden so that they could attend to other pastoral responsibilities.

The most prominent feature of the prayer offices is the use of psalmody, a use that far surpassed the use of psalms in the synagogue. James McKinnon has argued that there was "a psalmodic movement" in fourth-century Christianity in which the singing of the psalms became popular.[5] This led to a wider range of psalms even in the cathedral offices. Psalms also served as texts of versicles and responses, responsories, and supplicatory prayers known as suffrages. At this same time the development of schools of singers (*scholae cantorum*) increased musical resources in the church and honed skills that also became available to monasteries. Thus there was a mixing and blending of elements so that the distinction between monastic and cathedral offices became blurred. Nevertheless, this distinction has been useful in the contemporary retrieval of the liturgy of the hours for popular use.[6]

4. How did the liturgy of the hours develop throughout history?

The development of the liturgy of the hours throughout history is complicated and varied because it took shape both in monastic communities and in local churches in Eastern and Western Christianity. We can only offer here snapshots, mostly from the West, leading to our accustomed practices today in Roman Catholic and Protestant churches. However, I reference first the East Syrian and the West Syrian offices because, in their use in historical churches, they demonstrate respectively traces of the cathedral-type office (East Syrian) and a strong monastic influence (West Syrian/Byzantine). The untangling of these two types of prayer is important in the renewal of the prayer offices for use in congregations and Christian homes today.

A. The East Syrian Chaldean Office

The Assyrian-Chaldean Rite is used today by Christians in the Assyrian Church of the East, centered in Mesopotamia (modern Iraq) and by Catholic Malabar Christians in India. A synod held in Seleucia-Ctesiphon on the Tigris River south of Baghdad in 410 is the first known instance of a church decreeing that its liturgical rite is to be observed by all, although the Divine Office is not specifically mentioned. Canon 15 of the synod held under Catholicos George I at Darin in 676 required all the faithful to attend public morning and evening prayer.[7]

While this form of the office underwent monasticization like the forms in other ritual families, it is characterized by a retention of cathedral features. The early shape of the East Syrian-Chaldean office is not known, but many hymns survive in present-day usage from the illustrious hymnwriters in its history, including Ephrem (d. 373) and his contemporary Bishop Jacob of Nisibis, Narsai (d. 502), and Babai the Great (d. 608–609). Catholicos Simeon bar Sabba'ê (d. c. 341–344) is credited with having arranged the Daily Office into two "choirs" or "weeks," an arrangement still in use today. The form of the cathedral office in use today took shape in the reforms under Catholicos Iso 'yahyb III in 650–51 at the Monastery of Mar Gabriel in Mosul. The patriarch left the monks free to organize their own night vigil offices, but they were to respect the forms of the cathedral offices, which are still celebrated in the parishes.[8]

The Assyrian Night Vigil retains a similarity with the weekly Resurrection Vigil in Jerusalem as described by Egeria: the entrance of the bishop, three psalms or canticles with prayers, a procession to the sanctuary (in Jerusalem the procession was to the cross) with a hymn, a psalm with refrain, and a litany and concluding prayer. The evening service includes incensing, a hymn of praise, a Hallel psalm, fixed evening psalms (140, 141, 118:105-12), a litany, the Trisagion and its collect, and a blessing (prayer of inclination). The morning service includes fixed morning psalms with refrains (99, 90, 103:1-6, 112, 92), the Lauds psalms (148–150), Psalm 116 with a prayer to Christ the true light, hymns of light, Benedicite (on festivals) or Miserere (on ordinary days), Gloria in excelsis (on festivals) or a hymn (on ordinary days), Trisagion and Our Father, Trisagion prayer, blessing (prayer of inclination). These services are conducted from the bema, a raised platform in the middle of the nave, with the people gathered around. This was once also the case with the Byzantine offices.

B. The West Syrian-Byzantine Office

The West Syrian Rite is composed of Syriac elements, especially hymns, as well as Syriac pieces translated from the Greek. It was used in the churches of Antioch, Edessa, and Jerusalem. The Maronite Church of Lebanon, which was influenced by the Latin crusaders during the 1200s, also has an original Syriac base.[9]

The West Syrian Office provided the basis of the office used in the Great Church of Constantinople (Hagia Sophia), but that fell out of use after the Latin conquest of the city in 1204, and was gradually replaced by the monastic office of St. Saba. The "cathedral" tradition of Hagia Sophia had already been influenced by the work of the monastery of the Studion in Constantinople. Thus, unlike the Chaldean Rite, the Byzantine Rite is a form of the Divine Office that has been greatly influenced by monastic practice. Nevertheless, some "cathedral" elements remain, such as the lucernarium at Vespers (with the *Phos hilaron*) and incensations.

The cycle of eight daily prayer offices in the Byzantine Rite consists of the following:

Vespers (at sundown)
Compline (before sleep)
The Midnight Office (chanted in the middle of the night or early in the morning)
Matins (the longest of the day, which traditionally ends as the sun is rising)
First Hour (chanted at the rising of the sun)
Third Hour (chanted at the third hour of the day—approximately 9:00 AM)
Sixth Hour (chanted at noon)
Ninth Hour (chanted at the ninth hour of the day—approximately 3:00 PM)

On the great feasts of the liturgical year as well as on certain feast days (and in the Slavic tradition, on every Saturday night) there is a particularly solemn service called the All-Night Vigil that combines Vespers, Matins and First Hour, with special additions, into a single long service. This office has become known in the West through Sergei Rachmaninov's ethereal choral masterpiece *All-Night Vigil*.

The Byzantine Vespers in particular shows the merger of cathedral and monastic elements. At its heart is a lucernarium, Vespers psalms (140, 141, 129, 116) with incensation, three readings, a litany, and blessing, to which monastic psalmody has been prefixed.[10] The presidential prayers now bunched at the beginning of both Vespers and Orthros (Matins) were once scattered throughout the offices. The dangling doxologies that are now scattered throughout indicate the original places of these collects. The present Orthros or Matins is a compilation of four separate offices: the royal office (a brief service for the emperor celebrated in imperial monastic foundations, but really unrelated to the time of Matins), monastic nocturns, the cathedral vigil, and the morning office, which includes Lauds.

C. The Benedictine Office, c. 540
Of the many monastic rules in the West, such as that of Aurelian of Arles (fifth century), the Celtic *Rule of St. Columbanus* (c. 615), and the Visigothic *Rule for Monks* of Isidore of Seville (590–600), it was the *Rule of St. Benedict* that finally triumphed. This is because it provided a communal discipline that could be adapted to local conditions and provided a balance between work and prayer (*ora et labora*). The Benedictine prayer office is a combination of the office of the church of the city of Rome and the fifth-century Italian monastic *Rule of the Master*. The 150 psalms are spread fairly evenly throughout eight "hours" prayed seven days of week. The eight hours are: Vigil/Matins at 3 or 4 AM; Lauds at sunrise; Prime after breakfast; Terce at 9 AM; Sext at noon; None at 3 PM; Vespers at sunset; and Compline at bedtime. Prime and Compline seem to be original Benedictine inventions.

The psalms and canticles are sung with antiphons. The antiphons are brief verses, usually from the psalm or canticle, that introduce and conclude the psalm and bring out an emphasis in the text. Each psalm or cluster of psalms and canticle is concluded with the Gloria Patri. Benedict introduced Latin hymns into the liturgy of the hours and referred to them as "Ambrosian."

The Roman-Benedictine Office remained largely unchanged from the sixth century until the Second Vatican Council. Because of its importance I provide outlines of the offices here.

Matins on Sundays and Feasts at 3 AM
V/ O Lord, open my lips. R/ And my mouth shall proclaim your praise. (three times)
Psalm 95 with antiphon
Hymn
First Nocturn
six psalms with antiphons
versicle
blessing
four readings with responsory
Gloria Patri
Second Nocturn
six psalms with antiphons
versicle
four readings with responsory
Gloria Patri
Third Nocturn
three Old Testament canticles and alleluia
versicle
blessing
four readings with responsory
Te Deum (We praise you, O God)
Gospel of the day (omitted on nonfestival weekdays)
Te decet laus (It is right to praise you)
Concluding prayer
Benedicamus domino (V/ Let us bless the Lord. R/ Thanks be to God.)

Lauds
V/ O God, come to my aid. R/ O Lord, make haste to help me
Gloria Patri
Psalm 67 (solo)
Psalm 51
Two variable psalms
Canticle
Psalms 148–150

Epistle reading
Responsory
Hymn
Versicle
Benedictus with antiphon
Litany
Lord's Prayer (said aloud by the superior)

Structure of the "Little Hours" of Prime, Terce, Sext, None
O God, come to my aid . . .
Hymn
Three psalms
Short reading
Prayer

Vespers
O God, come to my aid . . .
Four consecutive psalms
Epistle reading
Responsory
Hymn
Versicle
Magnificat with antiphon
Litany
Lord's Prayer (said aloud by superior)
Concluding prayer
Benedicamus

Compline
O God, come to my aid . . .
Mutual confession of sins
Hymn
Psalm 4
Two other psalms
Short reading
Responsory
Versicle
Nunc dimittis with antiphon ("Protect us, Lord, while we are awake and safeguard
  us while we sleep, that we may keep watch with Christ and rest in peace")
Prayer
Blessing

D. Medieval Additions to the Divine Office

As with the sacramentaries, Roman office books (particularly the antiphonals, which contained the antiphons and responsories arranged for the hours and throughout the church year) were imported north of the Alps at the request of the Carolingian rulers. In this way the Roman Office was adopted throughout much of western and northern Europe. The Roman Office was similar to but not identical with the Benedictine Office. Synods held under the leadership of Archbishop Boniface of Mainz reinforced the chanting of the seven canonical hours "in a uniform manner and according to the usages of the Roman church" (Second Synod of Clovesho, 747, Canon 15).

The arrangement of the Roman Office underwent few changes from late antiquity until after the Second Vatican Council; there were only little modifications in the allotment of psalms. During the Middle Ages there were additions to the liturgy of the hours: additional proper offices for the sanctoral calendar (at the expense of the temporal cycle), a multiplication of votive offices (such as the Little Office of Our Lady and the Office of the Dead), and the addition of the office of the chapter after Prime (when the daily business of the monastery or the cathedral was conducted).

The reform of the clergy in the Rule of St. Chrodegang, Bishop of Metz (d. 766), reinforced the growing tendency to have secular clergy living together *canonice*, that is, grouped together in the church in which they served, rather than *vagi*, as isolated individuals.[11] Living together in a compound (such as the cathedral "close") in a celibate lifestyle, the obligation of the secular clergy with regard to the daily prayer offices was not too different from that of the monks.

E. The Invention of the Breviary

A major change occurred with the emergence of mendicant orders (e.g., Dominicans, Franciscans, Augustinians) in the twelfth and thirteenth centuries whose work took them outside cloistered compounds (e.g., preaching missions, work among the poor, teaching in schools and universities). These friars (brothers) could not gather in community to sing the prayer offices because they were on the road, begging for alms, working in hospitals, or studying in the universities. They drew upon the provision in the *Rule of St. Benedict* that anyone not present in choir for the singing of the hours should recite them privately. The breviary was invented as a means of facilitating this practice of the private recitation of the hours.

The breviary contained everything that was needed for the recitation of the Divine Office, just as the missal contained everything that was needed for the celebration of Mass. This includes the orders of the offices with their fixed and proper parts. Fixed parts would include opening versicles, Gospel canticles appropriate to the office, and concluding prayers. Propers would include psalms with antiphons, hymns, readings, and responsories. The propers would be arranged in the order of the church year with its seasons and festivals, days of devotion and saints' days. Additional votive offices would be included in appendices. Copying or printing out all this material in the order in which it was needed took up many pages. Not surprisingly, breviaries tended to be multivolume works, but small enough to fit in saddlebags or shoulder sacks.

F. Books of the Hours

By the late Middle Ages, pious laypeople also desired to have prayer books like the breviaries that they could use for their personal devotions. These books of hours (called *horae* in Latin) were individually compiled, copied, and illustrated at the order of laypeople of means who were also literate. Each book is therefore unique, and thousands of examples survive from the fifteenth and sixteenth centuries. Such books might be given to brides by their husbands or by mothers to their sons going off to battle. Books of hours were usually written in Latin, although there are many entirely or partially written in vernacular European languages, especially Dutch and French. The English term *primer* (or *prymer*) is usually now reserved for those books written in Old English.

As the original monastic prayer was simply an expansion of early Christian household prayer, so in the late Middle Ages Christian households borrowed elements form monastic prayer for their own devotions. The typical book of hours was an abbreviated form of the breviary that contained some of the offices recited in monasteries. It was developed for laypeople who wished to incorporate elements of monastic prayer into their devotional life. Reciting the hours typically centered upon the reading of a number of psalms and other prayers. Typical material in many books of hours includes:

> a calendar of church feasts
> an excerpt from each of the four Gospels
> the Little Office of the Blessed Virgin Mary
> the fifteen gradual psalms or Psalms of Degrees (120–134)
> the seven Penitential Psalms (6, 32, 38, 51, 102, 130, 143)
> the Litany of the Saints
> an Office for the Dead
> devotional prayers for use during Mass
> meditations on the passion of Christ
> Marian prayers
> various other prayers

However, each book contained the material specified by its owner.

G. The Quinoñes Breviary

There was a great desire for reform of the Divine Office by the late Middle Ages. The obligation of clerics to pray the daily prayer offices had become a burden because of the multiplication of offices, additional material, and increases in pastoral or other responsibilities. The choir offices had become sterile and new religious orders such as the Society of Jesus (the Jesuits) gave up the choral or communal celebration of the hours entirely.

Humanist reformers objected to the apocryphal and legendary hagiographic material in the readings of the breviary, the overgrowth in the sanctoral cycle, and the excess of votive offices.

There were numerous projects to reform the breviary in the sixteenth century. The most important of these was the effort undertaken by the Spanish Franciscan Cardinal Francisco de los Angeles de Quiñones (1482–1545), the minister general of the Franciscans, at the invitation of Pope Clement VII. He began this work in 1535 and it was issued in that year by Pope Paul III. A second recension followed in 1536. Quiñones suppressed votive offices, legends in the readings, as well as antiphons, responsories, hymns, and intercessions appropriate to a choral office; reduced Matins to one nocturn; spread the recitation of the psalter over a week, with no more than three psalms per office, and without repetition, and increased the length of the Scripture readings.[12]

This breviary was primarily intended for private use but (with permission) it began to be used in many religious houses and more than one hundred editions were printed between 1536 and 1566. However, it was subject to much criticism for its disregard of tradition and Pope Paul IV proscribed it in 1558.

H. The Divine Office in the Lutheran Reformation

Following the example of Martin Luther,[13] many Reformation church orders in the sixteenth century provided forms of morning and evening prayer (Matins and Vespers) that served as public congregational services in place of the daily Mass, if communicants were lacking. Hymn singing became a feature of the Lutheran office as a means of facilitating popular participation. The details of the offices varied from one church order to another to another, but all of them retained versicles, psalms, readings, hymns, canticles, and prayers—usually in that order.[14] Preaching was encouraged in the prayer offices and one of the few discrepancies in the orders was where to place the sermon (should it precede or follow the canticle?). In the construction of these offices elements of Matins and Lauds were joined into one morning office and elements of Vespers and Compline were joined into one evening office. The telltale sign of this was the provision for singing either the Te Deum Laudamus or the Benedictus at Matins and either the Magnificat or the Nunc dimittis at Vespers. The Te Deum was usually reserved for Sundays and festivals. The psalms and canticles could be sung in Latin by the choir or as chorale versifications by the congregation. The choral office was maintained in city churches with Latin schools, such as at the Thomaskirche in Leipzig. The Sunday worship schedule included Matins as the early service, the Holy Communion as the chief service, and Vespers in the afternoon.

I. Morning Prayer and Evening Prayer in the Book of Common Prayer (1549/1552/1559/1662)[15]

Archbishop Thomas Cranmer followed Martin Luther's recommendation that daily public morning and evening prayer replace daily masses in the churches. He followed the lead of some German Lutheran church orders in combining Matins and Lauds into one office of morning prayer and in combining Vespers and Compline into one office of evening prayer. The 1552 Prayer Book added a confession of sins, inspired by Prime. Cranmer drew upon the breviary experiments of the Spanish Cardinal Quiñones by eliminating antiphons and responsories and providing a course of psalmody in which all 150 psalms were spread over the course of a month. The Gloria Patri follows all psalms and canticles. A daily lectionary provided readings from the Old and New Testament (and Apocrypha) for both morning and evening prayer. The 1662 Prayer Book added an anthem (a setting of a biblical text) following the third collect ("In quires and places where they sing, here followeth the anthem."). In more recent versions of the *Book of Common Prayer* this is followed by other prayers. The Prayer Book provides no office hymns, reflecting the Reformed aversion to nonbiblical song, but a tradition developed after 1662 of singing hymns after the office proper.

Morning Prayer
Scripture sentence
Exhortation
Confession of sins
Declaration of pardon
Lord's Prayer (said aloud by the priest in the choir)
O Lord, open thou our lyppes. R/ And our mouth shal shewe forth thy prayse.
O God, make spede to save us. R/ O Lord, make haste to help us.
Glory be to the Father . . .
Psalm 95
Other psalms appointed in the table
Old Testament lesson
Te Deum or Benedicite opera omnia ("All ye works of the Lord, bless the Lord")
New Testament lesson
Benedictus or Jubilate Deo (Psalm 100)
Apostles' Creed (So-called Athanasian Creed used on thirteen festivals)
Salutation
Little litany
Lord's Prayer
Preces or Suffrages (psalm verses used as prayers)
Three collects: of the day; for peace; for grace

Evening Prayer
Lord's Prayer (said by the priest)
O Lord, open our lippes . . .
O God, make speed to save us.
Glory be to the Father . . .

The psalms appointed in the table
Old Testament lesson
Magnificat
New Testament lesson
Nunc dimittis or Meus misereatur (Psalm 67)
Three collects: of the day, for peace, against perils

J. Matins and Vespers in the Lutheran Common Service

The committee charged with drafting the Common Service of the Evangelical Lutheran Church (1888) had the task of deriving their orders from the "pure" Lutheran church orders of the sixteenth century, but putting it in English. They drew upon the language of the Prayer Book of The Episcopal Church in the U.S.A. as well as Anglican chant. The Common Service included orders of Matins and Vespers. These services were included in the English-language hymnals of various Lutheran synods. The *Service Book and Hymnal* (*SBH*) of 1958 was the culmination of the restoration of the historic Lutheran liturgy in English. We provide here the full development of these orders of Matins and Vespers in *SBH*.[16]

Matins

Versicles: O Lord, open thou my lips. R/ And my mouth shall show forth thy praise.
Make haste, O God, to deliver me. R/ Make haste to help me, O Lord.
Gloria Patri with Alleluia (omitted during Lent)
Invitatory: O come, let us worship the Lord. R/ For he is our maker.
Venite exultemus (Ps. 95:1-7a)
The Hymn (a morning hymn)
The Psalm (one or more psalms with the Gloria Patri after each one)
The Lesson (one or more readings)
After each reading: O Lord, have mercy upon us. R/ Thanks be to God.
A Responsory or Hymn may be sung.
A brief Sermon or Address may follow.
The Canticle:
Te Deum Laudamus (on Sundays except during Advent and Lent)
Benedictus (on weekdays and during Advent and Lent)
Benedicite, omnia opera (during Eastertide)
The Prayer: The Little Litany (threefold Kyrie)
The Lord's Prayer
The Salutation and Collect for the Day
Other collects
Collect for Grace with versicle: Let my mouth be filled with thy praise.
R/ And with thy honor all the day.
The Benedicamus and Benediction

Vespers
The Versicles (as in Matins)
The Gloria Patri with Alleluia (except during Lent)
The Psalm (one or more psalms with the Gloria Patri after each one)
The Lesson (one or more readings)
After each reading: O Lord, have mercy upon us. R/ Thanks be to God.
The Hymn (an evening hymn)
The Versicle: Let my prayer be set forth before thee as incense.
R/ And the lifting up of my hands as the evening sacrifice.
The Canticle:
Magnificat (proper at any time)
Nunc dimittis (proper at any time except the greater festivals)
The Prayer: The Little Litany (threefold Kyrie)
The Lord's Prayer
The Salutation and Collect for the Day
Other collects
The Collect for Peace with the versicle: The Lord will give strength to his people.
R/ The Lord will bless his people with peace.
The Benedicamus and Benediction

The *Common Service Book* (1917), *The Lutheran Hymnal* (1941), the *Service Book and Hymnal* (1958), and *Lutheran Worship* (1982) provided material for use in Matins and Vespers: proper invitatories and responsories for the seasons and festivals of the church year; tables of readings and psalms for use in Matins and Vespers on Sundays and festivals; a selection of morning and evening hymns in the hymnal portions of the book; morning and evening suffrages, which could be used as the form of the prayer in Matins and Vespers; and the great litany, which could be sung in place of the general prayer in the Sunday service (unless Holy Communion was celebrated) or as the form of the prayer in Matins and Vespers.

K. The Reformed Roman Office (1971)[17]

When the breviary of Cardinal Quiñones was proscribed, the Roman breviary reverted to what it had been before the Reformation. There was some pruning of the sanctoral cycle in the revised Roman breviaries under Pope Pius V in 1569 and Pope Pius X in 1911. The breviary of Pius X also reduced Matins from twelve psalms to nine, and assigned only one praise psalm each day of the week for Lauds rather than all three Lauds psalms. Psalms 51 (50) and 63 (62) were abandoned as fixed psalms at Lauds, as were the traditional canticles, except during Lent and for vigils.

The reform of the Roman Office after Vatican II was more radical than the reforms of Pius X. It involved a wholesale structural revision of the orders of Matins and Vespers, as follows:

Matins
Psalm 95 (94)
Hymn
Morning psalm
Old Testament canticle
Praise psalm
Scripture reading
Brief response
Benedictus
Prayers
Concluding collect
Blessing

Vespers
Hymn
Two psalms
New Testament canticle
Scripture lessons
Brief response
Magnificat
Intercessions
Concluding collect
Blessing

This is a much-simplified structure. Moreover, the amount of psalmody in the Divine Office is reduced and additional biblical canticles are assigned. Dissatisfaction comes from the fact that it is still regarded as a clerical, and indeed, as a private office rather than as the daily prayer of the whole church. Critics have suggested that the Roman Office can become popular only if cathedral-type elements are included.[18]

L. Morning Praise and Evensong (University of Notre Dame, 1973)
A major critic of the reformed Roman Office, William G. Storey, a professor of liturgy at the University of Notre Dame, set to work with his students to produce a form of the office that would include "cathedral" elements and have a popular character. An experiment with the office of Vespers or Evensong was conducted daily in the Log Chapel on the university campus and on Sundays in the Lady Chapel of the Basilica. Ordained graduate students took turns presiding and cantors and readers were recruited from among undergraduate students. David Wright, O.P., and Frank Quinn, O.P., provided musical settings so that the entire office could be sung.[19]

Especially noteworthy was that Vespers began with a lucernarium that included a procession with a lighted candle, a light hymn based on the *Phos hilaron*, and a thanksgiving for light translated from the *Apostolic Tradition* and the *Apostolic Constitutions*.

Incensing of the people was done during the singing of Psalm 141. Another psalm and a New Testament canticle were sung, followed by a time of silent reflection and a psalm prayer. After a brief reading there was again a time of silent reflection, followed by a brief homily on the reading. The Magnificat was sung and the altar was incensed on major feast days and Sundays. The prayer that followed was a Byzantine litany with the response sung in harmony by the congregation. Morning Praise was similar to the new Roman order of Matins. But for both offices brief readings were selected that related to the time of the day or the season in the church year.

M. Lutheran Book of Worship (1978)

The importance of this work done in the liturgical studies program at Notre Dame is reflected in the orders of Morning Prayer (Matins) and Evening Prayer (Vespers) in *Lutheran Book of Worship* (*LBW*) of 1978. The order of Evening Prayer is similar to the Notre Dame office, except that two additional opening versicles provide cover for a longer procession with the candle, a translation of the actual text of the *Phos hilaron* is sung, and a new thanksgiving for light was composed that has a paschal character (making reference to the pillar of fire that protected the ancient Israelites in their exodus from Egypt). The thanksgivings for light from the *Apostolic Tradition* and the *Apostolic Constitutions* are provided in the section of propers. A cathedral-type element was provided for Morning Prayer in the paschal blessing that may be done on Sundays at the end of the Matins with a gathering around the baptismal font. It consists of: versicle ("As many as have been baptized into Christ have put on Christ. R/ Alleluia"), resurrection Gospel, Te Deum Laudamus, collect, and blessing (with sprinkling of water).

In keeping with Lutheran tradition, an office hymn is sung after the psalmody in both Morning and Evening Prayer. Also, taking instruction from Anglican practice a pulpit office was appended to the prayer offices for occasions when a sermon is desired. The effort was to recover Matins and Vespers as prayer offices rather than preaching offices. For occasional preaching offices apart from the context of the Holy Communion, *LBW* provided a Service of the Word.

LBW provided seasonal invitatories for Matins and light versicles for Vespers but no responsories after the readings. The translation of the psalter is that of the 1979 *Book of Common Prayer* of the Episcopal Church in the U.S.A. But *LBW* provided a course of psalmody that related to the time of the day and the season of the church year rather than the thirty-day continuous recitation of psalms provided in the Episcopal Prayer Book. However, *LBW* did adopt the two-year daily lectionary of the Episcopal Prayer Book, providing for each day an Old Testament reading, an epistle reading, and a Gospel reading. This is a *lectio continua* lectionary and is not suitable for a cathedral-type office.

LBW also provided a full traditional office of Compline. While Compline originated in a monastic context, it has the character of a cathedral office because it is explicitly related to the time of the day at which it is prayed: before going to sleep at night.

LBW offices of Morning Prayer, Evening Prayer, and Compline were included in the worship books of the Lutheran Church–Missouri Synod, *Lutheran Worship* (1982) and

Lutheran Service Book (2006), along with the Common Service orders for Matins and Vespers. The basic *LBW* orders of Morning Prayer and Evening Prayer were also continued in *Evangelical Lutheran Worship* (*ELW*; 2006) of the Evangelical Lutheran Church in America. In *ELW*, however, the canticles and psalms avoid the use of masculine pronoun for God and sometimes get around this by addressing the verses of the psalms *to* God (therefore using "you") when the text is *about* God (for whom repetition of "God" or "the Lord" might call for "he"). More seriously, the Gloria Patri has been omitted from the Venite exultemus (Psalm 95) and the canticles, although it is inconsistently retained in the setting of Psalm 141 in Evening Prayer.

The Daily Prayer of the Church, edited by Philip Pfatteicher, provides all of the material needed for the singing of the *LBW* prayer offices in one thick volume, arranged like a breviary but clearly intended for communal use. Only the lectionary readings are missing.[20] This version, which includes antiphons for psalms and canticles and versicles before collects, serves well in retreats. It would have been helpful to provide musical settings for the antiphons.

N. An Order for Worship in the Evening (1979)

The *Book of Common Prayer* of The Episcopal Church in the U.S.A. (*BCP*) retains the orders of Morning and Evening Prayer in the Anglican tradition in both traditional and contemporary English. However, in keeping with the revived interest in cathedral-type prayer, it provides an order for worship in the Evening that draws upon cathedral-type elements.

> **The Service of Light**
> "Light and peace in Jesus Christ our Lord . . ."
> Brief reading
> Collect for light
> *Phos hilaron* or other hymn of light
> Psalmody
> Lesson
> Magnificat or other canticle
> Intercessions and Our Father
> Blessing and dismissal
> Sign of peace

5. How might daily prayer offices become daily once again?

The Anglican tradition alone among the Western Christian traditions has preserved the practice of daily public morning and evening prayer. In the cathedral and collegiate churches in Great Britain and in many other parts of the Anglican world, these offices are sung daily by trained choirs of boys (children) and men (adults). Morning and Evening Prayer in the *Book of Common Prayer* have been used in households as well as publicly in churches. Historical instances of this household use are during the Puritan Commonwealth in England when the Prayer Book was abolished and in colonial America in the absence of clergy or parish churches.[21]

The liturgy of time began as household prayer and if it is to become daily prayer once again this will take place only in the household. We cannot imagine that the whole Christian people ever gathered for daily prayer every day. Everyday secular life did not allow for this in the fourth century and it does not allow for it in the twenty-first. But the ancient Christian instinct to pray in the morning and in the evening has remained intact throughout the centuries. While Martin Luther did not provide explicit orders for morning and evening prayer, as he did with his orders of the Mass and orders of baptism, he made a lasting impression on evangelical household prayer with his orders of prayer in the *Small Catechism* upon arising in the morning and before retiring at night. The structure of this household office is as follows:

Invocation of the Trinity with the sign of the cross
The Apostles' Creed and Lord's Prayer (kneeling or standing)
A morning prayer/An evening prayer (original compositions still widely used)
In the morning, a hymn on the Ten Commandments "or whatever your devotion
    may suggest"

Lutheran Service Book (2006) provides fuller forms of "Daily Prayer for Individuals and Families"[22] and Concordia Publishing House prints laminated copies of these orders for use in homes.

Lutheran Book of Worship envisioned its public and communal orders being used in a pared-down way in households and among small Christian groups. Little red circles in the margins indicated items that could be extracted from the public offices to provide household offices.

A Lutheran breviary, *For All the Saints*, has been published in four volumes by the American Lutheran Publicity Bureau.[23] Compiled by Pastor Frederick Schumacher and members of St. Matthew Lutheran Church in White Plains, New York, these volumes includes the texts of the *LBW* orders for Matins, Vespers, Responsive Prayer, and Compline; opening prayers for each day plus special commemorative days appropriate to the season; the full Revised Standard Version text of the three Scripture readings for each day in the *LBW* and *BCP* daily lectionary; a fourth reading and a closing prayer for each day from one of the saints from the second to the twentieth century; and all 150 psalms following the thirty-day psalm course in the *BCP*, using the *BCP/LBW* translation with *LBW* psalm collects.

Finally, we would note that many Christians, including clergy and lay oblates of monastic communities, continue to use a traditional breviary in their home devotions. *Benedictine Daily Prayer* is called a "short breviary" because it does not include the patristic and other nonscriptural readings that the standard four-volume set of *Christian Prayer* does.[24] It does have readings for memorials, feast days, solemnities, and two Scripture readings to use at vigils or office of readings. In the proper of saints, the Benedictine calendar is followed, which is different from the Roman calendar. For the psalter, the breviary uses the inclusive-language Grail Psalms (inclusive language with regard to humans, not to God). The sing-song nature of the Grail Psalms (they are meant to be sung) may become monotonous through regular spoken use. The New Revised Standard Version of the Bible is used for the Scripture readings. This breviary is pretty much what is used at St. John's Abbey in Collegeville, Minnesota, currently the largest men's Catholic monastery in the world. The breviary provides two biblical readings for each day (usually other than from the Gospels) and nonscriptural readings for some of the feasts.

For further reading

Bradshaw, Paul F. *Daily Prayer in the Early Church: A Study of the Origin and Early Development of the Divine Office.* New York: Oxford University Press, 1982.
Gallen, John, S.J. *Christians at Prayer.* Notre Dame: University of Notre Dame Press, 1977.
Salmon, Pierre, O.S.B. *The Breviary through the Centuries*, trans. Sister David Mary, S.N.J.M. Collegeville: Liturgical, 1962.
Taft, Robert, S.J. *The Liturgy of the Hours in East and West: The Origins of the Divine Office and Its Meaning for Today.* Collegeville: Liturgical, 1986.

5

The Church-Year Calendar

1. *What is the fixed day of Christian worship?*
2. *What are the principal festivals and seasons?*
3. *What are the lesser festivals, days of devotion, and commemorations?*
4. *What do we do the rest of the time?*
5. *What is the difference between a feast and a fast?*

1. What is the fixed day of Christian worship?

Fixed days of worship are common in world religions. While worship is offered every day, and often multiple times during the day, certain days are regarded as especially holy. The fixed day of Muslim worship is Friday because on that day God created humankind. The fixed day of Jewish worship is Saturday, because it is the day on which God rested from all his labors of creation. The fixed day of Christian worship is Sunday, because Jesus rose from the dead on the first day of the week (the Roman day of the Sun).

A day of rest from ordinary work that could be devoted to worship and study is enshrined in the Decalogue: "Remember the sabbath day to keep it holy." The sabbath was a memorial of God's rest on the seventh day. For Jews, therefore, *Shabbat* is unquestionably on Saturday. Jesus' observance of the sabbath was criticized by the Pharisees in the Gospels. The Pharisees had defined "forty minus one" works to be abstained from on *Shabbat*, and Jesus and his disciples had been accused of breaking some of these customs during his ministry. Christians from very early times were conflicted about observance of the sabbath day. Colossians 2:16 suggests that early Christians had been judged by others in their traditions of eating foods and in observance of particulars of sabbath and festivals.

The first evidence that Christians gathered on the first day of the week, the day on which Jesus rose from the dead, rather than on the sabbath, appears in Acts 20:7 where the disciples met and "broke bread" together. John the Seer refers to the "Lord's Day" (*kuriake hemera*) in Revelation 1:10. *Kuriake*, meaning "the Lord's," later became the Greek word for Sunday. Some early Christians observed sabbath on Saturday, though resting on Saturday was prohibited by the church in 363 CE; over the first centuries an increasing number of Christians gathered for worship on Sunday. Justin Martyr reported to the Roman Senate that Christians assembled in one place around "the memoirs of the Apostles" and the Eucharist "on the day of the sun" in his *First Apology* 67.

The Roman calendar included the day of the Sun (Latin: *dies Solis*) for worship of the Invincible Sun (*Sol Invictus*). On March 7, 321, Emperor Constantine I decreed that Sunday would be observed throughout the Roman Empire as the day of rest. This decree, of course, would have favored worshipers of the Invincible Sun as well as Christians. It ordered:

> On the venerable day of the Sun let the magistrates and people residing in cities rest, and let all workshops be closed. In the country however persons engaged in agriculture may freely and lawfully continue their pursuits because it often happens that another day is not suitable for grain-sowing or vine planting; lest by neglecting the proper moment for such operations the bounty of heaven should be lost.[1]

Many Christians today consider Sunday to be sabbath, a holy day and a day of rest and church attendance. Denominations that observe Saturday as sabbath are called "Sabbatarians"; however, the name "Sabbatarian" has also been claimed by Christians, especially Protestants, who believe Sunday must be observed with just the sort of rigorous abstinence from work associated with *Shabbat*. For most Christians the custom and obligation of Sunday rest has not been as strict as the Jewish sabbath observance. It has been limited to the obligation to avoid work on Sunday. More recently in history, Christians in the Seventh-day Adventist, Seventh Day Baptist, and Church of God (Seventh Day) denominations (along with many related or similar denominations), as well as many messianic Jews, have revived the practice of abstaining from work and gathering for worship on Saturdays. For mainline Christians, however, Sunday is the fixed day for worship in honor of the resurrection and the new creation, whether it is a day of rest in civil society or not.

Christians inherited from Judaism the idea that the liturgical day begins on the eve of the day before. *Shabbat* starts on Friday night. In liturgical use, therefore, Sunday really begins on Saturday evening. This is the justification for the Roman Catholic practice of having an evening Mass on Saturday that fulfills the obligation of Sunday Mass attendance. Actually, a vigil Mass in anticipation of Sunday is a practice of long standing in the church. Vespers (evening prayer) on Saturday night is liturgically "first Vespers" of the Sunday. The same evening anticipation applies to other major festivals and commemoration.

In the Eastern Orthodox Church, Sunday begins at the Little Entrance of Vespers (or All-Night Vigil) on Saturday evening and runs until the Vespers on Sunday night.

During this time, the dismissal at all services begins with the words, "May Christ our True God, who rose from the dead . . ." Anyone who wishes to receive Holy Communion at Divine Liturgy on Sunday morning is required to attend Vespers the night before. Interestingly, a tradition developed among Lutherans in the late sixteenth century of attending Saturday Vespers, making a corporate confession and receiving individual absolution within that service, as a way of preparing to receive Holy Communion on Sunday.

Among Orthodox Christians, Sunday is considered to be a "Little Pascha" (Easter) and, because of the paschal joy, the making of prostrations is usually forbidden. Where Western Christians, for example, might kneel to receive communion even on Sunday, the Orthodox stand on the Lord's Day. The practice of standing to receive Holy Communion has been established in the Roman Catholic Church also since the Second Vatican Council.

2. What are the principal festivals and seasons?

In addition to a fixed day of weekly worship, world religions also observe special festivals that celebrate the central affirmations of their faith. The major Jewish holy days are:

Rosh Hashanah—The Jewish New Year
Aseret Yemei Teshuva—Ten Days of Repentance
Yom Kippur—Day of Atonement
Sukkot—Feast of Tents commemorating the wilderness wandering
Shemini Atzeret and Simchat Torah—Completing the annual cycle of Torah readings
Hanukkah—Festival of Lights
Purim—Festival of Lots
Pesach—Passover
Sefirah—Counting of the Omer
Shavuot—Feast of Weeks commemorating the giving of the Law

New holy days have been added to the Jewish calendar since the establishment of the state of Israel:

Yom HaShoah—Holocaust Remembrance Day
Yom Hazikaron—Memorial Day
Yom Ha'atzmaut—Israel Independence Day
Yom Yerushalaim—Jerusalem Day

Christianity also has festivals that mark the liturgical year. The two principal festivals are Easter (Pascha) and Christmas (Nativity of Our Lord). There is evidence in the New Testament that Pascha and Pentecost were being observed, not only in the Jewish

Christian communities but among Paul's Gentile congregations as well.[2] The Christians
of Asia Minor were definitely celebrating Pascha in the middle of the second century
on the 14/15 of Nisan. There is no certain attestation to Christmas before the fourth
century. We will discuss Christmas, Easter, and Pentecost more thoroughly in the next
three chapters. Here we note that the rest of the church year clusters around these days.
In the Western church the current calendar is as follows:

Advent—A four-week penitential season before Christmas that begins on the Sunday closest to St. Andrew's Day, November 30

Christmas—The Feast of the Nativity of our Lord on December 25 and the twelve-
day season that follows

The Epiphany of Our Lord—January 6, celebrating the visit of the Magi to the
Christ child

The Baptism of Our Lord—The Sunday after the Epiphany

The Presentation of Jesus and Purification of Mary—February 2 (forty days after
Christmas)

Ordinary Time or Time after the Epiphany, the length of which depends on the date
of Easter

Pre-Lenten Sundays—In the old calendar these were Septuagesima, Sexagesima,
Quinquagesima; they have been suppressed in the reformed new Roman Lectionary
(1969) and calendars and lectionaries based on it.

Ash Wednesday—The beginning of Lent

Lent—A forty-day penitential season, not including Sundays which are "in" but not
"of" Lent

Passiontide—In the old calendar the last two weeks of Lent (including Holy Week)

Annunciation to the Blessed Virgin Mary—March 25 (transferred to a Monday if it
falls on a Sunday or to the Monday after Easter if it falls during Holy Week)

Holy Week—The week beginning on Palm Sunday ending on Easter

Easter Triduum—The three days of Maundy or Holy Thursday, Good Friday, Holy
Saturday with its Great Vigil

Easter season—Easter Day and the Great Fifty Days ending on Pentecost

The Ascension of Our Lord—Forty days after Easter

Pentecost—The Fiftieth Day; end of the Easter season

Ordinary Time, Time after Pentecost, Time after Trinity, or Kingdomtide—Various
designations of the Sundays of the year, the length of which depends on the date of
Easter

Trinity Sunday—The Sunday after Pentecost

The Body of Christ (Corpus Christi)—The Thursday after Trinity Sunday, now usually celebrated on the following Sunday in American Catholic parishes.

The Sacred Heart of Jesus (in the Catholic tradition)—Friday in the third week after
Pentecost

The Assumption of Mary (Mary the Mother of our Lord)—August 15
All Saints' Day—November 1
All Souls' Day—November 2
Christ the King—The last Sunday of the church year

While this is a long list of festivals, the church year is really composed of three elements:

The Incarnation Cycle: the Advent and Christmas seasons through the Epiphany
The Paschal Cycle: the Lenten and Easter seasons through Pentecost
Ordinary Time or Sundays of the Year after the Epiphany and after Pentecost

These days and seasons constitute the temporal cycle of the church year. Alongside the temporal cycle is the sanctoral cycle or calendar of commemorations (saint's days), some of which have been included in the above and in the following lists. We will consider this calendar separately in the next section of this chapter.

The Eastern calendar varies only slightly from the Western. The church year begins on September 1. The other days in calendrical order are as follows:

Nativity of the Theotokos—September 8, the birth of Mary to Joachim and Anne (also observed by Roman Catholics)
Elevation of the Cross—September 14, the celebration of the rediscovery of what was believed to be the original cross on which Christ was crucified during the excavation for the Church of the Holy Sepulcher in Jerusalem c. 330 (also observed by Roman Catholics as the Triumph of the Cross and by Anglicans and Lutherans as Holy Cross Day)
Entrance of the Theotokos (Mary) into the temple at age three—November 21
Nativity of Our Lord and Savior Jesus Christ—December 25 (Christmas)
Theophany—January 6 (the Epiphany), celebrating the baptism of Jesus Christ
Meeting of Our Lord in the Temple—February 2
Great Lent—Eight weeks instead of six in order to account for forty days of fasting, since in the Eastern church Saturdays as well as Sundays are feast days
Annunciation of the Theotokos—March 25. In Eastern practice, should this feast fall during Holy Week or on Pascha itself, the Feast of the Annunciation is not transferred to another day. In fact, the conjunction of the feasts of the Annunciation and Pascha, known as "Kyriou-Pascha," is considered an extremely festive event.
Entry into Jerusalem—Sunday before Pascha
Holy Week
Pascha (Easter Day)
Pentecostarion—The Sundays of Pascha (Easter) through the Sunday after Pentecost, which is also called the Sunday of All Saints
Ascension—Forty days after Pascha

Pentecost—Fifty days after Pascha
Transfiguration of Our Lord—August 6
Dormition (falling asleep) of the Theotokos (i.e., Mary)—August 15

The chief Christian festival is Easter or Pascha. However, its date is calculated differently in the East and the West. All are agreed with the Council of Nicea in 325 that Easter is the first Sunday after the full moon that falls on or after March 21 (nominally the day of the vernal equinox). However, whereas Western Christians follow the Gregorian calendar in their calculations, the Orthodox calculate the fixed date of March 21 according to the Julian calendar, and observe the additional rule that Easter may not precede or coincide with the first day of the Jewish Passover. This is a nod to the ancient Quartodeciman (14 Nisan) practice in Asia Minor of not beginning the Christian paschal feast until the Jewish paschal feast on 14 Nisan was over at midnight.

3. What are the lesser festivals, days of devotion, and commemorations?

A distinction is made in the Christian liturgical traditions between greater festivals, lesser festivals, and days of devotion, using various nomenclature. Many of these are saints' days that are included in the sanctoral cycle of festivals and commemorations.

In all the churches Sunday as the day of resurrection has priority in celebrations. Only rarely would Sunday propers be suppressed in favor of another festival. This becomes especially an issue on the so-called green Sundays of Ordinary Time after the Epiphany and after Pentecost.

The Roman Catholic Church calls its principal holy days in the liturgical calendar solemnities. These usually commemorate an event in the life of Jesus, his mother Mary, or other important saints. The observance begins with the vigil on the evening before the actual date of the feast. In what is now the ordinary form of the Roman Rite feast days and memorials rank after solemnities and are called memorials. These are mostly commemorations of saints. Some of these are obligatory and others are optional. The Code of Canon Law allows conferences of bishops, with the prior approval of the Apostolic See, to suppress some of the holy days of obligation or transfer them to a Sunday. Among other differences, the Gloria and the Creed are said or sung at the Mass of a solemnity and a feast, but not at that of a memorial.

In Eastern Orthodoxy the ranking of feasts varies from church to church. The Russian Orthodox Church distinguishes between Great Feasts, All-Night Vigils, Polyeleos ("much oil" or, by connotation, "much mercy"), Great Doxology, Sextupple (having six stichera at Vespers and six troparia at Matins), Double (i.e., two simple feasts celebrated together), and Simple. The principle seen in other churches also applied in Russian Orthodoxy. The holy days are divided into two categories: the great feast days that commemorate events in the lives of Christ and the Theotokos (Mary); and holy days that commemorate the various events in the lives of the saints.

The Episcopal *Book of Common Prayer* distinguishes between Principal Feasts, Holy Days, Days of Special Devotion, and Days of Optional Observance ("Black Letter Days"). In a similar way *Lutheran Book of Worship* and now *Evangelical Lutheran Worship* distinguish between Festivals, Lesser Festivals, Days of Devotion, and Commemorations. Holy Days or Lesser Festivals include saints' days and special observances such as Reformation Day and the Day of National Thanksgiving. Days of (Special) Devotion include Ash Wednesday and the days of Lent and Holy Week, including Maundy Thursday and Good Friday. Days of Optional Devotion or Commemorations include commemorations in the calendar that are not holy days or lesser festivals. Lesser festivals and commemorations should not replace a Sunday. In actual practice some lesser festivals and days of devotion do replace Sundays (e.g., Reformation Day, All Saints' Day). Some Lutherans still observe lesser festivals, such as days of apostles and evangelists, when they fall on a Sunday in Ordinary Time.

The calendars of the various churches do not agree on what days fall into which categories. For example, days of Mary, Joseph, and John the Baptist (e.g., August 15, March 19, June 24, respectively) are ranked as solemnities in the Roman Catholic calendar; in the Anglican and Lutheran calendars they are holy days or lesser festivals, respectively. Many days ranked as feasts in the Roman Catholic calendar are ranked as holy days and lesser festivals in the Anglican and Lutheran calendars (e.g., the days of apostles and evangelists). Sometimes different observances are held on the same day. January 1 in the Roman Catholic calendar is Mary, Mother of God (an ancient Roman observance); in the Anglican and Lutheran calendars January 1 is observed as The Circumcision and Name of Jesus (a Gallican observance).

Many of the saints' days listed as memorials in the Roman Catholic calendar are similarly listed as days of optional devotion or commemoration in the Anglican and Lutheran calendars.

Each church has its own saints as well as the saints commemorated by all. The Roman Catholic calendar differentiates between saints who are commemorated universally and saints who are commemorated locally.

The Anglican and Lutheran calendars after the Reformation typically retained biblical saints: the apostles and evangelists, St. Stephen the First Martyr (December 26), the Holy Innocents (December 28), and such feasts as the Presentation of Jesus and Purification of Mary (February 2), The Annunciation (March 25), and The Visit of Mary to Elizabeth (May 31), which are Marian festivals as well as festivals of our Lord. *Lutheran Book of Worship* added Mary, Mother of our Lord, on August 15. *Evangelical Lutheran Worship* added Joseph, Guardian of Jesus, on March 19. The Lutheran books and the *Book of Common Prayer* (1979) greatly expanded the list of commemorations of other biblical and nonbiblical saints. It is not expected that every one of these saints would be commemorated with a special liturgy but that parishes would identify some saints who are of special importance to the parish because of its ethnic heritage or mission setting and who would serve as examples of faith to be emulated.

4. What do we do the rest of the time?

The times after the Epiphany and after Pentecost have come to be called "Ordinary Time," which is intended to be an English translation of the Latin *Tempus per annum* (literally "time through the year"). The designation *ordinary* comes from the same root as the word *ordinal*, and in this sense means "the counted weeks." In the Roman Catholic Church and in some Protestant traditions, these are the weeks that do not belong to a proper season. In Latin, these seasons are called the weeks *per annum*, or "through the year." In the current form of the Roman Rite adopted following the Second Vatican Council, Ordinary Time consists of thirty-four Sundays and is divided into two sections: the weeks after the Epiphany and the weeks after Pentecost.

The proper liturgical materials for the weeks in Ordinary Time are numbered, although several Sundays are named for the feast they commemorate, such as the Baptism of Our Lord (First Sunday after the Epiphany), Trinity Sunday (First Sunday after Pentecost) and the Feast of Christ the King (last Sunday in the church year), and for American Catholics, the Feast of Corpus Christi (transferred from the Thursday after Trinity Sunday to the second Sunday after Pentecost). The three-year lectionaries used in the Roman Catholic Church and several other churches are characterized by continuous readings of the Epistle and Gospel. There is no theme for these times; hence they are not really "seasons" in the sense that Advent or Lent are seasons.

While in the older lectionaries one could construe an Epiphany season with a theme of "God in Christ made manifest," there never has been a Pentecost season as such, with clearly defined thematic content. As we get to the end of the Time after Pentecost, however, the readings have an eschatological character. We will see in the next chapter that this had to do with the development of the Advent season in the Gallican Church. But the last Sundays in the church year have been called "Kingdomtide" in some traditions.

5. What is the difference between a feast and a fast?

The liturgical year developed with clear distinctions between times of fasting (preparation for the celebration of a festival) and the times of feasting (the festival day or season itself). Thus Advent and Lent are times of fasting and preparation; Christmas and Easter are times of feasting. It is based on the simple observation that one doesn't fast and feast at the same time. Times of feasting are preeminently times of celebrating the Eucharist. Thus Sunday is never a day of fasting, not even during Lent, because it is the day of resurrection and hence of the eucharistic feast. The Orthodox also do not fast on the sabbath (Saturday), except on the Great Sabbath (Holy Saturday). This distinction has been more carefully observed in the Eastern than in the Western traditions. In the East the Eucharist is forbidden on fast days, although communion might be administered from the presanctified elements.[3]

The ancient Roman Church observed four fasting seasons (*Quatuor Temporum*) during the year in the months of December, February, May, and August. These fasting times, which may have their origin in ancient Roman practice and were known and observed by Pope Leo the Great (440–461), were called Ember Days, from the German *Quatember*.[4] Proper prayers and readings were provided for the Wednesdays, Fridays, and Saturdays of the Ember Days. These would have been the usual fast days for Christians. This Roman tradition of the Ember Days spread to western Europe. The Roman Catholic practice of holding ordinations during the Ember Days goes back to Pope Gelasius I (492–496).

Four times of fasting are also observed in the Eastern church:

Great Lent, which is an intense time of fasting, almsgiving, and prayer, extending for forty days prior to Palm Sunday and Holy Week, as a preparation for Pascha

The Nativity Fast (Winter Lent), which is a time of preparation for the Feast of the Nativity of Christ (Christmas), extending for forty days (like the ancient Gallican Advent fast)

The Apostles' Fast, which is variable in length, lasting anywhere from eight days to six weeks, in preparation for the Feast of Saints Peter and Paul (June 29)

The Dormition Fast, which lasts for two weeks from August 1 to August 14 in preparation for the Feast of the Dormition of the Theotokos (August 15)

The liturgical year is so constructed that during each of these fasting seasons, one of the Great Feasts occurs, so that fasting may be tempered with joy.

The *Didache* indicates that by the end of the first century Christians were fasting on Wednesdays and Fridays. Orthodox Christians continue these weekly fast days throughout the year (and some Orthodox monasteries also observe Monday as a fast day). Certain fixed days are always fast days, even if they fall on a Saturday or Sunday (in which case the fast is lessened somewhat, but not abrogated altogether). These days are: The Decollation (beheading) of St. John the Baptist; the Exaltation of the Cross; and the day before the Epiphany (January 5). There are several fast-free periods, when it is forbidden to fast, even on Wednesday and Friday. These are: the week following Pascha (Bright Week); the week following Pentecost; the period from the Nativity of Christ until January the 5th (the eve of the Epiphany); the first week of the Triodion (the Sundays before Great Lent); and the week following the thirty-third Sunday after the Pentecost.

Rules of fasting played an important part in the development of the church-year calendar. It may be timely to reconsider the value of liturgical as well as ascetical fasting. Ascetic fasts are undertaken for the purpose of cultivating a spiritual discipline, such as subduing the flesh (putting down one's own desires) in order to focus on the word of God. This is why the monastic life is a perpetual fast.

Liturgical fasts mark out certain days, seasons, and celebrations. Friday has been a day of fasting since at least the beginning of the second century. It helps Christians to identify weekly with the passion of Christ. Fasting during Lent originated as a way of preparing for Holy Baptism. The *Didache* already encourages those who are able to fast along with the candidates for baptism. Rules of fasting also developed in connection with receiving communion. The ancient practice was to fast from midnight until the Eucharist or Mass that day, but as masses after noon and in the evening became common, this was soon modified to fasting for three hours. Current canon law requires merely one hour of eucharistic fast (nothing but water and medicine before receiving communion). Martin Luther admitted in his *Small Catechism* that fasting and other bodily exercises are good disciplines in preparation for receiving the sacrament, but the best preparation is believing the words of Christ "given and shed for you for the forgiveness of sins." Luther's teaching had the effect of discouraging the eucharistic fast in Lutheran and other Protestant traditions, but the practice is not unknown.

There has been a growing interest in fasting. Fasting for self-care or personal gain must be distinguished from fasting that focuses on heightening the experience of hearing the word of God and receiving the sacrament of Holy Communion. Moreover, Christian fasting has traditionally been accompanied by the other disciplines of prayer and almsgiving (Matthew 6). For example, fasting during Lent may be combined with almsgiving for world hunger. Fasting is not about "me"; it is about imitating Christ and serving the needy neighbor.

For further reading

Adam, Adolf. *The Liturgical Year: Its History and Its Meaning after the Reform of the Liturgy*, trans. Matthew J. O'Connell. New York: Pueblo, 1981.

Johnson, Maxwell E., ed. *Between Memory and Hope: Readings in the Liturgical Year*. Collegeville: Liturgical, 2000.

Nocent, Adrian, O.S.B. *The Liturgical Year*, 4 vols. Collegeville: Liturgical, 1977.

Pfatteicher, Philip H. *The New Book of Festivals and Commemorations: Toward a Common Calendar of Saints*. Minneapolis: Fortress Press, 2008.

Rordorf, Willy. *Sunday: The History of the Day of Rest and Worship in the Earliest Centuries of the Christian Church*, trans. A. A. K. Graham. Philadelphia: Westminster, 1968.

Schmemann, Alexander. *Celebration of Faith: The Church Year*. Introduction by John Jillions. Crestwood: St. Vladimir's Seminary Press, 1994.

6
The Church Year
Advent through Lent

1. Advent: Why do we begin at the end?
2. Christmas: What are the options for celebration?
3. The Epiphany: What are the riches of the observance?
4. Time after the Epiphany: Is there an Epiphany season?
5. Ash Wednesday and Lent: How do we practice penitence
   and catechesis?

1. Advent: Why do we begin at the end?

In the Western church calendar, Advent is the beginning of the church year. The season historically begins on the fourth Sunday before Christmas with apocalyptic warnings of the second coming of Christ to judge the living and the dead. This gives the impression that the church year places last things first. A case can be made that this is a very good place to begin: with a clear sense of where we are heading before we set out on the journey. But Advent was not always the beginning of the church year and these eschatological readings were in place before Advent became officially the beginning of the church year in the West in the tenth century.

In fact, the church year began at different times in different local churches, and it was not always correlated with the civil year even in the society of Christendom. New Year's Day in Rome at the time of the development of a Christian calendar was January 1. But the ancient Roman calendar actually started the year on March 1, which is still reflected in the names of some months that derive from Latin: September (seven), October (eight), November (nine), December (ten). The year used in dates during the Roman Republic and the Roman Empire was the consular year, which began on the day when consuls first entered office. This date was stabilized on January 1 by Julius Caesar in 45 BCE when he introduced the Julian calendar. January 1 was adopted as the date of the new year in much of Europe when the Julian calendar was revised under the authority of Pope Gregory XIII in 1582. However, there were other new-year days. The new year started on December 25 in Germany until the thirteenth century and in Spain from the fourteenth to the sixteenth century. The new year also began on March 25, the feast of the Annunciation, in many parts of Europe in the Middle Ages. This was the official start of the new year in England until 1752, although Scotland changed to January 1 in 1600. The rest of Great Britain changed to January 1 when the Gregorian calendar was adopted on September 3, 1752 (which became September 14 because of a loss of eleven days that year).

In the Eastern Orthodox Church, the civil New Year falls on Gregorian January 14 (January 1 in the Julian calendar). Many people in the countries where Eastern Orthodoxy is culturally dominant celebrate both the Gregorian and Julian New Year holidays, with the Gregorian day celebrated as a civic holiday and the Julian date, the "Old New Year," as a religious holiday. The Orthodox churches of Georgia, Jerusalem, Russia, Macedonia, and Serbia still use the Julian calendar. However, the Eastern Orthodox Church liturgical calendar begins on September 1.

The liturgical year in the West now begins on the first day of Advent, the Sunday nearest to St. Andrew's Day (November 30). According to the Latin Rite of the Catholic Church, the liturgical year begins at 4:00 PM on the Saturday preceding the fourth Sunday prior to December 25. This was formalized by the Congregation of Rites in the seventeenth century, but it had been observed in this way in the liturgical books since the tenth century. The same liturgical calendar is followed by the Anglican and Lutheran churches.

The Roman Church of late antiquity did not have a season of Advent. The Gelasian Sacramentary begins with prayers for the Vigil of the Nativity of Our Lord. The great classic Advent prayers are not Roman at all, but Gallican. The fact that some of them are addressed to Christ (e.g., "Stir up your power, O Lord, and come . . .") is a tell-tale sign of their Gallican provenance. Roman collects are addressed to God (the Father) through Jesus Christ our Lord. In *Evangelical Lutheran Worship* the prayers of the day for the first and fourth Sundays of Advent for all three years of the lectionary begin, "Stir up your power, Lord Christ, and come."

How did this season come about and why does it have an eschatological character? It has been postulated that in Gaul and Spain Epiphany was the second great day in the year for public baptisms because, like Easter, it had its forty days of preparation. Certainly there was a commercial relationship between the eastern and western ends of the Mediterranean Sea and Eastern influence on the far Western church. The Gallican and Hispanic churches observed a six-week season before Christmas that began close to November 11, the Feast of St. Martin of Tours, so it was called "St. Martin's Lent," or *Quadragesima sancti Martini*. It was like Lent because it was a time of fasting, although the fast was not as strict as the Lenten fast. It was observed only on Mondays, Wednesdays, and Fridays—not on all days except Sunday, like in Lent. A fast developed in the Eastern churches that was called "St. Philip's Fast" because it begins on the day after the

Feast of St. Philip the Apostle, November 14, and lasted until the Epiphany. While the Epiphany was a day for public baptisms in the East, no documentary evidence exists to substantiate the Epiphany as a day of public baptism in the West. We need to look to other explanations for this forty-day fast in the Western church.

The readings for this season in lectionaries of the sixth through eighth centuries, such as those of Wurzburg and Murbach, include themes of Christ's second coming and the ministry of St. John the Baptist with his call for repentance. In other words, "St. Martin's Lent" lacked readings that would lend themselves to catechetical purposes. They had more to do with the examination and change of behavior—readings that would be appropriate to the theme of judgment or rendering an account which would be appropriate during harvest time.

November and December were times of harvest and culling the herds in western Europe in preparation for winter. During such times, a kind of fasting was observed in that long days of labor did not allow much time for eating. Once the harvest was gathered in and the herd culled, there was time for relaxing and feasting. During such times, the church appropriately sounded warnings against excess and encouraged a sense of gratitude or thanksgiving. This would account for the kind of readings that we now have in the lectionary at the end of the church year.[1]

In Rome there were public fasts four times a year going back to pre-Christian times called Ember Days (or, in Latin, *quattuor anni tempora*, the "four seasons of the year"). As we have seen, these were four separate sets of three days within the same week—specifically, the Wednesday, Friday, and Saturday—roughly equidistant in the course of the year that were set aside for fasting and prayer (formerly known as the *jejunia quattuor temporum*, "fasts of the four seasons"). The December Ember Days came at the time of harvest and the fast was observed before the thanksgiving for the harvest. We have sermons from Pope Leo I that speak of these days and gather together the themes of thanksgiving, fasting, eschatological judgment. He says in Sermon XVII,

> there is also the solemn fast of the tenth month, which is now kept by us according to yearly custom, because it is altogether just and godly to give thanks to the Divine bounty for the crops which the earth has produced for the use of men under the guiding hand of Providence. And to show that we do this with ready mind, we must exercise not only the self-restraint of fasting, but also diligence in almsgiving, that from the ground of our heart also may spring up the germ of righteousness and the fruit of love, and that we may deserve God's mercy showing mercy to the poor.[2]

When the December Ember Days were over, the Roman Church observed two weeks in preparation for the Nativity of Our Lord on December 25, centered on the annunciation. Thus there were two different ways of observing the weeks before Christmas in the West: Gallican and Roman.

In the tenth century when German emperors forced the merger of Frankish and Roman liturgies throughout the Holy Roman Empire, a four-week Advent season emerged in which the themes were the second coming of Christ and the ministry of St. John the Baptist. The church year was reckoned to begin on the First Sunday of Advent. The eschatological readings of November carried over into Advent. The ministry of John the Baptist is a hinge linking repentance with anticipation of the coming of Christ. In the reformed Roman Lectionary of 1969, the Fourth Sunday of Advent is the annunciation of the angel Gabriel to the Virgin Mary. But even in this week of the annunciation there is a somber note sounded in the singing of the "O antiphons."[3]

The "O Antiphons" refer to the seven antiphons that are recited (or chanted) preceding the Magnificat during Vespers of the Liturgy of the Hours from December 17 to 23. The exact origin of the O Antiphons is not known. They were in use in Rome by the eighth century, but were probably recited at the Benedictine abbey of Fleury (now Saint-Benoit-sur-Loire) earlier. Like many of the texts coming out of Gaul in late antiquity (e.g., the Reproaches in the Good Friday Liturgy, the Exsultet in the Easter Vigil), the O Antiphons demonstrate a remarkable biblical typology and a christological reading of the Old Testament. Each antiphon highlights a title for the Messiah: *O Sapientia* (O Wisdom), *O Adonai* (O Lord), *O Radix Jesse* (O Root of Jesse), *O Clavis David* (O Key of David), *O Oriens* (O Rising Sun), *O Rex Gentium* (O King of the Nations), and *O Emmanuel*. Also, each title refers to prophecies of Isaiah.

It has been noted that if one starts with the last title and takes the first letter of each one—*I(E)mmanuel, Rex, Oriens, Clavis, Radix, Adonai, Sapientia*—the Latin words *ero cras* are formed, meaning "Tomorrow, I will come." In this acrostic the Lord Jesus, whose coming is prepared for in Advent and who is addressed in these seven messianic titles, says, "Tomorrow, I will come." Thus the O Antiphons not only bring intensity to the Advent preparation but bring it to a joyful conclusion.

The Advent hymn "O Come, O Come, Emmanuel" is based on the O antiphons. One of the few Advent hymns known and sung by many Western Christians, it was a translation and versification of the O Antiphons by John Mason Neale, first published in *Mediaeval Hymns* in 1851. Neale's original translation began, "Draw nigh, draw nigh, Emmanuel." It is believed that the traditional music stems from a fifteenth-century French processional for Franciscan nuns, but it may have an original Gregorian base. Many hymnals include only five stanzas. *The Hymnal 1982*, #56, includes all seven stanzas, with the first repeated as the eighth, thus covering all the days between December 17 and 23. This arrangement of the hymn was incorporated into *Evangelical Lutheran Worship*, #257.

The Advent season has received great emphasis in the Lutheran tradition, as demonstrated in the wealth of Advent hymnody generated in this tradition. Among German hymns we would note the chorale setting of Ambrose's "Savior of the nations, come" (*Nun komm, der heiden Heiland*) and Paul Gerhardt's "O Lord, how shall I meet you" (based on Jesus's triumphant entry into Jerusalem, the historic Lutheran Gospel reading for the First Sunday of Advent). Philipp Nicolai's great chorale, "Wake, awake, for night is flying," is often sung during the Advent season, but it is based on the parable of the wise and foolish virgins, which was read on the last Sunday after Pentecost (Trinity) in old Lutheran lectionaries. Advent is especially popular in Sweden. Among Swedish hymns are Laurentius Laurentii's "Rejoice, rejoice, believers" and Frans Mikael Franzén's "Prepare the royal highway."

Advent was also observed in the Anglican tradition, but there were no hymns related to Advent themes until Charles Wesley, because before Wesley congregational song in Reformed England was based almost exclusively on the psalter. But among Wesley's six thousand hymns are "Come, thou long-expected Jesus" and "Lo, he comes with clouds descending."

Reflecting the fact that Advent did not originate as a Roman observance, there was no proper preface for Advent in medieval and therefore also Reformation books. The first Advent preface in North America was in the Lutheran *Service Book and Hymnal* (1958). It was based on the Advent preface in the Scottish *Book of Common Prayer* (1929) and the 1940 *Book of Common Order* of the Church of Scotland. The Roman Sacramentary of 1969 provided two Advent prefaces: one for the first week through December 16, drawn from sources in the Leonine or Verona Sacramentary, and the other for December 17–24, drawn from a Christmas preface in the Verona Sacramentary (no. 1241).

A custom that has developed during the Advent season that also reflects the joy of anticipation is the Advent wreath. It is generally thought that a wheel or wreath of evergreens was a symbol in northern Europe long before the arrival of Christianity. The circle symbolized the eternal cycle of the seasons while the evergreens signified the persistence of life in the midst of winter. Some sources suggest the wreath—reinterpreted as a Christian symbol—was used in the Middle Ages, others that it was established in Germany as a Christian custom only in the sixteenth century, and others that the Advent wreath was not invented until the nineteenth century. This last theory credits Johann Hinrich Wichern (1808–1881), a Lutheran pastor in Germany and a pioneer in urban mission work among the poor, as the originator of the modern Advent wreath. During Advent, children at the mission school Wichern founded in Hamburg for juvenile delinquents (known as "The Rough House") would ask daily if Christmas had arrived. In 1839, he set up a large wooden cartwheel with nineteen small red and four large white candles. A small candle was lit successively every weekday during Advent. On Sundays a large white candle was lit. The custom gained ground among Lutheran churches in Germany and evolved into the smaller wreath with four candles known today. Roman Catholics in Germany began to adopt the custom in the 1920s, and in the 1930s it spread to North America. In Roman Catholic churches purple candles were used, except for pink on the third Sunday (*Gaudate*—"Rejoice," from the Introit, "Rejoice in the Lord always"), reflecting the liturgical colors. In Lutheran use white candles were used on all four Sundays. More recently, blue has become a liturgical color of Advent in Lutheran churches, and there have also been blue candles, or white candles with blue rings. Some Protestants, who think that red is a liturgical color for Christmas, use red candles. Originally a custom used in homes and schools, the Advent wreath has been brought into the churches and lighted during public worship. There is no prescribed liturgical use of the Advent wreath and there is no authoritative set of meanings for the candles. The Advent wreath is more properly the center for domestic devotions. Extensive devotions around the Advent wreath within the liturgy would not be appropriate.

We would note that the Feast of St. Lucia ("Sankta Lucia") on December 13 has become a popular observance in Swedish homes and is nearly as culturally important for Swedish immigrants as Our Lady of Guadalupe on December 12 is for Mexicans and Mexican Americans. Both of these saints' days influenced the understanding of Advent in their respective cultures.

The Swedish Sankta Lucia celebration is not so much a survival of a medieval custom after the Reformation as the resurgence of a cult of a saint in Protestantism in the eighteenth century. Whatever the impetus for this resurgence, the current tradition of having a white-dressed girl with candles in her hair appearing on the morning of the Lucia Day started in the area around Lake Vänern in the late 1700s and spread slowly to other parts of the country during the 1800s. In the celebration of Sankta Lucia a girl is elected to portray Lucia. The modern tradition of having public processions in the Swedish cities started in 1927 when a newspaper in Stockholm elected an official Lucia for Stockholm that year. The practice spread to other cities and even to the other Scandinavian and Baltic countries. Wearing a white gown with a red sash and a crown of candles on her head, she walks at the head of a procession of girls, each holding a candle. The girls are accompanied by star boys. The candles symbolize the fire that refused to take St. Lucia's life when she was sentenced to be burned. The women sing a Lucia song while entering the room, to the melody of the traditional Neapolitan song "Santa Lucia." Various Scandinavian lyrics have been fashioned to the tune, describing the light with which Lucia, "the queen of light," overcomes the darkness. The light shining in the darkness is appealing in the northern countries that are experiencing the longest nights of the year in mid-December. After finishing this song, the procession sings Christmas carols or more songs about Lucia and cookies and hot chocolate are shared. Sankta Lucia Day heralds the beginning of the Christmas festival.

The devotions leading up to and following from the feast day of our Lady of Guadalupe totally dominate the Advent season in Mexican and Mexican American practice.[4] The December 12 feast, together with the Feast of the Immaculate Conception four days earlier and the Feast of the Annunciation, provides a Marian focus for the entire Advent season. Novenas are devoted to the Virgin of Guadalupe from December 3 through 11. December 16 through 24 are the days for the *Las Posadas* Novenas, which consist of festive processions, songs, and ceremonies reenacting the search by Joseph and Mary for lodging in Bethlehem. Thus the focus of Advent for Mexican and Mexican

American Catholics is on the appearance of Mary "full of grace" and the nativity of Jesus. Here is a case where popular piety overwhelms the official liturgical celebrations of the church.

This does not mean that for Mexicans and Mexican Americans Advent (or Christmas) is lacking an eschatological character. Not only are the faithful able to invest their temporal hopes in the cult of the Virgin of Guadalupe, but the cult shares with all festivals the ability to lift people out of ordinary time. As Josef Pieper puts it, it sweeps them away from the here and now. Human beings need to live in both realities. We cannot escape the mundaneness of ordinary daily existence. But we need to be lifted out of it for a time, and that is what the festival offers. Pieper cites Athanasius, who wrote in his *Festal Letters*, "To us who live here our festivals are an unobstructed passage to that [other] life," and comments: "In celebrating festivals festively, man passes beyond the barriers of this present life on earth."[5]

The eschatological character of the festival of the Nativity of Our Lord is expressed in the Gelasian Sacramentary's collect for Christmas Eve: "O God, who made this most holy night to shine with the brightness of the true Light: grant, we beseech you, that as we have known on earth the mystery of that Light, we may also come to the fullness of his joys in heaven . . ."

The season of Advent looks to the coming of Christ the king in glory. But that glory was first set down in an obscure earthly setting. Even so, the celebration of the child born of King David's line in the city of David prompts consideration of the final fulfillment of the promises to David, that of his house and lineage there would be no end.

2. Christmas: What are the options for celebration?

Given the pervasive commercialization of Christmas in the modern world, which depends on a "white Christmas," Santa Claus (a version of Thor, the Nordic god of the hearth), and reindeer, one might think that it simply celebrates the winter solstice. And there is no doubt that the Christian festival is interlaced with pagan solstice celebrations. In fact, when Christians began celebrating the Nativity of Our Lord on December 25 or January 6, it was set down in the midst of a massive solstice celebration in the Mediterranean world. But this does not mean that Christmas was invented by Christians to compete with solstice celebrations or to encourage the spread of Christianity throughout the Roman world by making Christmas look like a pagan holiday.[6]

Actually, the emergence of the *Dies Natalis Solis Invicti* ("birthday of the unconquered Sun") occurred at about the same time as the earliest extant references to Christian observance of the Nativity of Jesus. The use of the title *Sol Invictus* allowed several solar deities to be worshiped collectively, including Elah-Gabal, a Syrian sun god; Sol, the god of Emperor Aurelian; and Mithras, a soldiers' god of Persian origin. Emperor Elagabalus (218–222) introduced the festival, and it reached the height of its popularity under Emperor Aurelian (270–275), who promoted it as an empire-wide holiday. This day had held no significance in the Roman festive calendar until it was introduced in the third century. The festival was placed on the date of the solstice because this was the day on which the sun reversed its southward retreat and proved itself to be "unconquered." Several early Christian writers connected the rebirth of the sun to the birth of Jesus. Clement of Alexandria mentions several putative dates of our Lord's nativity, but December 25 isn't among them.[7] But later authors comment on the relationship between the birth of Jesus and the winter solstice. Cyprian wrote: "O, how wonderfully acted Providence that on that day on which that Sun was born…Christ should be born." John Chrysostom also commented on the connection: "They call it the 'Birthday of the Unconquered.' Who indeed is so unconquered as Our Lord?"

A winter festival was the most popular festival of the year in many cultures. There was less agricultural work to be done during the winter, as well as an expectation of better weather as spring approached. Many Christmas customs are borrowed from pagan celebrations: gift giving and merrymaking from Roman Saturnalia; greenery, lights, and charity from the Roman New Year; and Yule logs and various foods from Germanic feasts. Pagan Scandinavia celebrated a winter festival called Yule, held in the late-December to early-January period. As northern Europe was the last part of Europe to be Christianized, its pagan traditions had a major influence on Christmas, giving us the Nordic Christmas Man and his reindeer. Scandinavians still call Christmas *Jul*. In English, the word *Yule* is also synonymous with Christmas.

But this does not mean that the festival of the Nativity of the "Sun of Righteousness" was invented to compete with the solstice festivals. The New Testament does not give a date for the birth of Jesus. In *Chronographai*, a reference work published in 221, Sextus Julius Africanus suggested that Jesus was conceived on the spring equinox. The equinox was March 25 in the Roman calendar, so this implied a birth in December. But the reason behind this suggestion was a Christian elaboration of a Jewish spiritual reckoning of time. Jewish tradition held that the world was created at Passover time. Christians reasoned that the new creation also began at Passover time, the Pascha of Christ from death to life. But the beginning of the new creation was the invasion of the Divine Word into human life in the annunciation of the Angel Gabriel to the Virgin Mary. The clearest references to this calendrical calculation of the birth of Christ are an anonymous tract (erroneously attributed to Chrysostom), *De solstitia et aequinoctia conceptionis et nativitatis domini nostri iesu christi et iohannis baptistae* ("Concerning the Solstice and Equinox Conception and Nativity of Our Lord Jesus Christ and John the Baptist"), and the writings of Augustine of Hippo. In *On the Trinity* (c. 399–419) he writes: "For he [Jesus] is believed to have been conceived on the 25th of March, upon which day also he suffered; so the womb of the Virgin, in which he was conceived, where no one of mortals was begotten, corresponds to the new grave in which he was buried, wherein was never man laid, neither before him nor since. But he was born, according to tradition, upon December the 25th."[8]

The earliest reference to the date of the Nativity of Our Lord as December 25 is found in the Chronography of 354, an illuminated manuscript compiled in Rome by the calligrapher Furius Dionysius Philocalus. This first known Christian calendar is an almanac of civil and religious feasts along with lists of bishops and consuls.[9]

In the East, early Christians celebrated the birth of Christ as part of Epiphany (January 6), although, as we shall see, this festival primarily emphasized celebration of the baptism of Jesus. Nevertheless, the Nativity of Our Lord was promoted in the Christian East as part of the revival of orthodoxy following the death of the pro-Arian Emperor Valens at the Battle of Adrianople in 378. The feast was introduced in Constantinople in 379 by Bishop Gregory of Nazianzus, and in Antioch in 380. The feast disappeared after Gregory of Nazianzus resigned as bishop in 381, but it was reintroduced by John Chrysostom about 400.

These two theories of the origin of Christmas—history of religions and calendrical calculation—are not mutually exclusive. It was not a foregone conclusion that the nativity of Jesus should be celebrated. In his Homilies on Leviticus in 245, Origen of Alexandria observed the propensity of the pagans to celebrate their birthdays and opined that "only sinners (like Pharaoh and Herod) celebrated their birthdays." But if calendrical calculation, even of a spiritual sort, put the birth of Jesus in proximity of the winter solstice, bishops of Rome especially could use such a celebration to counter the influences of the pagan celebrations, which lingered longer in the old capital than in other places. Even at the time of Pope Leo I there was a need to counter the pagan solstice celebration with the Christian festival, and the worship of the sun god with the true worship of the Sun of Righteousness. In Sermon XXVII he rails against

> the ungodly practice of certain foolish folk who worship the sun as it rises at the beginning of daylight from elevated positions: even some Christians think it is so proper to do this that, before entering the blessed Apostle Peter's basilica, which is dedicated to the One Living and true God, when they have mounted steps which lead to the raised platform, they turn round and bow themselves toward the rising sun and with bent neck do homage to its brilliant orb.[10]

Leo did not want Christians doing this because even if they were worshiping the Creator of the sun rather than the sun itself, it would mislead the pagans who still practiced sun worship. The pope was either unaware of the custom of Christians almost everywhere else to orient toward the east in prayer, toward "the dayspring from on high," or he sensed a need to counter lingering sun worship. Indeed, this aversion to orientation on Leo's part, and perhaps on the part of other popes as well, may account for the fact that apses in the old basilicas in Rome were on the west end of the building rather than the east end, as church buildings elsewhere usually were oriented.

The times of celebration in Rome may have been influenced by practices in the Holy Land in the fourth century. Egeria describes how the Christians of Jerusalem traveled to

Bethlehem on January 6, the Feast of the Epiphany, to attend the vigil during the night at the Grotto of the Nativity; then they returned to Jerusalem and at daybreak (the hour of the resurrection) gathered for a synaxis at the Anastasis (the shrine over the tomb of Christ); later on, they attended the regular liturgy of the day, the Eucharist, at the Martyrium (the main church). We know from the readings in the Armenian Lectionary as well as the location of the midnight vigil that in this place January 6 was observed as the Nativity of Jesus. Practices that pilgrims encountered in the Holy Land were brought back to their local churches and adapted. Although it was not a direct application, the practices of the Holy Land were applied to the December 25 celebration in Rome. The midnight vigil and Mass was celebrated at the Crib at St. Mary Major. A second Mass was added at dawn at the imperial church of St. Anastasia. The main Mass was celebrated at St. Peter's Basilica. There are thus three masses for Christmas day in the Roman tradition. This custom is peculiar to the Western church. From Egeria's description of Epiphany in the Holy Land, there was only one Eucharist. This continues to be the case in the Eastern churches—one Eucharist per day. During Charlemagne's reign, the Roman custom spread throughout his empire since the liturgical books he had imported into his realm contained propers for three masses on Christmas Day (beginning with the midnight Mass).

The Wurzburg Codex 62 provides the stations and epistle readings for the Roman Church as the Armenian Lectionary does for the Jerusalem Church. The Christmas readings in Rome were:

Vigil	St. Mary Major	Vigil readings; Romans 1:1-6; Matthew 1:18-21
Midnight Mass	St. Mary Major	Isaiah 9:2-6; Titus 2:11-15; Luke 2:1-14
Dawn Mass	St. Anastasia	Isaiah 61:1-3, 62:11-12; Titus 3:4-7; Luke 2:15-20
Daytime Mass	St. Peter's	Isaiah 52:6-10; Hebrews 1:1-12; John 1:1-14

These readings have remained stable in Western lectionaries. When the various current three-year lectionaries provide three sets of readings for Christmas, they are not for the three years of the lectionary but for these three services of Christmas. Thus, if a parish were to provide for the full historic celebration of Christmas, there would be a vigil Eucharist, a dawn Eucharist, and a midday Eucharist.

A more recent option has emerged for a vigil service: the Festival of Lessons and Carols. The format of this service is based on an order drawn up by Edward White Benson, later Archbishop of Canterbury, for Christmas Eve 1880 in the cathedral at Truro, Cornwall. It has since been adapted and used by other churches all over the world. In the United Kingdom, the service has become the standard format for schools' Christmas carol services (usually before dismissal for the holidays). It has become known throughout the world because of the annual broadcast from King's College, Cambridge, on Christmas Eve, featuring music by the famous Choir of King's College, Cambridge. The carols and other music vary from year to year, but the service usually begins with

"Once in Royal David's City" and ends with "Hark, the Herald Angels Sing." (Note: if this service were done during Advent, suitable Advent hymns should be used.) The nine readings are the same each year; each is read by a representative of the community and the church, often progressing up the ranks from a choir youth to the highest ecclesiastical minister. The order is:

Organ Preludes
Processional Hymn: "Once in Royal David's City"
Bidding Prayer and Lord's Prayer
Carol
First Lesson from Genesis 3:8-15, 17-19
Carol (usually "Adam Lay Ybounden"—words, fifteenth century)
Second Lesson from Genesis 22:15-18
Carol
Third Lesson from Isaiah 9:2, 6-7
Carol
Fourth Lesson from Isaiah 11:1-3a, 4a, 6-9
Carol
Fifth Lesson from the Gospel of Luke 1:26-35. 38
Carol (usually "I Sing of a Maiden"—words, fifteenth century)
Sixth Lesson from Luke 2:1, 3-7
Carol
Seventh Lesson from Luke 2:8-16
Carol
Eighth Lesson from the Gospel of Matthew 2:1-12
Carol
Ninth Lesson from the Gospel of John 1:1-14
Hymn
Collect and Blessing Hymn: "Hark! The Herald Angels Sing"
Organ voluntaries

Using this service on Christmas Eve should not preclude the Christ Mass or Holy Eucharist later at night. The tradition of a midnight Mass or late-night service seems to be waning and Christmas Day services are rare in Protestant churches. In fact, there is little tradition of Christmas Day worship in most Protestant churches. We recall that the English Puritans abolished Christmas. It was one of the reasons why the English people wearied of the Puritan Commonwealth and were happy to welcome back the king, bishops, and Prayer Book.

As the Advent wreath has come to dominate the liturgical decor of Advent, so the Christmas tree dominates the liturgical decor of Christmas. Francis X. Weiser argues that Christmas trees are "completely Christian in origin" and that "the Yule tree had

no direct pagan connotation . . ."[11] Indeed, one source of the Christmas tree may
have been the use of an evergreen tree as a prop for the late medieval Adam and Eve
mystery play, performed on December 24. The evergreen served as the tree of life and
fruit was hung on it. The Christmas tree as we know it seemed to emerge in Lutheran
lands in Germany in the sixteenth century. Although no specific city or town has been
identified as the first to have a Christmas tree, records for the Cathedral of Strassburg indicate that a Christmas tree was set up in that church in 1539 during Martin
Bucer's superintendency. It was not until the nineteenth century that the Christmas
tree spread beyond Germany, largely because of Queen Victoria's marriage to the
German Prince Albert.

Along with the Christmas tree, the Christmas crèche has become a part of the Christmas decor. The idea is attributed to St. Francis of Assisi, who did not think Christmas
had been celebrated as it should have been. The poverty of Christ had become lost in
the extravagance of the Christmas festivities. His idea to counter this affluence was to
erect a scene in a grotto with the Christ child lying on hay in a manger attended by his
poor parents and surrounded by ox and ass. Dressed in his deacon's vestments, Francis
sang the Christmas Gospel in this grotto and then preached a delightful sermon to the
people who stood around him, speaking about the nativity of the poor King and the
humble town of Bethlehem.

Another tradition of Christmas is the nativity pageant. The origin of the dramati-
zation of the nativity story goes back to the *Quem quaeritis/Quem vidistis* ("Whom do
you seek?/"What did you see?") tropes of Easter and Christmas attributed to Notker
Balbulus ("the stammerer") (d. 912). As with the Easter *Quem quaeritis*, the text of
Quem vidistis pastores is constructed in the form of a dialogue, which quickly can
suggest the alternation of choirs, and from there the dramatic rendition of a small
"scene" is a somewhat obvious step. In this case, the text alternates between the shepherds of the Christmas story in the Gospel of Luke, and some unnamed and anonymous bystanders who are questioning them. "What have you witnessed, shepherds?
Announce to us what happened to you." "We saw the birth, and a choir of angels
praising God!" "Tell us, what else do you see?" "They announced that the Christ is
born!" "Glory to the Father, the Son, and the Holy Spirit!" This little music drama in
the midst of Matins acted out by the choir boys was expanded in the miracle plays of
the late Middle Ages.

The practice continued in the Lutheran tradition, as witnessed in the fictionalized
account of Christmas Matins in the Nikolaikirche in Berlin in 1659.[12] The musical
forces amassed for this early Christmas morning service are impressive. The enacted
nativity story makes use of Martin Luther's song, "From heaven above to earth I come"
(with its fourteen stanzas). But the responsories and canticle (Te Deum Laudamus) are
all in Latin. The Christmas pageant was brought to America by German Lutheran and
Catholic immigrants in the mid-nineteenth century and has spread to churches in other
traditions. In the evangelical megachurches the pageant is enacted as a professional production attracting thousands of spectators. But there is no liturgical setting.

Finally, a custom has emerged in recent years of chanting or speaking the Proclamation of the Nativity of Christ at the beginning of the midnight Mass. The text of this Proclamation first appeared in the ancient Roman Martyrology and was sung in the office of Prime in the monasteries and cathedral chapters. The edition of the *Martyrologium Romanum* published in 2001 gives two options for the reading of the Proclamation: (1) during the celebration of the liturgy of the hours, where it is directed to be chanted/read after the oration (i.e., collect) of the day; and (2) as a devotion by itself, either in choir, in chapter, or at table. But it works well as a solemn beginning to the Christmas Eve or Christmas Day service, not unlike the Exsultet at the beginning of the Easter Vigil. The text of the Proclamation is as follows:

> In the five thousand one hundred and ninety-ninth year of the creation of the
> world from the time when God in the beginning created the heavens and the earth;
> the two thousand nine hundred and fifty-seventh year after the flood;
> the two thousand and fifteenth year from the birth of Abraham;
> the one thousand five hundred and tenth year from Moses and the going forth of
> the people of Israel from Egypt;
> the one thousand and thirty-second year from David's being anointed king;
> in the sixty-fifth week according to the prophecy of Daniel;
> in the one hundred and ninety-fourth Olympiad;
> the seven hundred and fifty-second year from the foundation of the city of Rome;
> the forty-second year of the reign of Octavian Augustus;
> the whole world being at peace,
> in the sixth age of the world,
> Jesus Christ the eternal God and Son of the eternal Father,
> desiring to sanctify the world by his most merciful coming,
> being conceived by the Holy Spirit,
> and nine months having passed since his conception,
> was born in Bethlehem of Judea of the Virgin Mary,
> being made flesh.
> The Nativity of our Lord Jesus Christ according to the flesh.

This Proclamation reinforces the idea of the incarnation as the glory of the Lord being set down in human history.

3. The Epiphany: What are the riches of the observance?

This festival has its origins in the Eastern Christian churches, in which it was a general celebration of the incarnation of Jesus Christ that included the commemoration of: his birth; the visit of the Magi ("wise men," as Magi were Persian priests) to Bethlehem; and Jesus' baptism in the Jordan River by John the Baptist; and even the miracle at the wedding of Cana in Galilee in which Jesus turned water into wine.

It seems fairly clear that the baptism was the primary event being commemorated. It has been suggested that the Egyptian Church began reading the Gospel of Mark at the beginning of the civil year in January, and the Gospel of Mark begins with the appearance of "the voice crying in the wilderness" and the baptism of Jesus.[13] The Egyptian Church followed this commemoration with a forty-day fast commemorating Jesus' time of fasting in the wilderness after his baptism before beginning his ministry.[14]

The earliest reference to Epiphany as a Christian feast was in 361 CE, by Ammianus Marcellinus. St. Epiphanius says that January 6 is *hemera genethlion toutestin epiphanion* (Christ's "birthday; that is, his Epiphany"). He also asserts that the miracle at Cana occurred on the same calendar day, and he associates it with the rite of drawing water from the Nile on that date. Later on John Chrysostom would derive the blessing of water on the Epiphany from the sanctification of water because of Jesus' baptism.

We have seen that about 385 the pilgrim Egeria described a celebration in Jerusalem and Bethlehem, which she called "Epiphany" (*epiphania*), that commemorated the Nativity of Christ. Even at this early date, there was an octave associated with the feast.

In a sermon delivered on December 25, 380, the second year in which the Roman Nativity festival was celebrated in Constantinople, Archbishop Gregory of Nazianzus referred to the day as *ta theophania* ("the Theophany," an alternative name for Epiphany), saying expressly that it is a day commemorating *he hagia tou Christou gennesis* ("the holy nativity of Christ"). He told his listeners that they would soon be celebrating the baptism of Christ. Then, on January 6 and 7, he preached two more sermons in which he declared that the celebration of the birth of Christ and the visitation of the Magi had already taken place, and that they would now commemorate his baptism. At this time, celebration of the two events was beginning to be observed on separate occasions, at least in Cappadocia where Gregory was from.[15]

We have seen that in Rome Christmas was celebrated on December 25 as early as 354. In Spain and southern Gaul, the Epiphany was observed on January 6, in conformity with Eastern practice. As these two festivals were adopted in both the Roman and the Gallican/Hispanic churches, the West observed a twelve-day festival, starting on December 25, and ending on January 5, known as Christmastide or the twelve days of Christmas. Some Christian cultures in Western Europe and Latin America extend the season to forty days, ending on the Feast of the Presentation of Jesus in the Temple and the Purification of Mary on February 2 (called Candlemas because of the blessing of candles on this day, from the Song of Simeon that proclaims Jesus as "a light for revelation to the nations").

Epiphany is a great day of blessing. We mentioned John Chrysostom's identification of the blessing of water with the baptism of Jesus, a practice continued in the Orthodox churches. The blessing is normally done twice: once on the eve of the feast—usually at a baptismal font inside the church—and then again on the day of the feast, outdoors at a body of water. Following the Divine Liturgy, the clergy and people go in a crucession (procession with the cross) to the nearest body of water (ideally a natural body of water).

In the Greek practice, the priest casts a cross into the water and divers try to recover it. The person who gets the cross first swims back and returns it to the priest, who then delivers a special blessing to the swimmer and his household.

In Russia, a hole will be cut into the ice so that the waters may be blessed. In such conditions, the cross is not cast into the water but is held securely by the priest and dipped three times into the water. The water blessed on this day is known as "Theophany Water" and is taken home by the faithful to be used with prayer as a blessing. People will not only bless themselves and their homes by sprinkling with Theophany Water but will also drink it. The Orthodox Church teaches that Theophany Water differs from regular holy water in that with Theophany Water, the very nature of the water is changed and becomes incorrupt, a miracle attested to as early as St. John Chrysostom.

Theophany is a traditional day for performing baptisms in the Eastern churches, and this is reflected in the Divine Liturgy by singing the baptismal hymn, "As many as have been baptized into Christ, have put on Christ. Alleluia," in place of the Trisagion. In the revision of the Roman Lectionary in 1969 the Sunday after the Epiphany was designed as "The Baptism of Our Lord," and various other lectionaries based on the Roman (such as the Revised Common Lectionary) follow this designation. The Sunday of the Baptism of Our Lord may also be a preferred time for public baptisms.

In addition to the blessing of water, frankincense, gold, and chalk are blessed. Chalk is used to write the initials of the three Magi over the doors of churches and homes. The letters stand for the initials of the Magi (named Caspar, Melchior, and Balthasar by the Venerable Bede), and also the phrase *Christus mansionem benedicat* ("May Christ bless the house").

The Epiphany remains a major celebration not only in the Eastern churches but also in Spain and some Latin American countries, where the day is called *El Día de los Reyes* ("The Day of the Kings"). In Spanish tradition, on the day of January 6 three of the kings, Melchor, Gaspar, and Balthazar, representing Europe, Arabia, and Africa, arrived on horse, camel, and elephant, bringing respectively gold, frankincense, and myrrh to the baby Jesus. Children (and many adults) polish and leave their shoes ready for the kings' presents before they go to bed on the eve of January 6. In Mexico, it is traditional for children to leave their shoes, perhaps filled with hay for the Magis' camels, along with a letter with toy requests for the Three Kings.

According to ancient custom, the priest announced the date of Easter on the feast of Epiphany. This tradition comes from a time when calendars were not readily available and the church needed to publicize the date of Easter, since the rest of the liturgical year depends on it. January 6 is actually the last day in the temporal cycle of the church year to have a fixed date. The proclamation may be sung or proclaimed at the ambo by a deacon, cantor, or reader either after the reading of the Gospel or after the post-communion prayer. The text is as follows (specific dates to be inserted each year):

Dear brothers and sisters, the glory of the Lord has shone upon us, and shall ever be manifest among us, until the day of his return. Through the rhythms of times and seasons let us celebrate the mysteries of salvation.

Let us recall the year's culmination, the Easter Triduum of the Lord: his last supper, his crucifixion, his burial, and his rising celebrated between the evening of the (date) of (month) (date of Holy Thursday) and the evening of the (date) of (month). (date of Easter Sunday)

Each Easter—as on each Sunday—the Holy Church makes present the great and saving deed by which Christ has for ever conquered sin and death.

From Easter are reckoned all the days we keep holy. Ash Wednesday, the beginning of Lent, will occur on the (date) of (month).

The Ascension of the Lord will be commemorated on the (date) of (month).

Pentecost, the joyful conclusion of the season of Easter, will be celebrated on the (date) of (month).

Likewise the pilgrim Church proclaims the passover of Christ in the feasts of the holy Mother of God, in the feasts of the Apostles and Saints, and in the commemoration of the faithful departed.

To Jesus Christ, who was, who is, and who is to come, Lord of time and history, be endless praise, for ever and ever.

R. Amen.[16]

4. Time after the Epiphany: Is there an Epiphany season?

The time after the Epiphany is elastic. How many Sundays there are depends on the date of Easter and therefore when Lent begins. Before the revision of the Roman calendar and lectionary in 1969, the lectionary included "Epiphany" events on the successive Sundays in which Christ's divinity is manifested: the boy Jesus instructing the scribes in the temple, the miracle of the wedding at Cana, healings and exorcisms. The most number of Sundays after the Epiphany there could be was six, because there were three pre-Lenten Sundays that preceded Ash Wednesday: Septuagesima, Sexagesima, Quinquagesima (the countdown to Lent). The revision of the Roman Lectionary in 1969 instituted continuous reading from the Gospel for the year (Matthew, Mark, or Luke).

There is no "thematic" season of Epiphany in the Roman and Revised Common lectionaries. But the time is framed in current lectionaries by the Baptism of Our Lord on the Sunday after the Epiphany and (except in the Roman lectionary) by the Transfiguration of Our Lord on the Sunday before Lent begins. The Transfiguration is certainly an "epiphany event" and was observed as such on the Sixth Sunday after the Epiphany in sixteenth-century Lutheran lectionaries.[17] In the current lectionaries it serves as a preview of Easter before Lent begins.

So there is no Epiphany season as such in various three-year lectionaries. But some of the Epiphany events proclaimed in the older one-year lectionary are still present in the three-year lectionaries, especially in Year C, which provides the stories of the boy Jesus in the temple on the First Sunday of Christmas, and Jesus' first sign in the Gospel of John of changing water into wine at the marriage feast in Cana on the Second Sunday after the Epiphany.

The Feast of the Presentation of our Lord and the Purification of Mary on February 2, forty days after Christmas, is sometimes regarded as the end of the Christmas season. Because of Simeon's song, the Nunc dimittis, which proclaimed Jesus as "a light to the nations" and "the glory of your people Israel," it has been customary to hold a candlelight procession and to bless the church's supply of candles. Hence, the feast has also been known as Candlemas.

5. Ash Wednesday and Lent: How do we practice penitence and catechesis?

Lent developed as a forty-day fast (*Quadragesima*) in imitation of Jesus' forty days of fasting in the wilderness after his baptism. The Egyptian Church observed a forty-day fast for this reason after the Epiphany, and this may have provided the idea for the forty-day fast that finally emerged in the rest of the church in the fourth century. Before the fourth century various lengths of fasting were observed in different local churches.

The season of Lent served two purposes: it was a time for electing the candidates for baptism at Easter (hence the candidates were called "electi"); and it was a time in which public penitents were prepared for reconciliation on Maundy Thursday. The season of Lent therefore acquired both catechetical and penitential features. Since the disciplines of fasting, almsgiving, and prayer (Matthew 6) were laid on both catechumens and penitents (and the faithful who joined them in these exercises), these disciplines became especially associated with Lent.

The days of Lent are therefore fast days on which Christians abstain as far as possible from meat, eggs, and dairy products. Some rules exempted fish and some exempted also fowl. Dispensations were granted for dairy products such as milk (for babies) and butter (for cooking). In the West Sundays were not included in the rules of fasting because Sunday is a feast day. In the East some fasting is observed even on Sundays during Lent. Thus all fifty-five days of their Lent are greater or lesser fasts. In some places, believers abstained from food for an entire day; others took only one meal each day, while others abstained from all food until 3 o'clock. Late afternoon is the time at which the Liturgy of the Pre-sanctified is celebrated in Orthodox churches (and in the Roman Catholic Church on Good Friday), so that believers may receive communion on fasting days. After communion and a meal, the fast resumes.

In the Roman Catholic Church, rules of fasting are established by national conferences of bishops, and they are quite relaxed in comparison with practices before the 1966 Apostolic Constitution of Pope Paul VI, *Paenitemini* ("On Penance"). It reduced the number of days of fasting and empowered episcopal conferences to substitute for the traditional abstinence on penitential days some other form of penance, especially works of charity and piety.[18] Many modern Protestants consider Lenten fasting to be a choice rather than an obligation. They may decide to give up a favorite food or drink (e.g., chocolate, alcohol) or activity (e.g., going to the movies, playing video games, etc.) for Lent, or they may instead take on a Lenten discipline such as devotions, volunteering for charity work, and so on. The Orthodox continue the practice of abstaining all animal products including fish, eggs, fowl, and milk sourced from animals (e.g., goats and cows as opposed to the milk of soybeans and coconuts) for the entire fifty-five days of their Lent. The Eastern churches also observe the distinction between fasts and feasts by not celebrating the Eucharist on the days of Lent; instead, the Liturgy of the Pre-sanctified provides opportunities for the faithful to receive Holy Communion, especially on the Wednesdays and Fridays of Lent.

Because Sundays are not included in the days *of* Lent, Lent begins on a Wednesday in order to account for forty days before Easter. Ash Wednesday derives its name from the practice of placing ashes on the foreheads of the faithful as a sign of repentance. At first only the public penitents were ashed as a sign of their enrollment into the order of penitents. By the tenth century all the faithful were being marked with ashes. The ashes used are typically gathered after the burning of the palm crosses from the previous year's Palm Sunday. In the liturgical practice of some churches, the ashes are mixed with the Oil of the Catechumens (one of the sacred oils used to anoint those about to be baptized), though some churches use ordinary oil. This paste is used by the minister who presides at the service to make the sign of the cross, first upon his own forehead and then on those in the assembly, with words making reference to the punishment of Adam and Eve after their fall into sin: "You are dust, and to dust you shall return." But the mark of the ashes is made in the sign of a cross, indicating that by the cross of Christ we are delivered from sin, death, and the power of the devil. In current liturgies a long litany of penitence precedes the imposition of ashes. The litany of penitence and imposition of ashes might occur at the beginning of the service or after the sermon, since both locations were places for penitential rites in medieval and Reformation Mass orders. The idea has been raised in recent years of not celebrating the Eucharist or receiving Holy Communion on Ash Wednesday because it is a fast day, one of the few fast days that might be observed by Protestants as well as Roman Catholics.

In recent years the practices of the adult catechumenate have assumed an important place on the Sundays in Lent. The First Sunday in Lent is the day on which persons are enrolled as catechumens. The Gospel readings from John in Year A in the lectionary for the Third, Fourth, and Fifth Sundays in Lent are especially appropriate for use with the catechumenate since they can be related to conversion (Nicodemus's encounter with Jesus at night), baptism ("living water"), and new life (the raising of Lazarus). Tradition-ally, the Gospels, the Creed, and the Lord's Prayer were handed over (*traditio*) to the catechumens on the Third and Fourth Sundays in Lent with the "return" (*redditio*) of the Creed and Lord's Prayer on the Fifth Sunday in Lent. In early Lutheranism there was preaching on the catechism during the week.[19] Midweek Lenten services offer a similar opportunity.

Many Protestant churches have held midweek services during Lent. Wednesday evenings have been an especially popular time for such services. The type of service var-ies greatly. It might be Holy Communion or evening prayer (Vespers). Sometimes it has been a form of corporate devotion such as the Stations of the Cross or Taizé Evening Prayer. The most typical Protestant midweek Lenten service is a Service of the Word with a five-week preaching series on a theme chosen by the preacher.

A custom of Lent since the Middle Ages is the veiling of crosses, pictures, and statues. This may go back to the veiling of the altar—the suspending of a Lenten veil or "hunger cloth" in front of the altar—from the eleventh century on. The veiling of crosses (a fasting of the eyes) was explained by Bishop William Durandus of Mende (1230–1296) in southern France as showing us that Christ veiled his divinity during his passion. The theologian observed that in the Gospel Jesus "hid himself and left the Temple."[20]

For further reading

Alexander, J. Neil. *Waiting for the Coming: The Liturgical Meaning of Advent, Christmas, and Epiphany*. Washington, DC: Pastoral, 1993.

Heinz, Donald. *Christmas: Festival of Incarnation*. Minneapolis: Fortress Press, 2010.

Johnson, Maxwell E. *The Virgin of Guadalupe: Theological Reflections of an Anglo-Lutheran Theologian*. Lanham: Rowman and Littlefield, 2002.

Merras, Merja. *The Origins of the Celebration of the Christian Feast of Epiphany*. Joensuu, Fin-land, 1995.

Roll, Susan. *Toward the Origins of Christmas*. Kampen, Netherlands, 1995.

Schmemann, Alexander. *Great Lent: Journey to Pascha*. Crestwood: St. Vladimir's Seminary Press, 1974.

See also "For further reading" at the end of chapter 5.

7
The Church Year
Holy Week

1. *How did the rites of Holy Week develop?*
2. *Palm/Passion Sunday: What is the relationship between palms and the passion?*
3. *Maundy Thursday: What is the relationship between foot washing and Lord's Supper?*
4. *Good Friday: What is the difference between liturgy and paraliturgical devotions?*
5. *Holy Saturday: How might the Great Vigil be structured?*

1. How did the rites of Holy Week develop?

Holy Week is the last week of Lent. It begins on what has been called Palm Sunday (now designated as the Sunday of the Passion in several calendars) and comes to a climax in the three days (Triduum) comprising Maundy Thursday (Holy Thursday), Good Friday, and Holy Saturday with its great Vigil of the Resurrection. In the Eastern church Holy Week is called Great Week and includes the Saturday before Palm Sunday, which is called Lazarus Saturday. Holy Week commemorates the last week of the earthly life of Jesus the Christ and focuses on his passover from death to life.

It is possible that already in the Gospel of John there is a demarcation of the last week in Jesus' life that reflects contemporary church practice. The supper at Bethany must have taken place on the Saturday, "six days before the pasch" (John 12:1-2), and the triumphal entry into Jerusalem was made from there next morning. Of Christ's words and deeds between this and his crucifixion we have a relatively full record.

Whether this feeling of the sanctity belonging to these days was primitive or not, it in any case existed in Jerusalem at the close of the fourth century because the diary of the Spanish nun Egeria, who made a pilgrimage to the Holy Land in the late 380s, contains a detailed account of the whole week, beginning with the service in the "Lazarium" at Bethany on the Saturday, in the course of which was read the narrative of the anointing of Christ's feet.[1]

The Holy Week rites that had developed in Jerusalem undoubtedly utilized the actual places where events in the life of Jesus had taken place. There was a kind of "acting out" of the Gospel narratives in processions and ceremonies. The assembly of worshipers, which was probably full of pilgrims from all over the Roman Empire and beyond, was given oral instruction on where to meet for each commemoration. Thus Egeria reports that at the beginning of Holy Week, "which they call here the 'Great Week,'" the archdeacon addresses a special reminder to the people in these terms: "Throughout this whole week, beginning tomorrow at the ninth hour, let us all gather in the Martyrium, in the major church."[2]

The commemoration of Christ's triumphal entry into the city took place the same afternoon. Great crowds, including even children too young to walk, assembled on the Mount of Olives and after suitable hymns, antiphons, and readings, they returned in procession to Jerusalem, escorting the bishop, and bearing palms and branches of olives before him. Special services in addition to the usual daily office are also mentioned on each of the following days.

On the Thursday the liturgy was celebrated in the late afternoon, and all received communion, after which the people went to the Mount of Olives to commemorate with appropriate readings and hymns the agony of Christ in the garden and his arrest, only returning to the city as day began to dawn on the Friday.

On the Friday again there were many services, and in particular before midday there took place the veneration of the great relic of the True Cross, as also of the title that had been fastened to it; while for three hours after midday another crowded service was held in commemoration of the passion of Christ, at which, Egeria tells us, the sobs and lamentations of the people exceeded all description. Exhausted as they must have been, a vigil was again maintained by the younger and stronger of the clergy and by some of the laity.

On the Saturday, besides the usual offices during the day, there took place the great Paschal Vigil in the evening, with the baptism of children and catechumens. But this, as Egeria implies, was already familiar to her in the West, so she doesn't provide as much information about it as we might wish.

The account just summarized belongs probably to the year 388, and it is of the highest value as coming from a pilgrim and an eyewitness who had evidently followed the services with close attention. Many of the ceremonies she witnessed in Jerusalem were undoubtedly carried by pilgrims back to their home churches to be implemented locally, including the procession with palms, the veneration of the cross, and the lighting of the great candle within the sepulcher at the beginning of the Paschal Vigil.

Still, the observance of Holy Week as a specially sacred commemoration must be considerably older. In the first of his festal letters, written in 329, Bishop Athanasius of Alexandria speaks of the severe fast maintained during "those six holy and great days [preceding Easter Sunday] which are the symbol of the creation of the world." He writes, in 331: "We begin the holy week of the great pasch on the tenth of Pharmuthi in which we should observe more prolonged prayers and fastings and watchings, that we may be enabled to anoint our lintels with the precious blood and so escape the destroyer."[3] From these and other references, for instance, in the *Apostolic Constitutions* and the sermons of John Chrysostom and Augustine of Hippo, it seems probable that throughout the Christian world some sort of observance of these six days by fasting and prayer had been adopted almost everywhere before the end of the fourth century. Indeed, it is quite possible that the fast of special severity is considerably older, for Dionysius of Alexandria (c. 260 CE) speaks of some who went without food for the whole six days. The week was also known as the week of the dry fast (*xerophagia*), while some of its observances were very possibly influenced by an erroneous etymology of the word *pasch*, which was current among the Greeks. "Pasch" really comes from the Hebrew *pesach*, meaning "passage" (of the destroying angel), but the Greeks took it to be identical with *paschein*, to suffer.

The rites of Holy Week continued to develop during the centuries. The Palm Sunday procession became especially popular in the Middle Ages. Maundy Thursday acquired three masses in the Roman Church: one for the reconciliation of the penitents (so that they could receive communion again that evening), another for the blessing of the oil (chrism) to be used to anoint the candidates for baptism at the Paschal Vigil, and the evening Mass of the Lord's Supper. Many ceremonies clustered around the veneration of the reserved sacrament during the Middle Ages.

In the Roman Catholic tradition Holy Thursday is regarded as the anniversary of the institution of the ministerial priesthood as well as the anniversary of the institution of the Eucharist. The practice has developed of priests concelebrating with their bishop at the Chrism Mass as well as at the Evening Mass of the Lord's Supper. Renewal of ordination promises is now part of the Chrism Mass.

The Good Friday liturgy was moved to the morning by the late Middle Ages in order to accommodate paraliturgical devotions that filled the rest of the day. The Paschal Vigil was also moved to the morning of Holy Saturday in order to accommodate all the confessions that needed to be made before the faithful could receive their Easter communion. By the time of the Reformation, the Triduum was hardly known in its ancient unity, and the Protestant Reformers uniformly rejected as superstitious the blessing of palms and the veneration of the cross.

In 1951 Pope Pius XII ordered the Paschal Vigil restored to its proper time of celebration in the evening. In 1956 he ordered the restoration and renewal of all the rites of Holy Week. At about the same time, Protestants also began to retrieve the rites of Holy Week. Lutherans, Anglicans, Methodists, and Presbyterians began providing these liturgies in their worship books and resources.[4] The first Lutheran resource was *Holy Week and Easter: Orders Supplementing the Service Book and Hymnal,* prepared by the Commission on Worship of the Lutheran Church in America in 1962. Full orders of the liturgies of Holy Week are in the *Lutheran Book of Worship* Ministers Edition (1978) and *Evangelical Lutheran Worship* Leaders Edition (2006).[5]

2. Palm/Passion Sunday: What is the relationship between palms and the passion?

Modern Western worshipers encounter a long and complicated liturgy on Palm Sunday, the Sunday of the Passion. It includes a festive procession with palms and then suddenly (and some think rather jarringly) turns somber and focuses on the passion of our Lord. This change in the character of the service can seem jarring to the contemporary worshiper, but the juxtaposition of palms and passion brings out that fact that Jesus rode on in majesty to die in abject humility.

Before the reform of the rites of Holy Week in 1956, this Sunday was known in the Roman Rite and other Western rites simply as Palm Sunday. The preceding Sunday was called Passion Sunday. From 1955 to 1970 Palm Sunday was called the Second Sunday in Passiontide or Palm Sunday. After 1970 it was called the Sunday of the Passion in the Roman Rite. Several Protestant traditions, especially in North America, followed the Roman lead. This is because the Gospel for the day is one of the Synoptic Gospel Passions: Matthew in Year A, Mark in Year B, and Luke in Year C. Before 1970 the Gospel for Palm Sunday was always the Passion according to Matthew. The other Passion narratives were read on other days during Holy Week: Mark on Tuesday, Luke on Wednesday, and John on Good Friday.

The Palm Sunday liturgy begins with the commemoration of the entrance of the Messiah into Jerusalem to accomplish his paschal triumph. The service begins with a reading of the Processional Gospel followed by the blessing of palm leaves (or other branches; for example, olive branches). The blessing ceremony, preferably held outside the church building, is followed by a procession or solemn entrance into the church, with the participants holding the blessed branches in their hands during the singing of the hymn of Theodulph of Orleans, "All Glory, Laud, and Honor" (c. 810).

Before the reform of the rite by Pope Pius XII, the blessing of the palms occurred inside the church within a service that followed the general outline of a Mass, with Collect, Epistle, and Gospel, as far as the Sanctus. The palms were then blessed with five prayers and a procession went out of the church, followed on its return by a ceremony for the reopening of the doors, which had meantime been shut. After this the usual Mass was celebrated. The fact that the old form of blessing looks like the complete set of propers of a Mass—Introit, Collects, Gradual, Preface, Thanksgiving, and Benedictus ("Blessed is he who comes in the Name of the Lord. Hosanna in the highest")—leads one to the conjecture that this may represent the skeleton of a consecration Mass formerly said at the station from which the procession started. Whether this is the case or not (the idea has been contested), it is probable that originally the palms were only blessed with a view to using them in the procession, but the later form of benediction seems distinctly to suppose that the palms will be preserved as sacramentals and carried about or hung behind crosses and religious pictures until the next Ash Wednesday, when they would be burned.

There were many local variants of the Palm/Passion Sunday liturgy. In the Sarum Use of the Roman Rite in medieval Salisbury, red vestments were used for the Liturgy of the Palms and the procession. Then the celebrant changed into the purple vestments of Lent. In Germany, and elsewhere on the Continent, the manner of the entry of Christ was sometimes depicted by dragging along a wooden figure of an ass on wheels (the Palmesel), and in other places the celebrant himself rode upon an ass. In England and in many parts of France the veneration paid to the churchyard cross or to the rood cross above the screen that divided the nave from the choir by genuflections and prostrations became almost a central feature in the service.

The only other noteworthy feature of the present Palm Sunday liturgy is the reading of the Gospel of the Passion. In the Middle Ages the Passions on Palm Sunday, Tuesday of Holy Week, Wednesday of Holy Week, and Good Friday were sung by three deacons who impersonate respectively the Evangelist, Jesus Christ, and the other speakers (*Synagoga*). This division of the Passion among three characters is very ancient, and it is often indicated by rubrical letters in early manuscripts of the Gospel. As time went on, the singing of the Passion became more musical and more dramatic, reaching the apex of this development in Lutheranism in the Oratorio Passions of Johann Sebastian Bach (St. Matthew, St. John). Bach interspersed the biblical texts with pietistic arias and chorales that reflected on the events being proclaimed in the Scripture. It is likely that these massive choral works were performed as part of the Good Friday service rather than on Palm Sunday. In any event, it has become customary to divide the script of the Passion into roles that are read by various ministers and members of the assembly, with the lines of the crowds being spoken by the congregation. There is also a value, however, in simply listening to the words of Scripture as read by the three ministers, as in the Middle Ages. Chorales might be sung by the congregation at the beginning and end of the Passion reading, and perhaps at a strategic point within the Passion narrative.

3. Maundy Thursday: What is the relationship between foot washing and the Lord's Supper?

Maundy Thursday, also known as Holy Thursday, Great Thursday, or Thursday of Mysteries, is one of the most ritually cluttered days in the calendar. In the ancient Roman Church, there were three liturgies on this day: the reconciliation of the penitents, the bishop's blessing of the oils for chrismation, and the evening liturgy of the Lord's Supper. The reason for the reconciliation of penitents on Maundy Thursday was so they could be restored to the eucharistic fellowship and be able to receive communion during Holy Week. The reason for the blessing of the oils was to use them in Holy Baptism at the Easter Vigil. The evening Mass of the Lord's Supper commemorated the institution of the Eucharist on the night in which our Lord was betrayed. To these basic liturgies were added other rites: the foot washing, the stripping of the altar after the communion, and the procession with the sacrament to an altar of repose, which would become a focus of adoration for the faithful and from which communion would be administered on Good Friday.

The evening Mass of the Lord's Supper actually initiates the three-day liturgy of the Easter Triduum, the three days of Friday, Saturday, and Sunday that commemorate the passion, death, and resurrection of Jesus. It is normally celebrated in the evening, when according to Jewish tradition Friday begins, as well as in imitation of the Last Supper of Jesus and his disciples before his betrayal, arrest, trial, and execution. It has become customary in some Lutheran churches to have an order of corporate confession and absolution with individual laying on of hands at the beginning of the Maundy Thursday service—a kind of adaptation of the historic liturgy of the reconciliation of the penitents.

The name *maundy* is a Middle English version of the Latin *mandatum*, the first word of the phrase *Mandatum novum do vobis ut diligatis invicem sicut dilexi vos* ("A new commandment I give to you, that you love one another; as I have loved you"), the statement by Jesus in the Gospel of John (13:34) by which Jesus explained to the apostles the significance of his action of washing their feet. We understand today that the Last Supper of Jesus was a kind of symposium, typical of the Greco-Roman world (also in Palestine), in which discussion accompanied the meal and drinking.[6] This discussion was sometimes provoked by a drama, poem, or song. In this case, Jesus' dramatic action of washing his disciples' feet at his Last Supper became a kind of last testament in which he bequeathed to the apostles his new commandment "to love one another, as I have loved you." This verse is used as the antiphon sung during the *Mandatum*, the ceremony of the washing of the feet, which may be held during Mass or at another time as a separate event, during which a priest or bishop (representing Christ) ceremonially washes the feet of others, typically twelve persons chosen as a cross-section of the community. In the Middle Ages the pope and other bishops often chose twelve beggars to have their feet washed, who were eager to volunteer because they were given coins for their trouble. As the ceremony has been revived today, it is often open to any people of any age in the assembly. Some have amended the tradition by having people in the assembly wash each others' feet, as the Mennonites do. But there is a value in seeing the presiding minister in the servant role that Jesus himself took on.

The Washing of the Feet is a widespread traditional component of the celebration in many Christian churches, including the Armenian, Ethiopian, Eastern Orthodox, Eastern Catholic, Brethren, Mennonite, and Roman Catholic churches, and is becoming increasingly popular as a part of the Maundy Thursday liturgy in the Anglican/Episcopal, Lutheran, and Methodist churches, as well as in other Protestant denominations.

In the Roman Catholic Church, the Mass of the Lord's Supper begins as usual, but the Gloria in excelsis is accompanied by the ringing of bells, which are then silent until the Gloria at the Easter Vigil liturgy.

The Washing of Feet may occur after the Gospel reading of John 13 and the homily, at which time the presiding minister removes outer vestments and kneels down on the floor in front of chairs or a bench on which those participating in the foot washing sit, having removed shoes and socks. The traditional hymn sung during the foot washing is "Where charity and love prevail" (*Ubi charitas et amor*).

The Maundy Thursday liturgy concludes after communion with a procession taking the Blessed Sacrament to the place of repose during which Thomas Aquinas's hymn for the Feast of Corpus Christi, "Sing my tongue the mystery telling," is sung. The altar is later stripped bare, as are any other altars in the church. In pre-1970 editions, the Roman Missal envisaged this being done ceremonially, to the accompaniment of Psalm 22, a practice that continues in many Anglican and Lutheran churches today. Since the liturgy of the Triduum continues on Good Friday, no benediction is given and the people depart in silence.

Since the 1960s growing numbers of Christian congregations have been holding Christian Passover seders. This is undoubtedly done with the idea of replicating the actual kind of meal Jesus celebrated with his disciples as his Last Supper. The Synoptic Gospels are clear that it was a Passover meal (although John 13:1 is just as clear that Jesus gathered with his disciples before Passover). In fact, the Passover at the time of Jesus cannot be replicated today because it involved the sacrifice of the Passover lambs in the temple. This is why pilgrims went to Jerusalem for the Feast of Passover. Moreover, the Jewish Passover seder (order) has undergone evolution, just as the Christian Eucharist has, and many of its features are medieval or modern. It surely is not respectful of Jewish practice for Christians to be doing a Jewish seder.[7]

4. Good Friday: What is the difference between liturgy and paraliturgical devotions?

Good Friday has also become a day with many options, owing to its "nonliturgical" character. By "nonliturgical" it is meant that the Eucharist is not celebrated on this day, since it is a strict day of fasting at the heart of the Triduum. The fast in the Latin Rite Church (Western church) is understood as having only one full meatless meal and two smaller repasts, which together do not equal one full meal. The liturgy is traditionally celebrated between noon and 3:00 PM. The Roman Catholic General Instructions (GIRM) recommend celebrating it at 3:00 PM, but in countries where Good Friday is not a day of rest from work the afternoon liturgical service is usually put off until a few hours after the recommended time.

The liturgy consists of three parts: the Liturgy of the Word, the Veneration of the Cross, and Holy Communion. The Liturgy of the Word consists of the reading of Isaiah 52:13—53:12, followed by the Psalm of the Passion (21/22), Hebrews 4:14-16, 5:7-9, and the Passion according to John, which is often divided between more than one reader or singer. The Liturgy of the Word concludes with a series of prayers called the bidding prayer, an ancient form of prayer in which a bid is announced by the deacon or assisting minister, silence is kept, and then the presiding minister offers a collect. The bids in the Roman Liturgy are for the church, the pope, the clergy and laity of the church, those preparing for baptism, the unity of Christians, the Jewish people, those who do not believe in Christ, those who do not believe in God, those in public office, those in special need. With some alterations similar bids are offered in Anglican/Episcopal, Lutheran, Methodist, and Presbyterian liturgies. In *Evangelical Lutheran Worship* the bids have been shortened to simple invitations to pray without additional explanations of what to pray for in each category. The traditional prayer for the Jews in the new Protestant worship books does not pray for their conversion but that the Jewish people may arrive at the fullness of the promise of the covenant.

The second part of the Good Friday liturgy is the Veneration of the Cross: a crucifix or old rugged cross, not necessarily the one that is normally on or near the altar at other times, is solemnly carried in procession and displayed to the congregation and then venerated by them, individually if possible, while special chants are sung. An old Gallican devotion before the cross is called The Reproaches. The Reproaches follow the pattern of Psalm 78, which rehearses God's continuing acts of faithfulness and Israel's repeated rebellion. Here, too, Protestant worship books (*The United Methodist Book of Worship*, *The Book of Common Worship*, *Evangelical Lutheran Worship*) have extended the people's acts of rebellion to the New Testament church. Theologically, the church is seen as a continuation of Israel. The New Testament references help the worshiper to see that the instances of rebellion are not applied only to the Jews. Each reproach follows a similar pattern, calling to mind God's saving acts and concluding with the same words: "but you have prepared a cross for your Savior." Following each reproach the congregation responds with a prayer for mercy, either simply "Lord, have mercy upon us," or with the traditional Trisagion ("the thrice holy" sung response from the Byzantine tradition). In the Protestant books the service may then conclude with an appropriate hymn or spiritual, and the worshipers depart in silence. However, the traditional custom was for the people to venerate the cross with a kiss as they departed while the hymn of Verantius Fortunatus, "Sing, my tongue, the glorious battle" (*Pange lingua, gloriosi*) was sung.

In Roman Catholic and Anglo-Catholic practice, the communion from the Blessed Sacrament on Good Friday follows. A cloth is spread on the bare altar and two candles are lighted. The order begins with the Our Father, but omits the ceremony of "Breaking of the Bread" and its related chant, the Agnus Dei. The Eucharist consecrated at the Mass of Holy Thursday is then distributed. Before the reform of Pope Pius XII, only the priest received communion in the framework of what was called the "Mass of the Pre-sanctified," which included the usual offertory prayers, with the placing of wine in the chalice, but which omitted the canon of the Mass. Lutherans and other Protestants would not administer the pre-sanctified elements because of different understandings of the sacrament. But in some Lutheran and Reformed churches in Europe (especially Germany), Good Friday is the biggest communion day in the church year. The full service of Holy Communion is celebrated with propers for Good Friday. This goes back to the late medieval custom of everyone receiving Holy Communion on Easter. The

Reformers, such as Ulrich Zwingli at Zurich, included Maundy Thursday and Good Friday as communion days in order to accommodate the whole city.

However the service ends, minsters and people depart in silence. The Triduum continues with the Easter Vigil.

This is the historic Good Friday liturgy that is part of the Triduum. But paraliturgical devotions are also crowded into this day. In the Roman Catholic Church, liturgy in the proper sense is the liturgy of the Mass, the Divine Office, and the sacraments. For hundreds of years, however, the Latin language, the clerical character of the liturgy, and the search for novelty have combined to produce forms of worship that are "paraliturgical," meaning that they lie outside the official liturgy, even though they may be promoted by the pope and the bishops themselves. The fact that these acts are also known as devotions or devotional practices means that they are accepted voluntarily and not from obligation. They are also sometimes referred to as "popular devotions" because they have elicited the emotional engagement of the people in ways that the official liturgy has not. As we shall see, Protestants are not lacking paraliturgical devotions that take place alongside of or sometimes in place of official liturgy.

The oldest form of paraliturgical devotion is the Way of the Cross. The pope traditionally leads this devotion at the Colosseum in Rome on Good Friday. The Way of the Cross, also called the Stations of the Cross, are often prayed either in the church or outside. In countries such as Italy, Mexico, Puerto Rico, Spain, and the Philippines processions with statues representing the passion of Christ are held. The *Via Crucis* is also enacted in Hispanic countries and cultures as a great pageant through the streets of the neighborhoods with people taking the roles of Christ and others in the Gospel Passion stories, complete with a "crucifixion."

The Stations of the Cross are not limited to Good Friday. It is a devotion that may be done at any time by groups or individuals. The Stations originated in pilgrimages to Jerusalem and a desire to reproduce the holy places in their own lands. Although several travelers who visited the Holy Land during the twelfth, thirteenth, and fourteenth centuries mention a "Via Sacra," that is, a settled route along which pilgrims were conducted, there is nothing in their accounts to identify this with the Way of the Cross, as we understand it. This devotion was likely developed by the Franciscans after they were granted administration of the Christian holy places in Jerusalem in 1342. Traditionally, fourteen stations were set up, often with pictorial displays of what is recounted at that station, with devotions in front of each. Pope John Paul II added a fifteenth station in honor of the resurrection. As devotees move from one station to another they may sing stanzas from the *Stabat mater* ("At the cross her station keeping/stood the mournful mother weeping"). The emotional appeal of the Stations of the Cross is such that some Anglicans and Lutherans have also retrieved this late medieval Franciscan devotion and have used it especially on Good Friday.

A Jesuit-inspired devotion that emerged in the seventeenth century has become popular in Protestant churches. This is the Three Hour ("Tre Ore") Service from noon to

3:00 PM. While no definite ritual is prescribed, the customary Tre Ore service on Good Friday is a series of homilies on the seven last words of Christ, along with appropriate hymns, periods for silent meditation. This service has provided a format for ecumenical community worship in which ministers from various churches preach on the "words." Franz Joseph Haydn's String Quartet on "The Seven Last Words of Christ" has become a popular vehicle for musical commentary.

Another form of service that has become popular in Protestant churches is the "service of shadows" ("Tenebrae"). The distinguishing feature of this service is the extinguishing of seven candles until the last lighted candle is removed from view. After a loud noise is made, representing the earthquake that rent the tomb of Christ, the candle is brought again into public view. The content between the extinguishing of candles varies and may include readings, meditations, and music. Actually, however, the historic office of Tenebrae is quite different from these Protestant devotions. Tenebrae is the name given to the service of Matins and Lauds belonging to the last three days of Holy Week. But this nocturnal/early-morning prayer office was sung shortly after Compline on the eves of Maundy Thursday, Good Friday, and Holy Saturday. The service was and properly is a prayer office of psalms. The fact that it is really anticipated Lauds is evident in the fact that the Lauds Psalms (148–150) are sung along with the canticle of Zechariah (the Benedictus), which are proper to Lauds.

Originally Matins was sung shortly after midnight, and consequently if the lights were extinguished the darkness was complete. The practice might go back to the seventh century since it is mentioned both in *Ordo Romanus Primus* and the Ordo of St. Amand published by Duchesne. On Friday the candles and lamps were gradually extinguished during the three Nocturns of Matins, while on Saturday the church was in darkness from beginning to end, save that a single candle was kept near the lectern to read by. It is not surprising that in the early Middle Ages the prayer office of these three days was treated as a sort of funeral service, or dirge, commemorating the death of Jesus Christ. Doing the prayer offices in this way, with the gradual extinguishing of lights, might have been suggested by the tradition that Christ laid in the tomb for three days. These obsequies thus came to be celebrated on each of the three separate days with the same demonstrations of mourning.

There is no doubt that Tenebrae is emotionally appealing. The lessons from the book of Lamentations have been set to music by many composers, of whom the most famous are Palestrina, Tallis, Lassus, Marc-Antoine Charpentier, François Couperin, Ernst Krenek (*Lamentatio Jeremiae prophetae*, op. 93) and Igor Stravinsky (*Threni*). In addition, the responses have been set by Lassus, Gesualdo, Victoria, and Jan Dismas Zelenka.

5. Holy Saturday: How might the Great Vigil be structured?

The climax of Holy Week is the Great Vigil of Holy Saturday. Also called the Paschal Vigil or the Great Vigil of Easter, it is a liturgy held in many Christian churches as the first official celebration of the resurrection of Jesus. Historically, it is during this liturgy that catechumens are baptized and received into full communion with the church. It is held in the hours of darkness between sunset on Holy Saturday and sunrise on Easter Day—most commonly in the evening of Holy Saturday—but is considered to be the first celebration of Easter Day, since the Christian tradition considers feasts and other days of observance where masses are celebrated to begin at sunset of the previous day.

The Vigil begins with a gathering around a new fire (usually outdoors) and the lighting of the paschal candle. Once the candle has been lit there follows the ancient and dramatic rite of the Lucernarium, in which the candle is carried by a deacon through the nave of the church, itself in complete darkness, stopping three times to chant the acclamation "The light of Christ" (*Lumen Christi*), to which the assembly responds "Thanks be to God" (*Deo gratias*). This ceremony was once common in the church, often occurred at Vespers and was retrieved by Lutherans (beginning with *Lutheran Book of Worship*) as the opening part of Vespers. As the paschal candle proceeds through the church, the hand candles of all present are lit from the paschal candle. As this symbolic "Light of Christ" spreads throughout those gathered, the darkness is decreased.

Once the candle has been placed on its stand in the sanctuary, the lights in the church are switched on and the assembly extinguish their candles (although in some churches the custom is to continue the liturgy by candlelight until the Gloria). The deacon or a cantor now chants the Exsultet (also called the "Easter Proclamation" or "Paschal Praeconium"), after which the people take their seats as the Liturgy of the Word begins.

The Liturgy of the Word historically consisted of twelve readings. In the restored Vigil under Pope Pius XII the number was reduced to four. The current Roman Rite has seven readings from the Old Testament, although it is permitted to reduce this number for pastoral reasons (if reduced, it is customary to use readings 1, 3, 5, and 7). The twelve readings in the fifth-century Armenian Lectionary used in the Jerusalem Church are as follows:

Genesis 1:1—3:24—the creation and fall
Genesis 22:1-18—the binding of Isaac
Exodus 12:1-24—the Passover meal
Jonah 1:1—4:11—the story of Jonah
Exodus 14:24—15:21—the crossing of the Red Sea
Isaiah 60:1-13—"Arise, shine, for your light has come"
Job 38:1-28—God speaking out of the whirlwind
2 Kings 2:1-22—the ascension of Elijah
Jeremiah 31:31-34—the new covenant
Joshua 1:1-9—the crossing of the Jordan into the promised land
Ezekiel 37:1-14—the vision of the dry bones
Daniel 3:1-90—the three young men in the fiery furnace

These readings are all types of resurrection and baptism (new creation). In modern lectionaries the story of Noah and the flood is included. The account of the Israelites' crossing of the Red Sea is given particular attention in the readings since this event is at the center of the Jewish Passover. The Vigil itself is the celebration of the passover of Christ from death to life. Each reading is followed by a psalm and a prayer relating what has been read in the Old Testament to the mystery of new life in Christ. The last canticle is the Song of the Three Children (*Benedicite opera omnia*) from the apocryphal addition to the book of Daniel (Daniel 3).

At this point there are different options for the structure of the Vigil. In *Lutheran Book of Worship*, this last canticle is sung during the procession to the font for the baptisms and renewal of baptism by the assembly. In the Roman Catholic order the baptisms follow the Gospel. Both structures are provided as options in *Evangelical Lutheran Worship*.

After these readings or after the baptisms the Easter Vigil proper is finished. The presiding minister or celebrant removes the cope, if one has been worn, and puts on a chasuble. Candles are lighted on the altar, and the first Eucharist of Easter begins. After the singing of the Kyrie, the Gloria in Excelsis Deo is sung for the first time since before Lent (with the possible exception of Holy Thursday), and the church bells and the organ, silent since that point on Maundy Thursday, are sounded again. If the crosses and statues in the church have been veiled during Lent they are unveiled at this time. The opening collect is read. A reading from Romans 6 is proclaimed. The Alleluia is sung for the first time since the beginning of Lent—a very solemn threefold alleluia. The Gospel of the Resurrection then follows, along with a homily.

At this point in the Roman Catholic order, the water of the baptismal font is solemnly blessed and any catechumens and candidates for full communion are initiated into the church, by baptism and/or confirmation, respectively. After the celebration of these sacraments of initiation, the congregation renews their baptismal vows and receive the sprinkling of baptismal water. The prayers of the faithful (of which the newly baptized are now a part) follow.

After the prayers, the Liturgy of the Eucharist continues as usual. This is the first Mass of Easter Day. During the Eucharist, the newly baptized receive Holy Communion for the first time. According to the rubrics of the Roman Missal, the Eucharist should finish before dawn. In most situations, it is finished before midnight because it begins around 8:00 PM. It is a growing custom to conclude the Vigil Eucharist with a breakfast or break-the-Lenten-fast party.

In the Eastern churches the Vigil and Divine Liturgy do last until dawn and the breakfast is a real breakfast. Following the dismissal from the Divine Liturgy, blessed eggs that have been dyed red are usually distributed to the people for the breaking of the Great Lenten fast, and baskets of food for the feast that follows are blessed with holy water. The service generally finishes around 4:00 AM and there is usually not a service on Easter Sunday morning. The faithful go home but may return on Easter

Sunday afternoon for a special Paschal Vespers, at which the Gospel is chanted in many languages (called "Vespers of Love" in some traditions).

It needs to be admitted that the restoration of the Triduum in Western churches during the course of the twentieth century bumps into other traditions that have developed. The Easter Vigil in particular has been slowly gaining popularity, but it is a long way from displacing the festival services of Easter Day, which continue to draw large crowds and which require all liturgical and musical resources of the congregation or parish. As with most restorations, however, it is successful if it meets the needs of the contemporary worshiping assembly. This will happen only as these ancient rites are adapted to contemporary styles of celebration. Late fourth-century Jerusalem is not likely to be retrieved, not even in twenty-first-century Jerusalem.

For further reading

Baldovin, John F., S.J. "Holy Week, Liturgies of," in Peter Fink, S.J., ed., *The New Dictionary of Sacramental Worship*, 542–52. Collegeville: Liturgical, 1990.

Bradshaw, Paul F., and Hoffman, Lawrence A., eds. *Passover and Easter: Origin and History to Modern Times*. Two Liturgical Traditions, vol. 5. Notre Dame: University of Notre Dame Press, 1999.

———, and ———, eds. *Passover and Easter: The Symbolic Structuring of Sacred Seasons*. Two Liturgical Traditions, vol. 6. Notre Dame: University of Notre Dame Press, 1999.

Davies, J. G. *Holy Week: A Short History*. Richmond: John Knox, 1963.

Tyrer, John W. *Historical Survey of Holy Week: Its Services and Ceremonial*. London: Oxford University Press, 1932.

See also "For further reading" at the end of chapter 5.

8
The Church Year
Easter and Beyond

1. Easter: How can a fifty-day celebration be maintained?
2. Pentecost: What happens on "the last and great day" of the feast?
3. Time after Pentecost: Should lesser festivals replace Sundays?
4. The Sanctoral Cycle: How do we commemorate the faithful departed?
5. Christ the King: How does the church year end?

1. Easter: How can a fifty-day celebration be maintained?

St. John Chrysostom said about the Easter (Paschal) season, "We have unending holiday." It was not entirely unending; the season lasted fifty days. The reason for a fifty-day celebration lies in the concept of emphasizing the importance of a feast by celebrating it for eight days, or repeating the celebration on the eighth day. Easter, as the chief Christian feast, would be an octave of octaves: seven times seven plus one. This was not a Christian invention. The Jewish feast of Passover was celebrated as an octave of octaves, ending on the fiftieth day: Pentecost or the Feast of Weeks.

One instance of the practice of emphasizing the importance of a feast by giving it an octave is seen in the eight-day celebration of the Feast of Tabernacles (Lev. 23:36) and the Dedication of the Temple (2 Chron. 7:9). Perhaps in imitation of this Old Testament example the dedication festivities of the basilicas erected under the auspices of Emperor Constantine I at Jerusalem and Tyre were observed for eight days.

There's no doubt that the practice of emphasizing the importance of major festivals by observing octaves complicated the calendar. Many of these octaves are no longer observed, but it is difficult to understand the development of the Christian liturgical calendar without knowledge of the concept. So, for example, while the Easter season was an octave of octaves, Easter Day itself acquired an octave known as "the week of white robes." Those who were baptized at Easter attended church every day wearing their white baptismal garments. On these days the bishops explained the meaning of the mysteries or sacraments of Holy Baptism and Holy Communion that newly baptized had just experienced. The readings of the first several Sundays of the Easter season still lend themselves to preaching on the sacraments.

By the late Middle Ages, Christmas, Easter, and Pentecost were celebrated with a shortened three-day octave, which must have been such an entrenched pre-Reformation holiday sequence that it passed almost without change into the Lutheran and Anglican calendars. The propers were even retained in the 1662 *Book of Common Prayer* long after any memory of Catholic practice had faded. Thus the first three days of Easter are retained in all three traditions with their propers.

On the Sunday following Easter Day, the newly baptized removed their white robes and joined the ranks of the faithful—the mixed crowd of sheep and goats, as Augustine referred to his congregation. Hence, the official Latin name is *Dominica in Albis [Depositis]*, "Sunday in [Setting Aside the] White Garments." ("White Sunday" is also the etymology of Whitsunday, which is another name for Pentecost). This Sunday also acquired other names: Thomas Sunday, from the Gospel reading concerning "doubting Thomas" in John 20:19-29; Low Sunday, from a corruption of the Latin word *Laudes*, the first word of the sequence of the day: *Laudes Salvatori voce modulemur supplici* ("Let us sing praises to the Savior with humble voice"), and not because of low attendance after the high attendance of Easter Day; and Quasimodo Sunday, from the Latin text of the traditional Introit for this day, which begins *Quasi modo geniti infantes...* ("As newborn babies . . ."), from 1 Peter 2:2, which is a reference to the newly baptized on this Sunday.

In the Roman Catholic Church, this Second Sunday of Easter has also become known as Divine Mercy Sunday. It is dedicated to the devotion to the Divine Mercy promoted by the seventh-century saint Faustina, and is based upon an entry in Faustina's diary stating that anyone who participates in the Mass and receives the sacraments of confession and Eucharist on this day is assured by Jesus of full remission of sins. This devotion was celebrated unofficially in many places for some years. On April 30, 2000 (Divine Mercy Sunday of that year), Pope John Paul II canonized St. Faustina and designated the Second Sunday of Easter as the Sunday of the Divine Mercy (*Dominica II Paschae seu de divina misericordia*) in the General Roman Calendar. He also decreed a plenary indulgence associated with this devotion. Pope John Paul II said he felt a closeness to St. Faustina when he was writing his second encyclical, *Dives in misericordia* ("Rich in Mercy"). He died during the vigil of Divine Mercy Sunday in 2005.

Lutherans have made a special devotion of Good Shepherd Sunday, the Fourth Sunday of Easter. The name derives from the Gospel readings on this day, which are taken from John 10. In this reading Christ is described as the Good Shepherd. It is customary to sing settings of Psalm 23, including the beloved hymn "The King of Love My Shepherd Is," among others. Many Lutheran church buildings in America have a painting of Christ the Good Shepherd above the altar.

Lutherans also designated the former Fourth Sunday after Easter *Cantate Domino*, "Sing to the Lord a new song" (Psalm 98), from the old Introit for the Fourth Sunday after Easter, as Church Music Sunday, now celebrated on the Sixth Sunday of Easter on which Psalm 98 is the appointed psalmody. Church Music Sunday is a day on which to recognize the music ministry of the congregation and give the various choirs and instrumentalists an opportunity to perform during the service.

The former Fifth Sunday after Easter was called Rogation Sunday because the Gospel reading for the previous Sunday included the passage "Ask and ye shall receive" (John 16:24), and it occurred in proximity to Rogationtide. The Rogation days in the calendar of the Western church were four days set apart for solemn processions to invoke God's mercy, especially on the seedtime as processions went through the fields singing psalms and litanies. These occurred at a time in the spring of the year when the seeds in the fields were springing to life. The custom may have arisen in Gaul during the fifth century after a time of pestilence and famine, but it was not introduced in Rome until the ninth century.[1] The Major Rogation Day is April 25, which coincides with St. Mark's Day but has no connection with it. This suggests that it has pagan roots, perhaps the ancient Roman festival of the Robigalia, a ritual involving prayer and sacrifice for crops held on April 25. The Minor Rogations are the three days preceding Ascension Day. More intense "days of asking" seem appropriate just before Ascension Day because one of the themes of Christ's ascension is his mediation between God the Father and the faithful on earth. These days were observed with processions through the fields (this will be described in chapter 11, below).

Ascension Day celebrates the ascension of Jesus to his Father in heaven forty days after his resurrection, according to Luke's chronology. The ascension is an article of the faith confessed in the creeds and has been one of the major festivals of the church year since the late fourth century. Like many other days in the church year, it owes its development to the practices of the Jerusalem Church. Christians gathered on the Mount of Olives, from which Jesus ascended to the Father in Acts 1, even before a church was built on the site. But the empress, Helena, erected a basilica over the site called "Eleona" (*elaion* in Greek means "olive garden").

Ascension Thursday was for a long time a holiday in the countries of Christendom. As it ceased to be such, and never has been in North America, the Roman Catholic Church in a number of countries has obtained permission from the Vatican to move observance of the feast from the traditional Thursday to the following Sunday, the Sunday before Pentecost. This is in keeping with a trend to move Holy Days of Obligation from weekdays to Sunday, to encourage more Catholics to observe feasts considered important. This particular move has been endorsed by the *Book of Common Prayer* of the Episcopal Church and *Evangelical Lutheran Worship*, but has not generally been picked up by Anglican parishes and Lutheran congregations. So Ascension Day may wind up not being observed at all, or else observed with only a small number of worshipers on Ascension Thursday.

The waning of this feast in popular observance does not reflect the importance of the ascension as an article of faith, since Christ's session at the right hand of God speaks of his rule over the universe and his intercession on behalf of his brothers and sisters. The custom of extinguishing the paschal candle on Ascension Day does not make sense unless it is done on the actual day. The more recent preference has been to keep it burning the full fifty days and extinguish it after the Pentecost liturgy.

2. Pentecost: What happens on "the last and great day" of the feast?

The Day of Pentecost is the last day, the fiftieth day, of the paschal celebration. In spite of the custom of replacing white or gold vestments and paraments with red, Pentecost does not begin a new season in the church year, even though by the later Middle Ages it was given its own octave, Trinity Sunday. Since the name of the day was already a Jewish feast (Acts 2:1), also called the Feast of Weeks, the intervening fifty days may have formed an octave of octaves of Passover. The day has also been called Whitsunday because of the custom of those baptized at Pentecost wearing their white robes. In the Roman tradition Pentecost was the second great day in the church year for solemn public baptisms. It may have served as a kind of "make-up" day for those who were not ready for baptism at Easter. In recent years, especially in Lutheranism, Pentecost has become a preferred day for the rite of confirmation (Affirmation of Baptism).

Like all the great festivals in the church year, Pentecost has a vigil. This has not been so universally restored like the Easter Vigil. But if the congregation or parish has baptisms to celebrate that could not be celebrated at the Easter Vigil, they might be celebrated at the Vigil of Pentecost. The Roman Lectionary provides four Old Testament readings for the Pentecost Vigil. With suggested psalms they are:

Genesis 11:1-9 (the confusion of languages at Babel) with Psalm 33
Exodus 19:3-8, 16-20 (the covenant between Yahweh and Israel) with Psalm 103
Ezekiel 37:1-14 (the Spirit of God gives life to the dry bones) with Psalm 42
Joel 2:28-32 (the Spirit poured out on all people) with Psalm 104, or the Song of the
    Three Children (*Benedicite opera omnia*).

The readings in the Eucharist are Romans 8:22-27 (the Spirit teaches us to pray) and John 7:37-39 (Jesus is the source of living water).

In the vigil structure collects are needed after the readings and psalms. I offer these, which I have adapted from several sources (Roman Sacramentary and *Lutheran Book of Worship* among them):

Genesis 11:1-9 with Psalm 33
God our Creator, earth has many languages, but your Gospel announces your love to

all nations. Make us messengers of the good news that, through the power of your
Spirit, everyone everywhere may united in one song of praise; through your Son,
Jesus Christ our Lord.

Exodus 19:3-8, 16-20 with Psalm 103

God our Maker and Redeemer, you have made us a new company of priests to bear
witness to your word. Enable us to be faithful to our calling to make known your
will to all the world; through your Son, Jesus Christ our Lord.

Ezekiel 37:1-14 with Psalm 42

Lord of hosts, you restore all things that are broken down, and preserve those things
that you have restored. Increase, we pray, the people who shall be regenerated in
your Name, that those who are washed in the waters of baptism may renewed by
your Spirit; through your Son, Jesus Christ, our Lord.

After Joel 2:28-32 the Song of the Three Children might be sung during a procession to the font. If Holy Baptism is celebrated after the Gospel and homily, the Gloria
in excelsis might be sung after the Joel reading, followed by the prayer of the day for the
Pentecost Vigil.

Like the Easter Vigil, the Pentecost Vigil should begin with a lucernarium: acclamations as the candle is carried into the assembly, a light hymn, and a thanksgiving for
light. The candle might be the paschal candle that had been lighted at the Easter Vigil
and continued to burn throughout the Great Fifty Days.

We noted above that late medieval calendars introduced a reduced three-day octave
for Christmas, Easter, and Pentecost that were retained in Roman Catholic and passed
into Lutheran and Anglican calendars. All three calendars have the same readings
for Pentecost Sunday, Monday, and Tuesday. The rest of the octave, including Ember
Wednesday, Friday, and Saturday were abolished by Lutherans and Anglicans. The
Ember Days reappeared without propers in the proposed 1928 *Book of Common Prayer*.

3. Time after Pentecost: Should lesser festivals replace Sundays?

Christ's resurrection and the outpouring of the Holy Spirit is the content of Sunday,
and recent liturgical renewal has emphasized Sunday as the major day in the Christian
calendar—every Sunday a little Easter—that should not be replaced by the content of
other lesser festivals. These would be transferred to Monday if they fell on Sunday. Yet
this theory is difficult to maintain in practice, because some of the lesser festivals that
fall during the time after Pentecost have acquired theological and cultural importance.
Indeed, some of these festivals are not "lesser" at all!

By the late Middle Ages, all the Sundays were designated "after Pentecost" or (especially in the northern countries) "after Trinity." Nevertheless, at this same time a trinity of festivals inaugurated the second half of the church year: Trinity Sunday, Corpus
Christi, and the Nativity of St. John the Baptist (June 24).

The Festival of the Holy Trinity was embraced throughout the Western church by the fourteenth century as the octave of Pentecost. A votive mass of the Holy Trinity was in medieval missals, but it was offered on various days. In the Frankish Kingdom this Mass of the Holy Trinity was usually celebrated on the Sunday after Pentecost. In 1334 Pope John XXII ordered this custom for the universal church and it became one of the principal festivals of the church year. (In the Eastern churches the Sunday after Pentecost is celebrated as All Saints' Sunday.) In the late Middle Ages in the West, a special devotion to the Holy Trinity developed in response to the plagues known as the Black Death. Hundreds of Trinity churches were dedicated throughout Europe during these times of pestilence.[2]

A historic feature of Lutheran practice has been the recitation of the so-called Athanasian Creed on Trinity Sunday, originally in Matins but sometimes in place of the Nicene or Apostles' Creed in the Holy Communion. This use is a survival of monastic use, since in the monasteries this creed was traditionally said at Prime on Sundays after the Epiphany and after Pentecost, as well as on Trinity Sunday. It was included in *Lutheran Book of Worship* (1978) as well as in *Lutheran Worship* (1982) and *Lutheran Service Book* (2006), but is not in *Evangelical Lutheran Worship* (2006). The Athanasian Creed was effectively dropped from the Roman Catholic liturgy following Vatican II. It was retained in the successive volumes of the *Book of Common Prayer* of the reformed Church of England from 1549 to 1662, which provided for its recitation on nineteen occasions each year. This practice continued until the nineteenth century, when vigorous controversy regarding its statement about "eternal damnation" saw its use gradually decline. It should be noted that the only persons "damned" are "those who have done evil." Otherwise, clinging to the catholic faith if one wants to be saved is simply a way of claiming one's baptism.

This creed, properly called *Quicunque vult salus esse* ("Whoever wishes to be saved"), was not written by Athanasius, who wrote in Greek rather than in Latin, the original language of this creed. Theologians have said that it is actually more a reflection of the trinitarian theology of Augustine of Hippo. In any event, in spite of its didactic quality, its opening sets out the essential principle that the catholic faith does not consist in the first place in assent to propositions, but that "we worship One God in Trinity, and the Trinity in Unity." All else flows from that orientation. Since, in the monasteries, it was chanted antiphonally, a way of reciting this creed in contemporary liturgical assemblies might be antiphonally by whole verse. In this way we are, in effect, teaching the faith to one another.

The Feast of Corpus Christi was established in the thirteenth century on the Thursday after Trinity Sunday as the delayed octave of Maundy Thursday. Its celebration on a Thursday is meant to associate it with Jesus' institution of the Eucharist during the Last Supper, commemorated on Maundy Thursday, and this is the first free Thursday after Paschaltide, which is an octave of octaves, and Trinity Sunday, which serves as an octave of Pentecost.

In the Ordinary Form of the Catholic Church, the feast is now officially known as the Solemnity of the Body and Blood of Christ. In many English-speaking countries, Corpus Christi is transferred to the Sunday after Trinity Sunday by Catholics and those Anglicans who observe it (it is not found in the calendars of all Anglican Prayer Books, although it is in the calendar of the Church of England). At the end of the Mass, it is customary to have a Procession of the Blessed Sacrament (often outdoors), followed by Benediction of the Blessed Sacrament.

The promulgation of Corpus Christi as a feast in the Christian calendar was primarily due to the petitions, over a forty-year period, of the thirteenth-century Augustinian nun Juliana of Cornillon (1193–1258) in Liège.[3] Juliana, from her early youth, had a great devotion to the blessed sacrament, and always longed for a special feast in its honor. This desire is said to have been increased by a series of visions of Christ between 1208 and 1228 in which she was told to establish a feast in honor of the Blessed Sacrament. She kept these visions a secret, but eventually reported them to her confessor, and he relayed her reports to the bishop. Juliana also petitioned the learned Dominican Hugh of St-Cher, Jacques Pantaléon (Archdeacon of Liège who later became Pope Urban IV), and Robert de Thorete, Bishop of Liège, to establish a feast in honor of the blessed sacrament. At that time bishops could order feasts in their dioceses, so in 1246 Bishop Robert convened a synod and ordered a celebration of Corpus Christi to be held each year thereafter. But the celebration of Corpus Christi became widespread only after both St. Juliana and Bishop Robert de Thorete had died. In 1263 Pope Urban IV investigated claims of a eucharistic miracle at Bolsena, in which a consecrated host began to bleed, and in 1264 issued the papal bull *Transiturus de hoc mundo* in which Corpus Christi was made a feast throughout the entire Latin Rite. However, Urban died later that year and the bull was not implemented.

It should be noted that the feast of Corpus Christi was promoted at a time when there were, on the one hand, heretical groups like the Cathari who denied the efficacy of the sacraments attracting a popular following, and, on the other hand, pious women like the Beguines whose devotion centered on the Eucharist and the humanity of Jesus, particularly his Passion. Both groups had attracted followers around Liège. Corpus Christi caught on as a response to this conflict of pieties during the thirteenth and fourteenth centuries. No less a theologian than Thomas Aquinas was commissioned to compose liturgical texts for this feast.

This liturgy has come to be used not only on the Feast of Corpus Christi itself but also throughout the liturgical year at events related to the Blessed Sacrament. The hymn Aquinas composed for Vespers of Corpus Christi, *Pange lingua gloriosi corporis mysterium* ("Now, my tongue, the mystery telling, of the glorious body sing"), is also used on Holy Thursday during the procession of the Blessed Sacrament to the altar of repose, thus tying Corpus Christi to Maundy Thursday. The last two stanzas of *Pange Lingua gloriosi corporis* ("Sing, my tongue, of the glorious body") are also used as a separate hymn, *Tantum Ergo* ("There we before him bending this great sacrament revere"), which is sung at Solemn Benediction of the Blessed Sacrament, thus tying together Corpus Christi and its procession with the blessed sacrament, with Solemn Benediction. *O Salutaris Hostia* ("O saving Victim"), another hymn sung at Benediction of the Blessed Sacrament, comprises the last two verses of *Verbum Supernum Prodiens* ("The Word descending from above"), Aquinas's hymn for Lauds of Corpus Christi. Aquinas also composed the propers for the Mass of Corpus Christi, including the sequence *Lauda Sion Salvatorem* ("Zion, praise your Savior"). This was the basis of Martin Luther's communion hymn, *Gott sei gelobet* ("O God, we praise you").

Corpus Christi became one of the most popular festivals in late medieval Europe, involving the whole town in its great procession. The procession was not an original part of the feast, and its inclusion has to be seen as part of the development of exposition and veneration of the Blessed Sacrament outside Mass.[4] The day continued with games, plays, eating, and drinking. It was so popular that it was hard for the Reformation to suppress it. It remained on some Lutheran calendars until the end of the sixteenth century. It would seem that, without the exposition or showing of the sacrament, the feast might be restored in Lutheran churches as a way of devoting a Sunday exclusively to preaching about the sacrament of the altar. The three years' readings in the Roman Lectionary provide suitable propers. Also, the prayer composed by St. Thomas, "Lord God, who left to us in a wonderful sacrament a memorial of your passion," has long been used as a post-communion prayer in Lutheran worship books, and could serve as a suitable prayer of the day.

The churches in North America have discovered that, as with the Feast of the Ascension, if Corpus Christi is to be observed it will have to be transferred to a Sunday. Thus, the U.S. Conference of Catholic Bishops has given permission to celebrate Corpus Christ—The Body and Blood of Christ—on the Sunday after Trinity Sunday.

4. The Sanctoral Cycle: How do we commemorate the faithful departed?

Along with the cycle of Sundays and seasons in the church year, there is a cycle of saints' days and other church festivals. Some saints' days, especially the days of martyrs, are among the oldest commemorations in the church-year calendar. Christians in the early centuries gathered at the graves of the martyrs of the day of their death, which was considered their birthday into eternal life. The Eucharist was celebrated on the mensa (table top) of the grave. Later on, altars were built to look like tombs and the relics of saints were interred within them.

Several saints' days of summer became universal throughout the church. The Feast of the Nativity of St. John the Baptist is celebrated on June 24 and is one of the oldest festivals of the Christian church. It was listed by the Council of Agde in 506 as one of that region's principal festivals. Like Christmas, it was celebrated with three masses: a vigil, at dawn, and at midday. It is also celebrated in the Eastern Orthodox churches as the Nativity of John the Forerunner with an All-Night Vigil ending with the Eucharist. It has an "after-feast" of one day. The feast always falls during the Apostles' Fast.

It occurs on June 24 because it is three months after the celebration on March 25 of the annunciation, when the Archangel Gabriel told the Virgin Mary that her cousin Elizabeth was in her sixth month of pregnancy, and six months before the Christmas celebration of the birth of Jesus. The date of June 24 rather than June 25 could have been arrived at because of the Roman custom of counting backwards from the next calendar; hence eight days before July, as Christmas would be eight days before January.

This purpose of the feast has been eclipsed by the Scandinavian Midsummer Day festival, which, with its maypole, bonfires, and dancing, may be a remnant of pre-Christian pagan midsummer festivals. Already in the seventh century, St. Eligius warned against midsummer activities and encouraged new converts to avoid them in favor of the celebration of St. John the Baptist's birth. However, we should note that because of inaccuracies in the calendar the summer solstice was in the middle of June before the adoption of the Gregorian calendar in 1582.

The Feast of Saints Peter and Paul was universally celebrated throughout the Western church on June 29. It commemorates the martyrdom in Rome of the apostles Peter and Paul. The celebration is of ancient origin, the date selected being either the anniversary of their death or of the translation (moving) of their relics. The date may also have usurped the celebration of the founding of Rome by Romulus and Remus on a date in late June or early July when a solar eclipse was calculated to have occurred, thus, in a sense, refounding Christian Rome on the two great apostles. For Eastern Catholic and Eastern Orthodox Christians, this feast also marks the end of the Apostles' Fast (which began on the Monday following All Saints' Sunday—i.e., the second Monday after Pentecost). It is considered a day of recommended attendance, whereon one should attend the All-Night Vigil (or at least Vespers) on the eve, and the Divine Liturgy on the morning of the feast (there are, however, no "Days of Obligation" in the Eastern church per se). For those who follow the traditional Julian calendar, June 29 falls on the Gregorian calendar date of July 12.

The Day of Peter and Paul has acquired ecumenical significance in recent times. On this day the pope and the Patriarch of Constantinople have officiated at services designed to bring their two churches closer to intercommunion. This was especially the case during the pontificate of Pope John Paul II, as reflected in his encyclical *Ut Unum Sint*. But it could also be a day of special significance for Roman Catholics and Protestants, whose churches have theologically appealed to Peter and Paul, respectively, as sources of authority.

By the late Middle Ages, the routines of the months of July, August, September, and October were broken by numerous holy days. The most universal of these was the Assumption of Mary on August 15. This feast was based on the belief held by Christians of the Roman Catholic, Eastern Orthodox, Oriental Orthodox, and some Protestant churches such as Lutheranism that the Virgin Mary at the end of her life was physically taken up into heaven. The Eastern churches call the day the Dormition or Falling Asleep of the Theotokos (God-bearer or Mother of God), and it is preceded by a fourteen-day fast. Eastern Orthodox Christians believe that Mary died a natural death, that her soul was received by Christ upon death, and that her body was resurrected on the third day after her death and that she was taken up into heaven bodily in anticipation of the general resurrection. Roman Catholic teaching also holds that Mary was "assumed" into heaven in bodily form. Some Catholics agree with the Orthodox that this happened after Mary's death, while some hold that she did not experience death. Pope Pius XII, in his apostolic constitution *Munificentissimus Deus* (1950), which dogmatically defined the Assumption, appears to have left open the question of whether or not Mary actually underwent death in connection with her departure but alludes to the fact of her death at least five times.

The first four Christian centuries are silent regarding the end of the Virgin Mary's life, though it is asserted, without surviving documentation, that the Feast of the Dormition was being observed in Jerusalem shortly after the Council of Ephesus. It spread from the East to the West, where it was championed especially by monks, particularly Bernard of Clairvaux. Martin Luther, who retained his devotion to Mary as the Mother of God and the great example of faith, was open to the idea of her assumption into heaven. The Feast of Mary, the Mother of Our Lord, is retained in Lutheran calendars as well as in the Anglican *Book of Common Prayer*.

Apostles' days and local patronal feasts were special holidays marked by fairs and entertainment. Every parish, diocese, province, religious community, town, city, region, and nation had its heavenly patron. The Feast of St. Michael and All Angels (September 29) marked the beginning of the fall term for the law courts and the universities in England. Most saints' days were celebrated locally and not universally. Since these were legal holidays as well as holy days, they were having a negative economic impact by the end of the Middle Ages by providing too many days off of work. Luther proposed that they be abolished and observed on the nearest Sunday. King Henry VIII in England decreed in 1534 that all saints' days that fall during harvest time between July 1 and September 29 be abolished, and exempted only the Feasts of St. Mary, of apostles, and St. George. This injunction abrogated seventeen national or local feast days in just these three months!

Lutheran practice has been to observe the lesser festivals that fall on Sundays on those Sundays, although *Evangelical Lutheran Worship* (2006) follows the Roman Catholic practice of transferring festivals that fall on a Sunday to Monday. But certain festivals are considered so important that they would not be transferred, such as the Nativity of St. John the Baptist, Saints Peter and Paul, and Mary, the Mother of Our Lord. All Saints' Day has been routinely observed on the Sunday after November 1 in many Protestant churches, especially in Lutheran churches that observe the Festival of the Reformation on the Sunday before Reformation Day, October 31.

Churches celebrate historic events that are important to their tradition.[5] The Orthodox celebrate the Triumph of Orthodoxy on the First Sunday in Lent, commemorating the resolution of the iconoclastic controversy in 843. The Roman Catholic Church celebrates the Chair of St. Peter on February 22, emphasizing the founding of the Roman Church on the apostle Peter. Anglicans celebrate the promulgation of the first *Book of Common Prayer* during the week of Pentecost. Churches East and West celebrate Holy Cross Day, called The Triumph of the Cross in the Roman Catholic calendar, on September 14. This feast commemorates the dedication of the Church of the Holy Sepulchre and the discovery of the true cross of Christ at Jerusalem during excavations for the foundation of the basilica—an event that electrified the Christian world.[6] Lutherans and some other Protestants celebrate the Festival of the Reformation on October 31, the date on which Martin Luther posted his Ninety-Five Theses on the door of the Castle Church in Wittenberg, Germany. A Reformation festival was already celebrated in Lutheran churches in the sixteenth century on various dates (usually the date on which the Reformation was legally adopted in the city of territory), but then the practice died out. In 1667 Elector John George II of Saxony ordered a Reformation festival on October 31. This practice caught on and has been the date of the Reformation festival ever since

In the Northern Hemisphere the months of October and November are times of harvest. Harvest times in agrarian societies have been accompanied by fasting during the time of harvest (taking only the food need for nourishment since the work hours are longer) and thanksgiving meals after the harvest to celebrate the bounty that has been gathered and the herds that have been culled for the winter. National days of thanksgiving are observed in Canada on October 13 and in the United States on the fourth Thursday in November. Protestant worship books, following the *Book of Common Prayer*, have provided propers for harvest festivals and days of thanksgiving.

The end of the Western church year is ushered in by the dual celebrations of All Saints' Day on November 1 and All Souls' Day on November 2, which occur during these times of harvest festivals with their attendant memories of the departed.

Feasts of All Saints in both the Byzantine and Roman churches originated in late antiquity as days to commemorate all the martyrs during the age of persecution. The Feast of All Martyrs was observed in the Byzantine calendar on the Sunday after Pentecost as a way of applying the saving benefits of Christ's paschal victory. This extended the paschal season with an octave of Pentecost.[7] This Feast of All Martyrs was expanded to a Feast of All Saints by Emperor Leo VI "the Wise" (886–911). His wife, Empress Theophano (who is commemorated on December 16), had lived a devout life. After her death, her husband built a church, intending to dedicate it to her. When he was forbidden to do so, he decided to dedicate it to "All Saints," so that if his wife were in fact one of the righteous, she would also be honored whenever the feast was celebrated.[8]

Following the theme of applying the benefits of the Christ's paschal victory to his followers, the Sunday following All Saints Sunday in the Byzantine calendar—the second Sunday after Pentecost—is set aside as a commemoration of all locally venerated saints, such as "All Saints of America," "All Saints of Mount Athos," and so forth. The third Sunday after Pentecost may be observed for even more localized saints, such as "All Saints of St. Petersburg," or for saints of a particular type, such as "New Martyrs of the Turkish Yoke."

In the West a festival of All Saints may be traced to the consecration of the Pantheon at Rome to the Blessed Virgin and all the martyrs on May 13, 609 or 610, by Pope Boniface IV. This Feast of the *Dedicatio Sanctae Mariae ad Martyres* has been celebrated at Rome ever since. May 13 had been a pagan observation of great antiquity, the culmination of three days of the Feast of the Lemures, in which the malevolent and restless spirits of the dead were propitiated.

A similar concern of converting a propitiation of evil or restless spirits lies behind the emergence of the Feast of All Saints as we know it on its current date (November 1). This date has several origins. One is the founding of an oratory (prayer chapel) in St. Peter's Basilica by Pope Gregory III (731–741) for the relics "of the holy apostles and of all saints, martyrs and confessors, of all the just made perfect who are at rest throughout the world." The day of the annual observance of this foundation was moved to November 1, probably to conform to a November 1 festival of all the saints that was already widely celebrated in the Frankish Empire during the days of Charlemagne. It was made a day of obligation throughout the Frankish Empire in 835, by a decree of Emperor Louis the Pious, issued "at the instance of Pope Gregory IV and with the assent of all the bishops," which confirmed its celebration on November 1.

It has been thought that the Celtic holiday of Samhain, which had a theme similar to that of the Roman Lemuria, and which was also a harvest festival, lies behind the choice of November 1. Samhain, like Lemuria, has aspects of a festival of the dead. Interestingly, it continued to be celebrated through medieval times, and is seen as contributing to the modern celebration of Halloween, such as carving heads from turnips or rutabagas (the origin of jack-o'-lanterns). Believing that the head was the part of the body that contained the spirit, the Celts used the "head" of the vegetable to frighten off harmful spirits. There was also a practice in western Europe generally of providing warmth and "treats" for the spirits of the dead as winter began to set in. It was believed that the dead lingered close to where their bodies were buried in cemeteries. But the spirits of the dead might "haunt" the living who had not carried out the provisions of their wills, or who had not arranged to reduce the time they had to spend in purgatory by paying for requiem masses to be celebrated. (Unlike modern ghosts, medieval ghosts haunted people, not places.) The church officially tried to counter this kind of folklore; yet on All Hallows' Eve many parish churches kept the church bells ringing all night to frighten the spirits to remain in their graves.[9]

The point of All Saints' Day had been to direct the attention of Christians away from evil spirits and toward the blessed dead who sleep in Christ. But are all the faithful departed "blessed"? Have all attained the "beatific vision"? Doubts about this led to the development both of the concept of purgatory and the Feast of All Souls as a special day for intercession for most of the faithful departed.

The earliest Christian view was that the dead in Christ await the resurrection when Christ comes again in glory to judge the living and the dead. The state of the person between death and the resurrection at the sound of the archangel's trumpet did not concern the New Testament or early Christian writers. But the importation of Greek ideas of the immortality of the soul during and after the third century led to speculation about the state of the dead. Augustine of Hippo contributed to the view that a judgment takes place at the time of death and the soul of the faithful needs to be purified before attaining the beatific vision. This led to the development of the doctrine of purgatory, which gained in popular imagination during the twelfth and thirteenth centuries.[10] The view that most souls go to purgatory after death to be purified to see the beatific vision contributed to the development of All Souls' Day.

A day of general intercession for all the faithful departed on November 2 was first established by Odilo of Cluny (d. 1048) at his monastery of Cluny in 998. From Cluny the custom spread to the other houses of the Cluniac order, which became the largest and most extensive network of monasteries in Europe. In fact, both of these holy days were popularized throughout Europe by the powerful network of the wealthy Cluniac monasteries, which venerated their founders and offered masses and prayers for their benefactors. The celebration was soon adopted in several dioceses in France, and spread throughout the Western church. It was accepted in Rome only in the fourteenth century. Thus All Saints' Day became a celebration of all the saints in heaven, marked in the churches by the display and veneration of whatever relics of the saints the local church possessed. All Souls' Day became a day of prayer for the souls in purgatory on which many requiem masses were offered.

While November 2 remained the official day of remembrance of all the faithful departed, in time the entire month of November became associated in the Western Catholic tradition with prayer for the departed. Lists of names of those to be remembered were placed in the proximity of the altar on which the sacrifice of the Mass is offered. This was a busy time for burial confraternities, which paid for requiem masses for their members and maintained the graves of their faithful departed members. It was precisely because so much needed to be done to care for the dead that the whole month of November was needed to do it. Pagan and Christian practice has been merged in these observances, as can be seen in the Mexican Day of the Dead celebrations in Mexico that claim indigenous Mexican or Aztec and Maya as well as Christian liturgical practices. Maintaining the distinction between the pure and those in need of purgation, November 1 honors children and infants, whereas deceased adults are honored on November 2. This is indicated by generally referring to November 1 as *Día de los Inocentes* ("Day of the Innocents") but also as *Día de los Angelitos* ("Day of the Little Angels") and November 2 as *Día de los Muertos* or *Día de los Difuntos* ("Day of the Dead").

The widespread observance of Armistice Day on November 11 in western Europe and North America has extended the commemoration of the dead (in this case the war dead). In the United Kingdom the second Sunday in November, the Sunday closest to

Armistice Day, is observed as Remembrance Sunday. In Canada Remembrance Day is observed on November 11 itself, and in the United States Veterans Day is observed on November 11. These days of remembering those who died in the armed services of their countries are often observed with church services, especially in the United Kingdom.

The Reformation had difficulty with the festivals of All Saints and All Souls on several grounds. All Saints' Day, with its display of relics (such as those collected by the Elector Frederick the Wise in the Castle Church in Wittenberg), fostered the cult of the saints, in which the faithful asked the saints to intercede on their behalf before God the Father, thus challenging the position of Christ as the sole mediator and advocate with the Father (1 Tim. 2:5; 1 John 2:1). All Souls' Day depended on the doctrine of purgatory, for which the Reformers could find no evidence in Scripture (or disagreed with the interpretations of certain texts on which the Catholic doctrine relied[11]). Nevertheless, the festival of All Saints was retained after the Reformation in the calendar of the Anglican Church and in many Lutheran churches. In the Lutheran churches it has assumed a role of general commemoration of all the faithful departed. In the Church of Sweden calendar, the observance takes place on the Saturday between October 31 and November 6, and is a national holiday. In many Lutheran and some Protestant churches, All Saints is moved to the first Sunday of November.

It should be noted that Halloween, which has become a major secular spin-off from All Saints'/All Souls' Days, has no liturgical or Christian content.

5. Christ the King: How does the church year end?

As we move toward the end of the church year in the Western church calendar, the readings have an eschatological character. This is a remnant of the Gallican-Visigothic six-week Advent with its emphasis on judgment. The theme of judgment, of rendering an account, fits in with the time of harvest during the month of November. The medieval Roman Rite provided no propers beyond the twenty-fourth Sunday after Pentecost until the twenty-seventh or last Sunday. It used readings from the eighth and ninth Sundays after the Epiphany if propers were needed and repeated the Introit and Gradual from the twenty-third Sunday after Pentecost. In the Lutheran Common Liturgy of the *Service Book and Hymnal* (1958), eschatological readings were appointed for the last three Sundays of the church year: Matthew 24:15-28 (the emergence of false messiahs in the last days and the coming of the Son of Man); Matthew 25:31-46 (the separation of the sheep and the goats at the last judgment); and Matthew 25:1-13 (the parable of the wise and foolish maidens).

The Festival of Christ the King did not emerge until the twentieth century, and at first it had nothing to do with the end of the church year. It was established by Pope Pius XI in 1925 to counter what he regarded as the destructive forces of the modern world and was celebrated on the last Sunday in October. Pope Pius's festival was promulgated in the wake of the rise of communism in Russia and fascism in Italy and Spain. In just a few years nazism would emerge in Germany. The intention was to oppose the rule of Christ to these regimes with their totalitarian claims on the lives of their people. We note that at least by coincidence the Festival of Christ the King also coincided with the Protestant celebration of the Festival of the Reformation.

In the reform of the Roman liturgy after the Second Vatican Council, the Festival of Christ the King was moved to the last Sunday of the church year. The new location served more than an ecumenical gesture. Located at this point in the church year with its eschatological emphasis, Christ the King proclaims Christ as "the goal of human history, the focal point of the desires of history and civilization, the center of humankind, the joy of all hearts, and the fulfillment of all aspirations" (*The Pastoral Constitution on the Church in the Modern World*, 45). For this reason, the Gospels in the three-year Roman Lectionary for the Mass present Christ not only as the Son of Man coming in glory in Year A (Matt. 25:31-46) but also as reigning from the cross in years B and C (John 18:5-8; Luke 23:35-43). Eschatological texts are retained for the other readings.

Lutherans, Anglicans, and others who use the Revised Common Lectionary also observe Christ the King on the last Sunday of the church year. Out of feminist concerns about "kingship" it has sometimes been restyled "The Reign of Christ." Yet the themes of the original Christ the King of Pius XI linger on, and these themes are worth considering. The last judgment is not just a judgment on individuals; it is a judgment on human history. The dialogue between Pontius Pilate and Jesus the Christ in John 18 demonstrates the struggle between the kingdoms (and republics) of this world and the kingdom of God and of his Christ. This gospel, which is not about Christ's second coming, confronts the believer with a decision about political claims to which we will be answerable at the last judgment. To which kingdom (or republic) do we owe our ultimate allegiance? If we want to get "in" with the coming administration of Christ the King, we had better come to terms with the witness of Revelation: that the one seated on the throne is the Lamb who was slain, and that self-giving love is the agenda throughout his dominions.

For further reading

Baldovin, John, S.J. "On Feasting the Saints," "All Saints in the Byzantine Tradition," and "The Liturgical Year: Calendar for a Just Community," in *Worship: City, Church, and Renewal*, 37–76. Washington, D.C.: Pastoral, 1991.

Brown, Peter. *The Cult of the Saints: Its Rise and Fall in Latin Christianity*. Chicago: University of Chicago Press, 1981.

Ruben, Miri. *Corpus Christi: The Eucharist in Late Medieval Culture*. Cambridge: Cambridge University Press, 1991.

Weiser, Francis X. *Handbook of Christian Feasts and Customs*. New York: Harcourt, Brace, and World, 1958.

See also "For further reading" at the end of chapter 5.

9
Life Passages

1. *How does the church make new Christians?*
2. *How do Christians affirm and live out their baptism?*
3. *How does the church make ministers?*
4. *How does the church solemnize marriages?*
5. *How does the church militant transfer members to the church triumphant?*

1. How does the church make new Christians?

Tertullian of Carthage famously said that "Christians are made, not born." Jesus told Nicodemus, "One must be born again of water and the Spirit" (John 3:5). A ritual process of Christian initiation developed in the ancient church whose outlines we already see in Acts 2. In response to Peter's proclamation that the crucified Jewish Messiah was raised from the dead by God, the people in Jerusalem asked what they should do. Peter replied: "Repent, and be baptized every one of you in the name of Jesus Christ so that your sins may be forgiven, and you will receive the gift of the Holy Spirit" (Acts 2:38). Receiving the gospel message, forgiveness of sin, invocation of the name (of Jesus in Acts, of the Holy Trinity in Matthew 28:19 and *Didache* 7:1), immersion in water, infusion of the Holy Spirit—these comprise the complex of activities that together make up the rite of Christian initiation.

The details of the rites varied from place to place and over time.[1] However, certain elements became inextricably connected with Christian initiation in the first five or six centuries: enrollment as a catechumen; a time of catechetical instruction; election as a candidate for baptism; the water bath itself; anointing before and after the bath; the laying on of hands with prayer for the gift of the Holy Spirit; first communion; mystagogy, or instruction in the mysteries or sacraments.

The heart of Christian initiation is the water bath called Holy Baptism. A bath requires water and we have archaeological evidence of many ancient fonts in the

Mediterranean world. The literary sources comment on the symbolism of the fonts as the tomb of death and resurrection and the womb of new birth. The hexagonal and octagonal shapes of bath houses called baptisteries may also refer to Christ's death on the sixth day and resurrection on the eighth day (the eschatological day of the Lord). The three steps into and up out of the font were also given symbolic interpretations. The archaeological evidence shows that immersion was the mode of baptism. The candidates went down into the font and stood in water. The candidate turned to the west to renounce Satan and all his works and pomps (honors), then faced east to confess faith in God the Father, Son, and Holy Spirit. The candidate was immersed three times. What is not so certain is whether immersion implies submersion. Everett Ferguson argues, in his massive study of baptism in the early church, that the dominant practice was that the candidate stood hip-deep in water and the minister put his or her (deaconesses for women) hand on the candidate's head and dipped him or her into the water. He notes that the depths of fonts varied (Western fonts being generally shallower than Greek fonts), and pouring and sprinkling were not unknown in exceptional circumstances. However, he argues that it would be possible for candidates to bend over and the minister's hand on the head indicates that the candidate was pushed below the water.[2] However, if the cultural backdrop of Christian baptismal practice is Mediterranean bathing practice, I think actual submersion is unlikely. In the bathhouses the bathers sat in the pools and slaves poured water over their heads. The minister's hand on the head of the candidate is a gesture of blessing, perhaps even of manumission of sins. In Roman society the laying on of hands was the gesture used by the master to indicate the granting of freedom to the slave, who then entered the service of the patron as a client. In the waters of baptism, we are freed from slavery to sin in order to serve Christ.

The rites of Christian initiation clearly envisioned a norm of adult baptism. Yet infants were baptized in the ancient church and in the society of Christendom during the Middle Ages infant baptism became the usual practice. This became controversial at the time of the Reformation and has become even more controversial since then. The practice of infant baptism continues to be questioned today by Baptists, many evangelicals, and Pentecostals, and they form a sizeable block of the religious landscape in the United States and now also around the world. But with the solitary exception of Tertullian, the practice wasn't questioned in the early church.

The Scriptures do not specifically enjoin the baptism of infants, but neither is such baptism forbidden. Rather, the church is commanded to baptize "all" peoples (Matt. 28:19), and there are examples in the book of Acts of whole households being baptized (e.g., Cornelius's household in Acts 10). Granted, the suggestion of paedobaptists that the households in Acts might have included children is an argument from silence. There is no specific mention of infant baptism in the first two centuries. But by the beginning of the third century there is the indirect testimony of Tertullian, who discouraged the practice—which means that it was being done. In *On Baptism* 18 he cites Matthew

19:14, "Forbid them not to come to me." "So let them come," he writes, "when they are growing up, when they are learning, when they are being taught what they are coming to: let them be made Christians when they have become competent to know Christ. Why should innocent infancy come with haste to the remission of sins?" If the *Apostolic Tradition* does not represent the practice of the Roman Church in the early third century, as used to be thought, we lose that source as a testimony to the fact that children were being baptized at the beginning of the third century and even how it was done. But Origen and Cyprian are witnesses to it. Without going so as far as Augustine later on in developing the doctrine of original sin, Origen appealed to Old Testament examples of ritual defilements in need of purification and extended baptismal forgiveness of sin to ritual impurity associated with childbirth. Ferguson insightfully comments, "Origen's statements indicate that infant baptism preceded this justification for the practice. As has often been true in Christian history, the practice preceded its doctrinal defense."[3] In other words, infant baptism was a practice in search of a theory.

When we come to Augustine of Hippo, Ferguson is careful to note that the great North African father did not defend infant baptism on the basis of original sin but taught a doctrine of original sin on the basis of the fact that children were baptized. This is a typical patristic appeal to the *lex orandi* as the basis of the *lex credendi*. In the context of the Pelagian controversy, Augustine repeated his emphasis in the Donatist controversy that baptism is regeneration, but new life is possible only if sins are forgiven. Since infants are baptized forgiveness of sin must also apply to them. Since infants are not capable of sinning, the sin forgiven must refer to the original sin inherited from Adam and Eve. Later on it might have been argued that infants should be baptized because they are born in original sin, but that is not how Augustine argued. Infants were already being baptized. They were also being baptized in the East, which did not develop a doctrine of original sin.

So we return to the question: Why did the church baptize infants and small children? Ferguson rejects Joachim Jeremias's appeal to Jewish proselyte baptism, Kurt Aland's proposal of changing perceptions of children and acceptance of the doctrine of original sin, Johannes Leipoldt's suggestion of the initiation of children in the mystery cults (children were initiated, but not infants), Joseph R. Moore's case for the example of the old Punic practice of child sacrifice (since infant baptism found its strongest support in North Africa), and David Wright's theory of the extension of child baptism to baby baptism. Instead, after examining inscriptions on tombstones (baptismal dates and death dates in close proximity), Ferguson suggests that "when a child of Christian parents (or of catechumens) became seriously ill, there was a natural human concern about the welfare of the child's soul and a desire to make every preparation for the afterlife. Request from parents or family members for the baptism of a gravely sick child would have been hard to refuse."[4]

This theory of emergency baptism holds through the fifth century when most candidates for Holy Baptism were adults. Some even delayed baptism until they were on their deathbed (e.g., the emperor Constantine). However, after the fifth century the high infant-mortality rate, which was exacerbated by declining social conditions in the West, prompted parents to rush their children to the font as quickly as possible. At that point in the West the doctrine of original sin would provide a justification for the growing normalcy of the practice of infant baptism.

Nevertheless, the church in antiquity never found a reason not to baptize infants and small children. Once the practice became more customary, church fathers like Augustine could develop views about the efficacy of the sacrament even with regard to the faith of the infant. As he wrote to Bishop Boniface in Numidia with regard to the pastoral issue of Christian parents desiring to have their child baptized, "even if that faith that is found in the will of believers does not make a little one a believer, the sacrament of the faith itself, nonetheless, now does so. For, just as the response is given that the little one believes [the response of the parent at the child's baptism], he is also in that sense called a believer, not because he assents to the reality with his mind [the infant cannot assent] but because he receives the sacrament of that reality." [5]

The discussion of the relationship between baptism and the doctrine of original sin emerged in the heat of the Pelagian controversy. But we should step back and look at baptism in the light of Augustine's less polemical writings, especially his *Confessions*. Augustine was enrolled as a catechumen on his eighth day. His mother, Monica, was a baptized Christian; his father, Patricius, was a Christian catechumen. This was a normal arrangement at the time. Women were more likely to receive the water bath than men because they did not have public responsibilities that might compromise the gospel values. Augustine became seriously ill when he was a bit older and his mother made arrangements for an emergency baptism. But he recovered and the baptism did not take place. He delayed his own baptism until the age of thirty when he was under the influence of Ambrose of Milan. Yet, between his enrollment as a catechumen and his baptism and first communion, Augustine regarded himself as a Christian. He had received the sign of the cross at his enrollment, which he counted among the many *sacramenta* that were included in Christian initiation. This leads me to argue that baptism was regarded as a ritual process that, in some instances, could last a lifetime. One could present oneself as a candidate for election and complete the process at any point before death. The process extended from enrollment through mystagogia. If baptism is understood as including everything in this process, and infants were enrolled as catechumens, "infant baptism" was being practiced far more regularly than we have assumed if we think of baptism only as the water bath.

When we come to the end of the period of antiquity in the West, we see the full rite of Christian initiation in the Gelasian Sacramentary (mid-eighth century) and *Ordo Romanus XI* (late eighth century). The prayers of the sacramentary and the rubrics of the ordo indicate the practice of the scrutinies of the elect on the Third, Fourth, and Fifth Sundays in Lent; blessing and giving of salt; the exorcism over the elect; the exposition of the Gospels and the introduction of the creed and the Lord's Prayer to the elect (in either Latin or Greek, depending on the language spoken by the catechumen); the blessing of the oil on Maundy Thursday; the final exorcism on the morning of Holy Saturday; the readings and their accompanying prayers in the Easter Vigil (which are all leading up to baptism); and then the blessing of the font; profession of faith in God the Father Almighty, in Jesus Christ his only Son our Lord, and in the Holy Spirit; the triple dipping in the water; the chrismation by the presbyter; the vesting of the newly baptized with *stola and casula* (in the ordo, but not the sacramentary); the prayer for the sevenfold Spirit and laying on of hands by the bishop; and the episcopal anointing, with presumably first communion to take place at the Mass.[6]

The growing prevalence of infant baptism (really "emergency baptism") also led to dislocations in the rite of Christian initiation in the West (but not in the East).[7] We note the following:

• Baptism ceased to be performed only at the Easter Vigil, although that remained the preferred time for solemn public baptism (thus Pope Leo I the Great).
• The postbaptismal ceremonies (laying on of hands, second anointing or sealing) were to be done only by the bishop (thus Pope Innocent I in his letter to Bishop Decentius of Gubbio). When baptisms were not performed in the bishop's church at the Easter Vigil, these episcopal ceremonies were separated from the water bath, sometimes by years, until the baptized could be taken to the bishop or the bishop visited the local community. This is the origin of the separate sacrament of confirmation in the Western church (see next section). However, the evidence suggests that the episcopal administration of this sacrament was sometimes irregular, depending as it did on episcopal visitation.
• Infants who could not chew and swallow the bread were communed with the wine alone. This was acceptable under the doctrine of concomitance, which held that the entire Christ is received under either species. But when the Fourth Lateran Council in 1215 decreed that the cup should normally be withheld from lay communicants for fear of spilling the blood of Christ and that all who have reached an age of discretion (age seven) should make a confession before receiving communion, this effectively ended infant communion in the Western church (although not in the Eastern church). The Utraquists (followers of Jan Hus) in Bohemia held out for infant communion just as they did for communion in both kinds.

In the sixteenth century, Martin Luther revitalized the place of baptism in Christian life and teaching. He saw it as the ritual sign of justification by grace through faith and made baptism the basis for the reform of church and society, especially in his doctrine of vocation. He taught that baptism is a "means of grace" through which God creates and strengthens "saving faith" as the "washing of regeneration" (Titus 3:5) in which infants and adults are reborn by water and the Spirit (John 3:3-7). Since the creation of faith is exclusively God's work, it does not depend on the actions of the baptized, whether infant or adult. Even though baptized infants cannot articulate that faith, Lutherans believe that it is present all the same. Because it is faith alone that receives these divine gifts, Lutherans confess in the words of Luther's *Small Catechism* that baptism "works forgiveness of sins, delivers from death and the devil, and gives eternal salvation to all who believe this, as the words and promises of God declare." In the section on infant baptism in his *Large Catechism*, Luther argues that infant baptism is God-pleasing because persons so baptized were reborn and sanctified by the Holy Spirit, as their lives have shown.

Luther rendered the order of baptism in the vernacular in 1523. This order was based on the Magdeburg Agenda of 1497. He revised this order in 1526, eliminating all duplications as well as all signs that in his view were likely to lead to misunderstandings or were superfluous: the breathing on the water at the beginning, the salt, the final exorcism, the signing of the cross with chrism after the baptism, the christening candle. What is left in the 1526 *Baptismal Booklet* is the following:[8]

The baptismal party is met by the pastor at the church door for a remnant of the ancient catechumenal rite
The little exorcism
The sign of the cross
A prayer for God's acceptance of the candidate
The "flood prayer" (based on the Gelasian consecration of the font)
The big exorcism
The Gospel of St. Mark 10 ("At that time they brought little children to Jesus . . .")
The Our Father
The baptismal party then processes to the font with the verse of Psalm 121:8, "The Lord preserve your going in and your coming out from this time forth and forevermore."
The renunciation of the devil and all his works and ways
The confession of faith in God the Father, in Jesus Christ, and in the Holy Spirit
The baptism in the triune name
The vesting of the child in the baptismal gown
The prayer for strengthening with grace
The peace

Luther's order, together with Osiander's Order for Nuremberg in 1524,[9] were influential on later German church orders and on the *Book of Common Prayer* (*BCP*) through Thomas Cranmer, who visited often in Osiander's home and married the pastor's niece before returning to England. The Anglican Prayer Books also preserved Luther's "flood prayer," so called because of its typological comparison of baptism in the church and Noah and his family preserved in the ark.

The Reformed tradition did not depart significantly from Luther in the practice of baptism, but in the order of baptism the sign of the cross, exorcism, and any suggestion of the blessing of the water were eliminated. Luther advocated the immersion (of infants), and medieval fonts were still large enough to accomplish this. As these were replaced in Protestant traditions, the tendency was to place the fonts in a visually more prominent place in front of the congregation, the size of fonts was reduced, the amount of water used was reduced, and pouring or sprinkling because customary.

The sixteenth-century Anabaptists ("rebaptizers") and seventeenth-century Baptists promoted adult baptism, or "believer's baptism." Early Anabaptists were given that name because they rebaptized persons who they felt had not been properly baptized, having received infant baptism, sprinkling, or baptism of any sort by another denomination. They performed baptisms indoors in a baptismal font if one were available, but more usually outdoors in a creek or river because of their lack of access to church buildings. Baptists see baptism as an act identifying one's acceptance of Jesus Christ as personal Savior. This is what regeneration or being born again means. There is no confidence in the efficacy of the ritual act as a means of grace that accomplishes regeneration because of the command and promise of Christ's word.

In the liturgical renewal of the twentieth century, there was a concern to restore the ancient order of baptism seen in the ancient church orders such as the *Apostolic Tradition*. This came to fruition in *Lutheran Book of Worship* (*LBW*) (1978), which has the following order:

Baptism is located after the sermon in the Service of Holy Communion
A hymn is sung during the procession of the font
Statement about the meaning of baptism
Presentation of the candidate(s)
Admonition to the sponsors (of children and adults)
Intercessions (for that day's liturgy, including prayers for the baptized)
Thanksgiving over the font
Renunciation of evil, the devil, and all his empty promises
Threefold profession of faith (Apostles' Creed)
Baptism in the name of the Trinity
Psalm or hymn sung as the baptismal party moves to before the altar
Laying on of hands and prayer for the sevenfold gifts of the Holy Spirit
Anointing and sign of the cross
Presentation of the lighted baptismal candle
Prayer for the parents of small children
Welcome into the congregation/community of faith

Two improvements were made in this order in *Evangelical Lutheran Worship* (*ELW*) (2006). The renunciation was given a triple expression to match the triple profession of faith. The thanksgiving over the font was juxtaposed with the water bath. A rubric also allows for the vesting of the candidate(s) in a white robe after the water bath.

The so-called form and matter of confirmation (the laying on of hands and anointing) are restored to the Liturgy of Holy Baptism in these orders. Of course, the Roman Rite has maintained the distinct tradition seen already in the *Apostolic Tradition* of a double anointing after the baptism: one by the presbyter and a second by the bishop. This provides continuing justification for episcopal confirmation (see the next section).

The other significant development in the twentieth century was the Roman Catholic Rite of Christian Initiation of Adults (RCIA) in 1972.[10] This rite envisions a unified process of making Christians that comprises four stages:

Enrollment into the catechumenate
Election and final preparation for baptism (normally during Lent)
Baptism and first communion (normally at the Easter Vigil)
Mystagogy

Intended at first for use in the mission fields of Africa, Asia, and Latin America, the restoration of the adult catechumenate has also proven fruitful to missionary work in North America and Europe. Many Roman Catholic parishes have carefully implemented the RCIA. Organizations have been formed such as the Forum on the Catechumenate and much literature has been developed to support the efforts of parishes. Its success has been noteworthy. Episcopal/Anglican and Lutheran churches have also prepared materials for the adult catechumenate, and have even sought to integrate the preparation of adult and child candidates for baptism.[11] *ELW* includes an order called "Welcome to Baptism," which can serve as a rite of enrollment into the catechumenate.

2. How do Christians affirm and live out their baptism?

The rite of confirmation has developed in the Western church as the primary means by which Christians baptized as infants can affirm their baptism. Separated from baptism because of assertion of episcopal prerogatives of bishops to be the minister of Christian initiation, confirmation became a rite in search of a meaning. It was construed as a strengthening of the gift of the Holy Spirit given in baptism. In a Pentecost sermon preached c. 450, Faustus of Riez said: "In baptism we are born anew for life, after baptism we are confirmed for battle; in baptism we are washed, after baptism we are strengthened."[12] The Fourth Lateran Council required all who reached an age of discretion to be confirmed. It should be accompanied by catechesis. But the administration of this sacrament tended to be haphazard because of the irregularity of episcopal visits. In *The Babylonian Captivity of the Church* (1520) Martin Luther called it "monkey business" (*Apfenspiel*) that served no good purpose. It was not a sacrament ordained by Christ but an ordinance of the church.[13] He retained and improved the catechetical instruction but abandoned the rite.

Confirmation came into Reformation churches through Martin Bucer in Strassburg. Bucer needed to respond to the Anabaptist accusations that the magisterial Reformation lacked church discipline. In the interest of providing church discipline, Bucer developed a rite of confirmation that would serve, after catechetical instruction, as a way for those baptized as infants to affirm their baptism. Bucer also made first communion a goal of the rite of confirmation.[14] This remained one of the purposes of the rite of confirmation in Protestantism.

The rite of confirmation in the Anglican Prayer Book shows the influence of Bucer through the 1543 Consultation of Archbishop Hermann of Cologne, which had been prepared by Bucer and Melanchthon. The *BCP* also included a catechism and subsequent editions of the *BCP* have continued to include a catechism.

In Lutheranism the rite of confirmation was restored under Pietism and in the age of Enlightenment as a way for persons to make a personal confession of faith rather than merely confessing the faith of the church by rote memorization. Confirmands might write their own personal faith statements. Confirmation was even seen as superior to baptism. In the culture religion of Christendom, confirmation became a rite of passage into adulthood. In the kingdom of Prussia, confirmation was even required for those going on to high school, apprenticeship, or the army. Immigrants brought these cultural trappings to America (and other places of German emigration).

In the renewal of the late twentieth century, there was an effort to recover the premier role of baptism in Christian life. Confirmation was construed as an affirmation of Baptism, perhaps even one affirmation among others.[15] *LBW* envisioned the order of Affirmation of Baptism being used for confirmation, reception of new members from other denominational traditions, and restoration to church membership after a lapse. However, the confirmation blessings with the imposition of hands was retained for that one use. Nevertheless, the rite of Affirmation of Baptism in *LBW* and *ELW* is clearly designed to relate to baptism by repeating the questions and promises made at Holy Baptism. Similar efforts are seen in other traditions, such as Anglican, Methodist, and Reformed. But Anglicans, who value the visit of bishops to the parishes, and Lutherans, who have a solid tradition of pastoral relationship with the youth in catechetical classes, are loath to abandon this rite. Some Roman Catholics also question what confirmation confers that isn't given in baptism.[16] Confirmation is a practice in search of a theory.

Martin Luther said that the real issue in baptism is not the momentary, one-time rite but the ongoing Christian life. The water of baptism signifies, he said in the *Small Catechism*, "the old Adam in us together with all sins and evil lusts, should be drowned by daily sorrow and repentance, and be put to death, so that the new Adam should come forth daily and rise up, cleansed and righteous, to live forever in God's presence."[17] Because sin is ever trying to get us back in its power, and often succeeds, we need, as Luther never tired of reiterating, confession and absolution. In his catechisms he taught that confession and absolution is a return to baptism (by which he meant individual confession to the pastor).

The problem of sin after baptism concerned many of the church fathers. The ancient church saw the development of an order of penitents that paralleled the order of catechumens. Tertullian already attested to such as *ordo poenitentium* in his treatise *On Penance* at the turn of the third century. Augustine also encouraged a life of penance as a way of living out baptism. In the ancient Roman Church the reconciliation of the public penitents occurred on Maundy Thursday (so they could be welcomed back to the table that night or for Easter), just as the baptism of the catechumens occurred at the Easter Vigil. The life of baptism is a penitential life.

This canonical public penance waned and died out sometime after the fifth century. New forms of individual confession emerged in the Celtic monasteries and caught on as a pastorally practicable way of dealing with sin. The Fourth Lateran Council decreed that all who reached an age of discretion (age seven) should make a confession to a priest before receiving communion, and that all should receive communion at least once a year, at Easter. This decree may have contributed to pushing the Easter Vigil to Holy Saturday morning, because clearly priests were busy during the Triduum hearing confessions.

Individual confession continued to be practiced in Lutheran churches after the Reformation. In time it was attached to Saturday Vespers, and a global absolution was given to all who had come to confession. Eventually, this practice also died out and all that was left was a brief Order for Confession before the beginning of the Service of Holy Communion—the Reformation's congregational adaptation of the prayers at the foot of the altar in the medieval Mass. This brief order is really a preparation for worship (note the Collect for Purity) and not an effective way of dealing with real sin. Efforts are being made, for example, by the Society of the Holy Trinity, to recover individual confession for pastors and by pastors for congregants in their parishes. An Order for Individual Confession and Forgiveness is provided in *LBW* and subsequent worship books.

There is yet another way Christians may affirm their baptism: by receiving Holy Communion. Holy Communion is also a sacrament of initiation. In fact, inclusion in the eucharistic fellowship is the goal of Christian initiation. It is the promised land reached after the long journey of the catechumenate. This was signified by including cups of milk and honey in first communion in ancient church orders. There is no historical or theological justification for reversing the order of font to table, even out of concerns to show hospitality to unchurched visitors.[18] The proper way to welcome and include the unchurched is to invite them to join the church by being baptized or by affirming their baptism.

Finally, the daily prayer offices provide a way of remembering baptism by reciting the Apostles' Creed. The Creed is included in the morning and evening suffrages, which may be the form of prayer for Matins (Morning Prayer) and Vespers (Evening Prayer). Luther's catechisms instruct the Christian to make the sign of the cross and recite the Apostles' Creed upon rising in the morning and retiring at night.

3. How does the church make ministers?

The New Testament does not give us much information on how leaders were set aside for their ministry. The apostles were handpicked by our Lord and their office as witnesses of the risen Christ was not transferable. The gifts of the charismatic prophets and teachers (1 Cor. 12:28) were simply recognized. The overseers (*episcopoi*) were at first appointed by the apostles and later, with the servants (*diakonoi*), were elected by their community. The elders (*presbyteroi)* were somehow recognized by their community. In Acts appointment of ministers was by laying on of hands associated with prayer for the Holy Spirit (Acts 13:2; 20:28). In the pastoral epistles the imposition of hands is also the means of designating and recognizing those who exert leadership and ministry in the community (1 Tim. 4:14; 5:22; 2 Tim. 1:6; 4:1-8). This pattern formed the core of the ordination rites that developed in the church.

Some have speculated that Moses' "ordination" of Joshua by the laying on of hands (Num. 27:22-23; Deut. 34:9) provides a model both for later Jewish ordination of rabbis and for Christian ordination of ministers. Lawrence Hoffman disputed any direct connection from the Torah to either tradition, and in fact suggested that Christian practice could just as easily have influenced Jewish practice in the early common era.[19]

The *Didache* at the end of the first century reflects a situation in which the charismatic and itinerant prophets and teachers are dying out and the community must elect bishops and deacons who will perform the liturgy (15). The *Apostolic Tradition* and related church orders provide for the election of bishops by the local church and the ordination of the bishop by three neighboring bishops; the ordination of presbyters by the bishop with the participation of fellow presbyters; and the ordination of deacons by the bishop alone (since the deacon assists the bishop in his ministry). Prayers are provided for each of these offices. Subdeacons and readers are appointed by handing them the book. The charism of healers is simply recognized by the community.

In the fifth and sixth centuries, ordination prayers for bishops, presbyters, and deacons are found in the Roman Verona (Leonine) Sacramentary and rubrics for the ordination services are found in *Ordines Romani XXXIV-XL*. It is noteworthy that in the ordination prayers the Christian ministers are seen more as successors of the Old Testament priesthood than of the New Testament apostolate. The bishop is seen as the successor of Aaron, the high priest, and as the ruler of the church (as indeed he is also in ordination prayer in the *Apostolic Tradition*). The presbyters are depicted as the successors of the Levites, of the seventy wise men appointed by Moses, and as the sons of Levi. They are to be counselors to the bishop, teachers of the faith, and virtuous colleagues. The deacons are the sons of Levi, devoted to ministry.

It does not serve our purpose here to go into the job descriptions of the various ministries; our question is how ministers are made. In this connection it is noteworthy that the tenth-century Roman-German Pontifical from Mainz includes an inquiry into the worthiness of the candidate, an anointing of the head, hands, and thumbs of the bishop and of the hands of a presbyter, and the presentation of the instruments of the order being conferred. The anointing is to sanctify parts of the body that will touch holy things. In the case of anointing the head of the bishop there is a reference to the anointing of Aaron the high priest.

Between the tenth and thirteenth centuries, Gallican and Roman material was combined, producing some duplications in the rites (in effect, ordaining a person first in the Roman fashion and then again in the Gallican fashion). In the thirteenth-century Pontifical of William Durandus, there is a formal presentation of the candidate for bishop, followed by a review of the duties of the office, an examination, and profession of faith. The ordination prayer is interrupted by the singing of *Veni Creator Spiritus* while the head of the bishop is anointed. After the ordination prayer the hands of the new bishop are anointed and he is presented with the crozier (shepherd's crook), ring (symbol of authority), and gospel book. In the rite for the ordination of a presbyter there is also a presentation and examination of the candidate. The ordination prayer is preceded by the imposition of hands and followed by the vesting of the new priest. A chalice and paten is then presented. A second imposition of hands follows the communion and is accompanied by a declarative formula, *Accipe Spiritum Sanctum*...("Receive the Holy Spirit . . ."), and the power to forgive and retain sins. This reflects the medieval idea that the form of the sacrament is expressed by a declarative act rather than by prayer of blessing and invocation. Similar procedures (vesting in stole and dalmatic, presentation of the gospel book, *Accipe* formula) are found in the ordination of a deacon. The rites of ordination took place before the portion of the Mass at which the ordinand would exercise ministry: between the Epistle and Gospel for bishops and deacons so that they could proclaim the gospel and before the offertory for the presbyters so that they could offer the sacrifice of the Mass. Usually, however, the new priest concelebrated with the bishop and celebrated his own first Mass at a later time. These rites of ordination are substantially the same in the Roman Pontifical of 1595 and continued in use in the Roman Catholic Church until 1968.[20]

In spite of revitalizing the concept of the priesthood of believers, the sixteenth-century magisterial reformers and the Council of Trent were in agreement that ministers of word and sacrament are needed in the church. For the Protestants this is because all things should be "done decently and in order" and because the appointment of ministers is commanded by Christ. The Reformers typically stripped away anything they considered unbiblical in the ordination rites. Lutheran, Reformed, and Anglican ordination rites typically emphasized the election and examination of a candidate, prayer, and the laying on of hands (although the Reformed were in some disagreement over this).[21] Declarative formulas expressing the bestowal of office were preferred to prayer for the Holy Spirit. Vesting, anointing, and presentations of implements fell away, except for the presentation of a Bible.

In recent ordination rites prayers imploring rather than declarations imparting the Holy Spirit have been restored.[22] The *Roman Pontifical, Occasional Services: Lutheran*

Book of Worship, and the Episcopal *BCP* rites of ordination have similar elements.[23] The rite takes place within the Mass/Service of Holy Communion/Holy Eucharist. Candidates are presented, the duties of office are reviewed, the candidates are questioned, and promises are made. Intercessory prayer is offered for the candidates; in the Roman Pontifical it is the Litany of the Saints. In the Lutheran and Episcopal orders, the *Veni Sancte Spiritus* or *Veni Creator Spiritus* hymn is sung. The ordaining minister(s) lay hands on the head of the candidate. The accompanying ordination prayers are in the form of a thanksgiving that invokes the Holy Spirit on the ordinand rather than a declarative formula. The ordinands are vested and the implements of office are presented. The Roman Rite adds the anointing of the hands and the *Veni Creator* is sung at this point. The new ministers are then presented to and acclaimed by the people. Today they are usually greeted with applause. In the Greek Orthodox tradition when the newly ordained are presented to the people by the bishop, they will exclaim, "*Axios! Axios! Axios!*" ("worthy") to show their approval.

4. How does the church solemnize marriages?

The church solemnizes marriage with "many customs" in "many lands," as Luther wrote in the introduction to his 1529 *Order of Marriage for Common Pastors*.[24] The Bible has a lot to say about marriage and the marital relationship, but gives few ritual clues about how marriage was celebrated.

Christianity did not come into the world with a marriage rite of its own. Kenneth Stevenson is convinced that Jewish Christians continued to observe Jewish marriage customs. He hypothesized that the kind of blessings we see in Tobit and that became the seven blessings in the later Talmud developed in a Christian form in the first two centuries (comparable to the development of Christian eucharistic prayers from the *Birkat ha-mazon*).[25] However, typical elements of Jewish marriage rites, such as the signing of the written contract, the canopy, and the blessing of a cup of wine, did not come into the Christian marriage service.

On the other hand, a number of elements of rite were retained in emerging Christian marriage celebrations from Roman culture: betrothal at the home of the bride, placing the ring on the fourth finger of the bride's left hand, a banquet bringing together the families of the bride and groom, the bride's wearing of a girdle (symbol of virginity), a veil, and a floral crown on the wedding day, reciting of solemn promises before witnesses, the joining of hands, the wedding banquet, the bride taken to her new home and carried over the threshold by the bridegroom, and the blessing of the marriage bed. In Roman culture the bride offered a sacrifice to the god of the hearth. The idolatrous nature of the Roman marriage rites brought Christian bishops into the rites to replace the pagan officials. They witnessed the exchange of vows, pronounced a prayer of blessing, and celebrated the Eucharist in place of the pagan sacrifices.[26] However, the ancient church orders give us no liturgies of Christian marriage.

Much more information emerges from the literature of late antiquity, especially from the homilies of the church fathers and from canons of regional synods and ecumenical councils. In the Eastern church the betrothal rite took place in the church narthex or vestibule. The couple then processed into the church building for the crowning by close relatives while the priest recited the nuptial blessing. This was important enough for the entire marriage rite to be called "the crowning." The canons of the Council of Laodicea at the end of the fourth century indicate a growing tension between what the church would allow and what families wanted. One canon that had lasting effect was the ban on weddings during Lent. Councils in the West also indicate a reluctance to solemnize marriages during Advent and Lent and a desire to curb lewd and rowdy activities at the wedding celebrations (probably with little effect). An interesting difference is that the West emphasized the wearing of the bridal veil and did not develop a tradition of crowning the couple.

The sacramentaries of the sixth through eighth centuries provide texts for nuptial masses: proper readings, psalms, nuptial blessings. The civic or legal aspect of the marriage rite, with the exchange of vows and rings, was performed on the church porch. Then there was a procession into the church for the nuptial mass. The sacramentaries also provide blessings of the marriage bed. We must question whether every couple went through the entire complex of rites offered by the church or even had their vows witnessed in the church. Nuptial masses may have been for the nobility and well-to-do. It is also evident in marriage legislation that the desire of the church (e.g., for keeping peace between warring families) often clashed with the desires of families.[27]

Luther and the Protestant Reformers actually devoted a lot of attention to marriage. In part this was because marriage had become so entangled in church law. They denied that marriage was a sacrament but recognized that it was of divine institution. They turned over the regulation of marriage to the civil government (which they believed is also of divine institution) but preferred to keep the solemnization of marriage in the church building (which was a public facility). In Luther's view this was a way to emphasize the goodness of marriage, which had been demeaned in the spiritual elevation of monastic vows. It also prevented clandestine (i.e., Romeo and Juliet) marriages, a move that won the support of parents. It was in response to the Protestant insistence that weddings be held in church buildings that the Council of Trent also decreed that weddings should take place in the parish church and should be registered by the priest in the parish records. The registration was also a way to ensure that godfathers were not marrying their goddaughters.[28]

Luther severely simplified the marriage service. He kept the medieval custom of announcing the banns on three Sundays before the wedding and the performance of the marriage rite itself on the church porch. Then, during the singing of Psalms 127 and 128, the wedding party processed to the altar where Genesis 1:26-28 was read, sometimes a catena of other readings combined with exhortation, a homily given, and a blessing pronounced. In time this simple liturgy at the altar was expanded with music such as hymns and choir motets.

In time the marriage rite itself was moved into the church building, although a distinction continued to be made between the "civil" aspects of marriage (betrothal, exchange of vows) and the blessing at the altar. The Reformed and Anglican traditions, like the Lutheran, continued the announcement of the banns on three Sundays before the wedding. The Reformed tradition rejected the giving as well as the blessing of rings.

Luther did not provide for a nuptial mass because it was a votive mass (a Mass offered for special intentions). However, Martin Bucer at Strassburg encouraged the celebration of weddings on Sunday at the congregation's Sunday Service of Holy Communion so that the bride and groom could receive communion. This practice was also encouraged in the *BCP*. But Sunday weddings gave way to Saturday weddings during the Puritan regime, because the Puritans disapproved of having joyous celebrations (with inevitable poor behavior) on Sundays or at the Eucharist.

The French Revolution brought a radical change to wedding practice in Europe. Marriage was placed under civic law. The civil rite was performed in a civic setting such as a courthouse. Couples who wanted their marriage solemnized by the church then went to a church for a nuptial Eucharist. This practice continues today.

In the U.S.A. marriage laws are regulated by the fifty states. But clergy are given a license to officiate, in effect, as the magistrate for the occasion. Many couples still prefer to celebrate their wedding in a church building, and with the growing number of unchurched (or those whose church building is not "traditional") the practice of "renting" church buildings and even clergy has increased. Many clergy respond by requiring premarital counseling and some kind of commitment to the church. The problems of cultural pluralism, mixed marriages, and mobility (family and friends coming from afar for the celebration) have added to the age-old clergy burden to balance what couples want with what the church should provide. Often there is a tug-of-war over what kind of music is appropriate for the marriage service.

Current marriage rites reflect a response to this situation. The introductory rites may include a statement of the reason for the gathering, statements of intent by the bride and groom (the old betrothal), and expressions of support from family and friends. The service of readings is placed before marriage rite, and the responsible pastor will include at least a brief homily applying the readings. In premarital sessions the couple may even select the readings, with pastoral guidance. After the exchange of vows and rings and the nuptial blessing, intercessions will typically include petitions for all families as well as this new family, thus placing this marriage within a larger social framework. Holy Communion may be celebrated, but with the proviso that as a sacrament of the church it must be open to all who are eligible to receive with the bride and groom.

The mystery/sacrament of marriage is Christ and the church (Eph. 5:32). Unlike in the West, where the bride and groom are viewed as the celebrants of marriage, the Orthodox East sees the church as the celebrant. The betrothal in the vestibule is the civic aspect of marriage as it is in "this world," but the crowning at the altar signifies marriage as it is fulfilled in the kingdom of God—"that ultimate Reality of which everything in 'this world'—whose fashion is passing away—everything has now become a sacramental sign and anticipation."[29]

5. How does the church militant transfer members to the church triumphant?

The church did not come into the world with its own funeral rites any more than it had its own marriage rites. However, the central proclamation of Christianity—the resurrection of Christ—and the promise of the resurrection of the dead and eternal life with Christ for all who are baptized into Christ affected the church's appropriation of funeral and burial customs.

From the Roman world, the custom of the *viaticum*, or last meal for the dying, became reception of Holy Communion. The singing of psalms and alleluias replaced the lamentations and dirges in the funeral procession. The church fathers inveighed against black (clothes made dirty by rolling on the ground in an expression of grief) in favor of white garments. Cremation was rejected; the body was buried "in sure and certain hope of the resurrection." The *refrigerium*, or meal with the dead on the mensa of the grave, became the celebration of the Eucharist on the grave, especially the graves of the martyrs and saints. This influenced the development of Christian altars later on. The Eucharist came to be celebrated on the seventh and thirtieth days after death, and annually.

In the ancient world burial usually occurred within a day of death and cemeteries were located outside of cities to avoid defilement. The new Christian attitude toward the dead body was upsetting to pagans because Christians brought relics of the dead into their churches and eventually even practiced burial in the churches or the churchyard.[30] Many great basilicas, like St. Peter's at the Vatican, were built on necropolises or cemeteries, over the tomb of the saint.

The sacramentaries of the sixth through eighth centuries provide prayers at the time of death, at the conclusion of the wake, psalms to be sung during the procession from the house to the church and from the church to the place of interment (23, 32, 115, 116), readings for use in the prayer office (Matins and Vespers) and the Eucharist (if celebrated), and prayers for the interment. These prayers sum up the practice of the ancient church in transferring its members from the church militant to the church triumphant.

But significant changes occurred in the Middle Ages, due in large part to the doctrine of purgatory, which was envisioned as a place of purification for the heaven-bound soul before it could come into the divine presence. Death became something to mourn rather than to celebrate. Black replaced white as the color of death. Penitential psalms replaced the psalms of comfort and praise in the prayer offices. The sequence hymn, *Dies irae* ("Day of wrath"), replaced the Alleluia in the votive mass for the dead (named "Requiem" from the Introit, *Requiem aeternam dona eis, Domine, et lux perpetua luceat eis*—"Rest eternal give them, O Lord, and let light perpetual shine upon them"). The

Requiem Introit has no Gloria Patri. Other omissions include the use of incense at the Introit and the Gospel, the kiss of peace, lit candles held by acolytes when a deacon chants the Gospel, and blessings. There is no Gloria in excelsis Deo or Creed, but this was due to the fact that requiems were not celebrated on Sundays or festivals.

The Reformation questioned the whole concept of purgatory. The Requiem Mass was the most frequently celebrated votive mass and the spearpoint of a whole ritual industry that was designed to provide, in John Bossy's words, "charity for the dead."[31] The demand for Requiem masses became so great in the fourteenth and fifteenth centuries (the period of "Black Death") that priests were ordained who did no other work than to offer these masses, for a stipend. The view of the Reformers was that the purpose of funerals was to provide comfort for the living, and that included the comfort of God's promises to his baptized people of eternal life with Christ.

Nevertheless, the early Lutherans retained many of the pre-Reformation practices: prayers at the home of the deceased, the procession to the church for a short prayer office, the procession to the cemetery, and the interment. Luther even provided German translations of the hymn *In media vita* ("In the midst of life"), sung during the procession to the grave, as well as the *De profundis* ("Out of the depths," *Aus tiefer Not*—Psalm 130). Otherwise, Luther produced no burial service as he had done for baptism and marriage. Not surprisingly, there is considerable variety in the church orders.

In the Reformed tradition the body was interred "without any ceremony," and a service was held afterward in the church that consisted of psalms, reading, sermon, and prayers.[32]

The *BCP* burial office was influenced by the German church orders, especially Cologne, but also used material from the pre-Reformation Sarum Use and the Dirges of English Reformation Primers. The 1549 Prayer Book provided propers for the celebration of Holy Communion when there is a burial of the dead, and that custom continued here and there even though it was not provided for after 1552. The Prayer Book does not otherwise provide an order of service for use in the church. However, this order was arranged in the American Prayer Book (1790) so that the first part, with psalmody and readings, could be done in the church building. After the readings the rubric in the 1892 book states, "Here may be sung a Hymn or an Anthem; and, at the discretion of the Minister, the Creed, and such fitting Prayers as are elsewhere provided in this Book, may be added."[33] Then the service continued at the grave.

The Lutheran Common Service (1917) provided a form of the chanted Office of the Dead, as follows:[34]

The service may begin with a hymn
Invocation
Kyrie (sixfold)
Psalm 130 with antiphon
Psalm 23 with antiphon
The Lesson(s)

Responsory: *Si bona suscepimus* ("If we receive good") (Other historic responsories
  are provided)
Sermon or address
Hymn
Canticle: Nunc dimittis with antiphon
Little litany
Our Father
Prayers
The service of committal at the grave

This order was retained in the *Service Book and Hymnal* (1958).

The 1614 *Rituale Romanum* provided the first universal Roman Catholic funeral rite.
The ritual simplified monastic burial rites, but otherwise preserved the overall tone of
fear of the last judgment in the medieval rites. Significant reforms in the Roman Catholic funeral rites were enacted after the Second Vatican Council in the *Ordo Exequiarum*
of 1969.[35] There is an effort to relate Christian death to the paschal mystery, especially
in the choice of readings. But the suppression of the Gloria Patri and the Alleluia seems
incongruous with this new emphasis, especially in view of the fact that in the early
Christian ages the Alleluia was regarded as especially appropriate to funerals, and still is
in the Christian East. In the ordinary form of the Roman Rite (the Mass of Paul VI) the
priest wears purple or black vestments, and the coffin is covered by a white pall. There is
a fashion among some of the more progressive clergy to wear white vestments, and the
bishops in England and Wales have allowed it. In the Tridentine form of the Roman
Rite, the historic Requiem Mass is celebrated and the priest always wears black vestments, and the pall is black. In 1969 the absolution of the dead was removed from the
ordinary form of the Roman Rite, and replaced with the Commendation. However, the
absolution of the dead continues to remain part of the funeral service of the Tridentine
Mass. The absolution is not of sins committed by the deceased but a prayer that the sins
forgiven will not be punished in purgatory. The *Libera me, Domine* is sung while the
priest incenses the coffin and sprinkles it with holy water. The *In paradisum* is sung while
the body is carried from the church.

At the place of interment, the tomb or burial plot is blessed if it has not been blessed
previously. This blessing consists of a single prayer, after which the body is again sprinkled with holy water and incensed. Apart from this, the service at the graveside is very
brief. The priest intones the antiphon "I am the Resurrection and the Life," after which
the coffin is lowered into the grave and the canticle Benedictus with its antiphon is
recited or sung. Then the Lord's Prayer is said silently, while the coffin is again sprinkled
with holy water. Finally, after one or two brief responses and prayers, the priest concludes the burial service with the final petition, "May his/her soul and the souls of all
the faithful departed through the mercy of God rest in peace."

The reformed Catholic Rite of Christian Funeral influenced Protestant, especially Lutheran and Episcopal, rites. The paschal theme is emphasized. The paschal candle is lighted and placed at the head of the coffin in the church. The coffin is covered with a white pall. Episcopal priests wear white vestments. Lutherans, however, use the color of the day or season. Both the *LBW* and the *BCP* cast the Order for the Burial of the Dead as a liturgy of the word rather than a prayer office and Holy Communion may be celebrated. At the end of the service in the church, there is a commendation of the faithful departed that has brought great comfort to mourners. Cremation is allowed. A memorial service may be held some time after the burial or disposition of the body in place of a funeral service. This allows time to gather people and resources for a celebration of the life of the deceased. But the inclusion of the deceased's life within the life of Christ should be emphasized.

For further reading

Baptism
Ferguson, David. *Baptism in the Early Church: History, Theology, and Liturgy in the First Five Centuries.* Grand Rapids: Eerdmans, 2009.
Kavanagh, Aidan. *The Shape of Baptism.* New York: Pueblo, 1978.
Johnson, Maxwell E., ed. *Living Water, Sealing Spirit: Readings on Christian Initiation.* Collegeville: Liturgical, 1995.
———. *The Rites of Christian Initiation: Their Evolution and Interpretation.* Collegeville: Liturgical, 1999.
Neunheuser, Burkhard. *Baptism and Confirmation*, trans. John Jay Hughes. Freiburg: Herder, 1964.

Confirmation
Austin, Gerard. *Anointing with the Spirit: The Rite of Confirmation: The Use of Oil and Chrism.* New York: Pueblo, 1988.
Fisher, J. D. C. *Confirmation Then and Now.* London: SPCK/Alcuin Club, 1978.
Kavanagh, Aidan. *Confirmation: Origins and Reform.* New York: Pueblo, 1988.
Repp, Arthur C. *Confirmation in the Lutheran Church.* St. Louis: Concordia, 1964.
Truscott, Jeffrey A. *The Reform of Baptism and Confirmation in American Lutheranism.* Lanham: Scarecrow, 2003.

Penance
Clerk, Paul de. "Celebrating Penance or Reconciliation," The Clergy Review 68 (1983): 310–23.
Dallen, James. *The Reconciling Community: The Rite of Penance.* New York: Pueblo, 1986.
Poschmann, Bernhard. *Penance and the Anointing of the Sick*, trans. and rev. Francis Courtney, S.J. New York: Herder and Herder, 1964.

Senn, Frank. "The Confession of Sins in the Reformation Churches," *Concilium: The Fate of Confession*, ed. Mary Collins and David Power, 105–16. Edinburgh: T & T Clark, 1987.

Ordination
Bradshaw, Paul F. *Ordination Rites of the Ancient Churches East and West*. New York: Pueblo, 1990.
Lawler, Michael G. *Secular Marriage, Christian Sacrament*. Mystic: Twenty-Third, 1985.
Hatchett, Marion J. *Commentary on the American Prayer Book*. San Francisco: HarperCollins, 1995. 503–32.
Pfatteicher, Philip H. *Commentary on the Occasional Services*. Philadelphia: Fortress Press, 1983. 165–243.
Porter, H. Boone, Jr. *The Ordination Prayers of the Ancient Western Churches*. London: SPCK, 1967.
Vos, Wiebe, and Geoffrey Wainwright, eds. "Ordination Rites: Papers Read at the 1979 Congress of Societas Liturgica." *Studia Liturgica* 13, nos. 2, 3, 4 (1979).

Marriage
Hatchett, Marion J. *Commentary on the American Prayer Book*. San Francisco: HarperCollins, 1995. 427–40.
Meyendorff, John. *Marriage: An Orthodox Perspective*. Crestwood: St. Vladimir's Seminary Press, 1975.
Pfatteicher, Philip H. *Commentary on the Lutheran Book of Worship*. Minneapolis: Fortress Press, 1990. 455–73.
Stevenson, Kenneth. *Nuptial Blessing: A Study of Christian Marriage Rites*. Alcuin Club Collections 64. New York: Oxford University Press, 1983.
Stevenson, Kenneth. *To Join Together*. Studies in the Reformed Rites of the Catholic Church 5. New York: Pueblo, 1987.

Burial
Aries, Philippe. *Western Attitudes toward Death: From the Middle Ages to the Present*. Baltimore: Johns Hopkins University Press, 1974.
Hatchett, Marion J. *Commentary on the American Prayer Book*. San Francisco: HarperCollins, 1995. 477–500.
Pfatteicher, Philip H. *Commentary on the Lutheran Book of Worship*. Minneapolis: Fortress Press, 1990. 474–507.
Rowell, Geoffrey. *The Liturgy of Christian Burial*. London: Alcuin Club/SPCK, 1977.
Rutherford, Richard. *The Death of a Christian: The Rite of Funerals*. New York: Pueblo, 1980.

10
The Liturgical Arts

1. What are "psalms and hymns and spiritual songs"?
2. How are hymns and other music selected for worship?
3. What is the role of bells?
4. How is the liturgical space arranged?
5. What do ministers wear for the liturgy?

1. What are "psalms and hymns and spiritual songs"?

Paul refers in Colossians 3:16 and Ephesians 5:19 to singing "psalms and hymns and spiritual songs." The material in both letters in these chapters is similar, even verbatim. It is possible that Ephesians was copied from Colossians, or both were copied from some other document. But the material in both letters concerns Christian life, particularly relationships in the household. So the "psalms and hymns and spiritual songs" may refer to what we might call "household devotions" rather than public worship.

Is there a distinction between psalms, hymns, and spiritual songs? Whatever the author intended by this phrase, distinctions can be made. In the Christian context, "psalms" refers to the biblical psalms. In the context of ancient cults "hymns" refer to songs addressed to a deity. "Songs" are what people sing to one another for encouragement or to express certain sentiments (such as love songs).

There are no specific references to the singing of psalms in Christian public worship before the fourth century. Jesus and his disciples sang a psalm after the Last Supper (in the Passover context probably one of the Hallel psalms, 113–118) before they went out into the night (Matt. 26:30; Mark 14:26; Luke 22:31). The psalter was the hymnbook of the second temple. We don't know what role psalmody played in synagogue prayer in the first century. However, it is likely that Christians sang psalms in their homes and from there the psalmody found a natural inclusion in the prayer offices. Psalms were sung in the public liturgies of the basilicas during processions at the entrance, the offertory, and communion, and in processions through the streets from one station to another.

Other biblical songs with psalm-like character, such as canticles, attained use in Christian liturgy. Non-psalm biblical canticles are sung in the prayer offices. The Roman Breviary takes seven Old Testament canticles for use at Lauds in place of a fourth psalm, as follows:

On Sundays and Festivals, the "Canticle of the Three Children" (Dan. 3:57).
On Mondays, the "Canticle of Isaiah" (Isaiah 12).
On Tuesdays, the "Canticle of Hezekiah" (Isa. 38:10-20).
On Wednesdays, the "Canticle of Hannah" (1 Sam. 2:1-10).
On Thursdays, the "Canticle of Moses" (Exod. 15:1-19).
On Fridays the "Canticle of Habakkuk" (Hab. 3:2-19).
On Saturdays, the "Canticle of Moses" (Deut. 32:1-43).

Two others (Isa. 26:9-20 and Jon. 2:2-9) are added for Friday and Saturday respectively.

The Greek Orthodox Church has the same nine canticles at Matins, although not assigned to the same days as in the Roman Breviary.

From the New Testament the breviary takes the following:

At Lauds, the "Canticle of Zachariah" (Luke 1:68-79), commonly referred to as the Benedictus (from its first word).
At Vespers, the "Canticle of Mary" (Luke 1:46-55), commonly known as the Magnificat (from its first word).
At Compline, the "Canticle of Simeon" (Luke 2:29-32), commonly referred to as the Nunc dimittis (from the opening words).

These are all biblical songs. Early Christians also developed *psalmi idiotici* ("private psalms"), that is, compositions by individuals in imitation of the biblical psalter. One of the best known is the Gloria in excelsis Deo, "Glory to God in the highest." This prose hymn begins with the words that the angels sang when the birth of Christ was announced to shepherds in Luke 2:14. Other verses were added very early, forming a doxology, which in the fourth century became part of morning prayer, and is still recited in the Byzantine Rite Orthros (morning) service. The Latin translation is attributed to Hilary of Poitiers. It became the standard Sunday and festival canticle of praise in the Roman Mass.

Another important nonbiblical canticle is the Te Deum Laudamus. It was traditionally ascribed jointly to Ambrose and Augustine, but more likely it originated in southern Gaul in the fifth century. Like the Gloria in excelsis, it begins addressed to God ("We praise you, O God . . .") but then changes to an address to Christ ("You, Christ, are the king of glory . . ."). With its references to the prophets, apostles, and martyrs, it may have been sung in procession to the baptismal font. It was also sung as a song of thanksgiving for deliverance. More routinely, it is sung at the end of Matins on all days when the Gloria is said at Mass; those days are all Sundays outside Advent and Lent, on all feasts (except the Triduum), and on all weekdays during Eastertide. Psalm verses were added later and came to be regarded as part of the canticle.

We don't know how the psalms were chanted in the ancient church. But eight Gregorian plainchant tones, one for each musical mode, developed in the early Middle Ages to which any of the psalm texts could be recited. They were devised so that the antiphon that is sung between verses or at the beginning and ending of the psalm or canticle transitions smoothly into the psalm tone. Anglican chant was developed at the time of the English Reformation and appears to be an adaptation of the plainchant method for singing the psalm texts in English. A system of chanting psalms, not unlike the method of Anglican chant, was devised in the monastery at Taizé, France, after 1955 by Jacques Berthier (1923–1994). *Lutheran Book of Worship* (p. 291) and *Evangelical Lutheran Worship* (pp. 337–38) also provide a collection of tones for chanting the psalms and canticles.

Form critics have detected in the New Testament the citation of early Christian hymns, specifically in John 1, Philippians 2:5-11, and Revelation 4–5. The earliest known Christian book of hymns, psalms, or odes is the *Odes of Solomon*, c. 100 (no relationship to the ancient Israelite king). Pliny the Younger, in his letter to the emperor Trajan (c. 112), reports Christians gathering before dawn "to recite a hymn [*carmen*] antiphonally to Christ, as to a god."[1]

The earliest Christian hymn still in use is "Shepherd of Tender Youth," attributed to Clement of Alexandria (c. 170–c. 220), best known in English in a translation by Henry M. Dexter (1821–1890). Another third-century Greek hymn is the *Phos hilaron*, "Joyous Light of glory," sung in Vespers.

Strophic hymns and spiritual songs became popular in Syria in the fourth century, especially those composed by Ephrem the Syrian (c. 306–373). Over four hundred hymns attributed to Ephrem are extant; there were undoubtedly others that are lost. Ephrem wrote hymns because Bardaisan and Mani composed hymns. His hymns were meant to teach the faith and strike against heresy. Stanzas with a repeating melody made the song easy to learn. Another great Eastern hymnwriter was John of Damascus (c. 676–749), a Syrian Christian monk and priest who was born and raised in Damascus and died at his monastery, Mar Saba, near Jerusalem. Some of his Easter hymns, such as "Come, You Faithful, Raise the Strain" and "The Day of Resurrection," are sung in Western churches in the translations of John Mason Neale.

Hilary of Poitiers (d. 367) is mentioned by Isidore of Seville as the first to compose Latin hymns. Ambrose of Milan (c. 337-340–397) is considered the father of Latin hymnody. He clothed Christian ideas in classical phraseology, yet appealed to popular tastes. Several of his hymns are still sung, such as "Savior of the Nations, Come" and "O Splendor of the Father." Other great Latin hymn lyricists were the Spanish Christian poet Aurelius Clemens Prudentius (348–c. 413), who has left us "Of the Father's Love Begotten" (Christmas) and "Earth Has Many a Noble City" (Epiphany), and Verantius

Honorius Fortunatus (530–609), who penned "Welcome, Happy Morning" (Easter) and "Hail, Thee, Festival Day" (stanzas for Easter, Ascension, and Pentecost).

While strophic hymns found a welcome place in Eastern liturgies, in the West they were primarily confined to the prayer offices. Strophic songs came into the Mass liturgy during the Middle Ages as sequences to the Gradual and Alleluia (the popularity of sequences was discussed in chapter 2). In the Latin Mass of the Middle Ages, it became customary to prolong the last syllable of the Alleluia, while the deacon was ascending from the altar to the ambo to chant the Gospel. This prolonged melisma was called the *jubilus* because of its jubilant tone. It was also called *sequentia*, "sequence," because it followed (Latin: *sequere*) the Alleluia. Notker Balbulus (c. 840–912) developed sequence hymns by setting words to this melisma in rhythmic prose for chanting as a trope (so that these hymns were also called "proses"). The name sequence came to be applied to these rhythmic prose and rhymed texts.

Sequences continued to be composed throughout the Middle Ages and were sung on major festivals. One of the reforms of the Roman Missal of Pius V (1570) reduced the number of sequences for the entire Roman Rite to four: *Victimae paschali laudes* (eleventh century) for Easter; *Veni Sancte Spiritus* (twelfth century) for Pentecost; *Lauda Sion Salvatorem* (c. 1264) for Corpus Christi, and *Dies Irae* (thirteenth century) for All Souls and in Masses for the Dead. In 1727 the thirteenth-century *Stabat Mater* for Our Lady of Sorrows was added to this list. In 1970 the *Dies Irae* was removed from the Requiem Mass of the revised Roman Missal and was transferred to the liturgy of the hours to be sung *ad libitum* ("at will") in the week before the beginning of Advent.

In Germany vernacular carols were added for the congregation to sing in connection with the Latin sequences. For example, to the sequence for Easter, *Victimae paschali laudes* ("Christians to the paschal victim offer praises"), usually attributed to the eleventh-century Wipo of Burgundy, was added the vernacular carol *Christ ist erstanden* ("Christ is arisen"). This became the basis of Martin Luther's *Christ lag in Todesbanden* ("Christ lay in death's strong bands").

The sequences, both Latin and vernacular, became one of the first sources of Lutheran Reformation spiritual songs. It is simply not true that Luther made use of tunes from the beer hall. Most of his tunes were based on Gregorian chant; others drew upon the *Meistersinger* tradition of German art song. Luther wrote thirty-six German hymns and spiritual songs and encouraged others to do so as well. Lutheran hymnody flourished in the post-Reformation period. German Catholic hymnody also flourished after the Reformation (e.g., "Lo, how a Rose e're blooming," "Holy God, we praise thy Name").

Luther also promoted the work of noted contemporary composers such as Josquin des Prez (c. 1450–1521). Music for choirs (chorale settings, motets, cantatas) continued to be composed for Lutheran worship, reaching a high point in the Baroque era in the church music of Johann Sebastian Bach (1685–1750). Bach's cantatas were based on the Gospel reading or hymn of the day and were located in the liturgy around the sermon.

In Roman Catholicism there was a reaction to polyphonic liturgical music after the Council of Trent and Giovanni Pierluigi da Palestrina (c. 1525 or 1526–1594) developed a chaste polyphony, in which the text was not obscured, that was influential on later composers of Catholic Mass settings. Catholic composers produced innumerable settings of the Mass.

In Anglicanism, cathedral and college choirs sang settings of the psalms and canticles in morning and evening prayer. In the Restoration period choirs also sang anthems at the end of Evensong that, in keeping with the Reformed tradition, were settings of biblical texts but had their origin in the Marian antiphons sung in English cathedrals after Vespers.[2] They are called "anthem" from "antiphon."

The Reformed tradition embraced congregational song but confined it to versifications of biblical psalms and canticles. Most famous are the settings of the French composer Louis Bourgeois (c. 1510–1560), who set the texts of the Geneva Psalter. This tradition first moved beyond this restriction in the songs of Isaac Watts (1674–1748), who is credited with 750 hymns. Charles Wesley (1707–1788) penned about six thousand hymns and songs.

After Wesley, hymn singing became a standard part of Protestant worship. Spurred on by Watts and Wesley, many nonconformist churches produced lively popular hymns that expressed one's personal relationship with God. Later songs came to be used in the revivals that occurred between 1800 and 1920. Songs such as "Washed in the Blood of the Lamb" came from the hymnbook of Dwight Lyman Moody (1837–1899) and Ira David Sankey (1840–1908).

The Negro spiritual is an indigenous contribution of American American slaves to the revival tradition. The lyrics of these spirituals often referenced symbolic aspects of biblical images, such as Moses and Israel's exodus from Egypt in songs like "Michael Row the Boat Ashore," which expressed the slaves' aspirations for freedom.

Gospel music has a complex religious and musical history. Gospel songs developed in the revivals, especially in the cities, and drew on both European and African roots. In recent times gospel song has become a style associated especially with African American worship. This may be attributed to the legacy of Thomas A. Dorsey in Chicago in the 1930s, best known as author of the song "Precious Lord, Take My Hand," who had spent the 1920s writing secular music, turned full time to gospel music, established a publishing house, and invented the black gospel style of piano music.

In the 1960s both Roman Catholics and evangelical Protestants turned to popular genres of music to provide songs for Christian worship. Roman Catholic songs tended to follow the folk idiom, using acoustical instruments such as guitar and flute, whereas evangelical Protestants turned to rock music, using electronic instruments. The contemporary Christian music industry in Nashville developed from Christian popular music. The use of Christian popular music was promoted by the church-growth movement to reach the unchurched and has become ubiquitous, not only in North America but also throughout Asia.[3] While music in the church has drawn upon the musical styles of the various cultures through which Christian liturgy has passed, there has not been the intentional effort to use popular styles such as we see in evangelistic circles today. Indeed, "popular" music forms a new genre that is neither art music nor folk music, and it is closely associated with the commercialism of the mass media.[4]

New hymns and songs have been composed in East Africa, southern Africa, Asia, the Caribbean, and Latin America that utilize indigenous musical styles. Some of these have found places in Western hymnals and become popular in North America. Examples include "Christ has arisen. Alleluia" (East African), "We are marching in the light of God" (South African), and "Cantad al senior un cantico nuevo" (Brazilian).

Instrumental music, often associated with pagan cults, was forbidden by early church fathers. This has remained the rule in Eastern Orthodox worship. Pipe organs first appeared in church buildings in the fourteenth century. They were used at first for ceremonial occasions and not to accompany congregational singing. Lutherans retained and expanded organs to introduce and later to accompany congregational hymns and chants. The Reformed tradition, beginning with Ulrich Zwingli, removed organs from churches. Puritans in England also removed organs from Anglican churches, but they were restored during the Restoration period. Choral and instrumental music, including organs, came back into the Reformed tradition in force during the revivals because of music's ability to stir the emotions.

2. How are hymns and other music selected for worship?

Hymns and other music are selected for use in orders of service according to their function and relation to the church-year festivals and seasons and the biblical readings in the liturgy. As hymns and songs have taken the place of psalmody in the Western family of rites, congregational songs are sung at the entrance, during the offertory, during communion, and at the exit or sending. Lutherans have the tradition of a hymn of the day, historically sung between the Epistle and Gospel but now sung before or after the sermon. The choir may sing at any of the places the congregation sings, either for the ordinary or the locations mentioned above.

The entrance hymn sets the mood for the liturgy and is often used to accompany a procession. It should generally be a song of praise, have a familiar tune, and be easy to process with. Likewise, the sending hymn should generally be one that gives praise to God, or reinforces the themes in the readings and sermon, or encourages people to go out into the world as Christian disciples. It should be easy to process with. The Lutheran hymn of the day will be specifically chosen to proclaim the readings, especially the Gospel. If there is a hymn during communion, it might be quiet and meditative, but also express joyful thanks for the gift of communion.

Many times the hymns and songs and choir music chosen will relate to the church year and reflect the character and content of the season: for instance, more solemn for Lent, more joyful for Easter. The hymns in many current denominational hymnals are grouped according to the seasons of the church year. There are also sections for particular lesser festivals.

Hymns chosen for the prayer offices should reflect the time of the day or the season of the church year. Organ or instrumental music should also be chosen according to location within the liturgy and the church year. The Lutheran tradition of choosing pre-service organ music and voluntaries based on the hymn of the day or other hymns and songs sung in the liturgy certainly may be commended to other traditions as well.

Contemporary Christian worship has its own character and liturgical dynamics. The Vineyard Christian Fellowship has established carefully considered principles for the praise medley. The songs selected by the worship team would lead the assembly in a certain direction. Thus gathering songs might lead to praise songs, which would lead to more meditative songs before the reading of Scripture and the message. Traditions that follow the church year and the lectionary will choose music appropriate to the season and the readings. Whether in liturgical or free-church traditions, there needs to be planning between the music team and the pastor so that the service has a unified character.[5]

There are some principles that apply to all worship situations. First and foremost, all music chosen for the assembly or choir should be within the capabilities of the group that is singing. Pastors and musicians have to know their people.

Whether the music is traditional or contemporary, classical or popular, there are some things that just should not be put before the assembly because some music doesn't lend itself to group singing. Some songs have been written with a soloist in mind. Some hymns and songs have easily learned refrains but stanzas that are irregular. The stanzas can be sung by cantors or choirs while the people sing the refrain. Responsorial singing is an old practice in the history of liturgy that can make worship more dynamic. It is often used today in Roman Catholic liturgy as a means of singing psalms and canticles.

3. What is the role of bells?

Bells have played a varied and important liturgical role. Used in liturgical music, bells can be a powerful musical support. Small peals of handbells were used in the choirs of large medieval churches (located behind the rood screen or in a gallery). They can still be seen in the *coro* of some Spanish churches. In the Use of the Sarum Rite, these bells were rung in changes during the Te Deum and the Sequence hymn. Used as part of liturgical music, bells are a welcome respite from the dominance of big instrumental sound in the liturgy. They are used to sound the tones for the chanting of psalms so that the pitches don't have to be played on the organ or piano. Handbells can mark the ends of half-verses and verses when chanting psalms. They can also be used to mark the beginning and ending of periods of silence.

Large bells have also been used to accompany singing. A tolling bell may well have been used rhythmically during the *Dies Irae* in Requiem masses. There is strong evidence that bells were used for musical effect as well: the sixteenth-century English composer, John Taverner, wrote a setting of the *Ave Maria* that was designed to be coordinated with the ringing of the Angelus. Some churches with steeple bells have rung them during the Lord's Prayer—seven tolls for the seven petitions.

Bells have been used to announce what is happening in the liturgy. During the Middle Ages, bells known as Sanctus (or sacring) bells were rung during the Sanctus to announce that the consecration was taking place. This was because at High Mass the choir was still singing the Sanctus when the celebrant, reciting the canon silently, got to the words of institution. The people, who no longer frequently received communion, wanted to see the host elevated and the bells announced that this was happening.

A recent practice has been to invite people to bring handbells to the Easter Vigil and to ring them joyously at the announcement of the resurrection. For example, at the end of the vigil of readings the announcement is made, "Christ is risen. Alleluia! R/ He is risen indeed. Alleluia!" Then during the singing of the canticle ("Glory to God in the Highest" or "Worthy Is Christ") people ring their bells enthusiastically.

Bells are a fascinating part of Christian tradition. They are actually quite deeply connected with the whole worldview organized around traditional Christianity. They were used to ward off evil. Handbells were rung for this purpose when the sacrament was carried to the sick. In medieval England steeple bells were rung during the night of All Hallow's Eve to chase away evil spirits.

Large bells in towers have been rung to call people to worship, to toll exits from the church at funerals, and to ring out joy at the exits of wedding parties. In traditional societies people regulated their lives by the ringing of church bells as they called out the times of prayer.

In recent years a whole new issue has arisen with bell choirs. There is no doubt that they are popular and can give people an opportunity to participate in music making who might not do so otherwise. But with their typical front-and-center position bell choirs take on an ethos of concert performance that is not conducive to liturgy. In fact, any musical group that occupies a front-of-the-stage position in the worship space projects a concert-performance ethos.

4. How is the liturgical space arranged?

We have made references throughout this book to different architectural spaces for the liturgical assembly throughout history: the house church, the Roman basilica, the Romanesque fortress, the Gothic hall, the Baroque theater, the meeting hall, the auditorium. What is important is that the assembly has a meeting place and the furniture necessary for its essential acts: proclaiming the word, baptizing, and sharing the meal. The following places of liturgical action are noted here.

Altar

The altar is a table on which bread and wine for Holy Communion are placed. It may be built of wood or marble and should be the focal point toward which the assembly is oriented. In fact, the altar has traditionally been placed at the east end of the nave (hence, "orientation") since it was the practice of the ancient church to face east for prayer, toward the rising Sun of righteousness. The space around which the main altar in a church is located is called the "sanctuary" ("holy place"). The sanctuary is often separated from the body of the church by railings (hence the area may also be called the "chancel," from *cancelli*, or railings) and screens (in the case of Orthodox churches, by an iconostasis which forms a complete visual as well as physical barrier). The sanctuary is usually the most ornately decorated part of a church, emphasizing the altar area as the visual focus of the church building. The altar table will be covered with a fair white linen and perhaps also a parament covering or frontal in the color of the day or season. Two candles are placed on the table top (mensa) and/or six candles above or around the altar. A cross is placed above or behind the altar, also serving as a visual focus.

Font

The place for baptism is towards the western end of the nave, near the main entrance into the worship space because baptism signifies entry into the community of the church. Sometimes, in Gothic churches, the font was located in a circular area to the side of the west end (the baptistery). The font could also be located directly in the path of those entering the nave. Today, especially in Roman Catholic churches, shallow baptismal pools are being installed around which one passes to come into the nave. In Baptist churches and those traditions that practice full submersion, a deep baptismal pool is located behind the pulpit area. Many Protestant churches place a small font in the front of the church so that the assembly can see the baptisms taking place. It may be stored on the side and moved into place for a celebration of Holy Baptism. The symbolism of the west end, toward which the candidates turn to renounce evil, commends itself, and the congregation is surely able to turn around to face the west end.

Ambo

Standing toward the front of the nave is a desk or lectern from which the Holy Scriptures are read. In some churches this takes the form of an eagle that supports the book on its outstretched wings and is the symbol of John the Evangelist. There may be a separate rostrum or pulpit from which the sermon is preached and the biblical readings are expounded. The pulpit might be of marble or wood, and may be a simple structure or a highly elaborate carved pedestal decorated, for example, with the winged figures of a man, a lion, a bull, and an eagle, representing the Gospel writers, Matthew, Mark, Luke, and John. In many churches today a single ambo is preferred for reading and preaching that serves as a focal place for the proclamation of the word.

Choir

Historically, musical forces have been placed in a position from which they could lead singing: on a bema or platform in the middle of the nave (e.g., Hagia Sophia and Greek basilicas), in a divided choir formation within a screened-off chancel (e.g., Gothic churches), in side galleries (e.g., St. Mark's, Venice; Kreuzkirche, Dresden), or in rear galleries (e.g., Baroque churches). In these various positions choirs and instruments have driven liturgical participation without becoming the focus of attention. In revival-inspired Protestant churches, however, the choir is often arranged above the pulpit area surrounding the organ console and visible to the assembly. In contemporary services, the singers and instrumentalists (the worship team) are actually the leaders of worship and in this approach to worship they are on the stage in front of the assembly.[6] The advantage of placing musical forces within, alongside of, behind, or above the congregation is that all the leadership of worship is not located up front. This is a hierarchical arrangement even in contemporary services. The musicians become the priests.

Nave

The nave is the body of the church building in which the people gather. Naves were once wide-open spaces with aisles for processions. Since the fourteenth century naves in Western churches have been filled with benches, pews, and chairs, which restrict movement and interaction. It is probably not possible to do without seating, but of the various options moveable chairs allow for the most flexible seating arrangements.

Narthex

The narthex of a church is the entrance or vestibule, located at the opposite (west) end of the nave from the church's main altar. Traditionally, the narthex was not considered part of the church proper. Its purpose was to allow those not eligible for admittance into the general congregation (particularly catechumens and penitents) to hear and partake in the service. The narthex is thus traditionally a place of penitence. Penitents in the ancient church sat in the vestibule asking the faithful to pray for them. In Eastern churches some penitential services, such as the Little Hours during Holy Week, are celebrated there instead of in the main body of the church. In the Russian Orthodox Church funerals are traditionally held in the narthex. Today they are lobbies in which people congregate before or after the service and places where processions can be formed.

5. What do ministers wear for the liturgy?

In many, perhaps most, Christian traditions, the clergy and leaders of worship wear distinctive garb that designates their function and connects the contemporary assembly with the founding of their community. In the Torah God gave explicit instructions on the vestments of the high priest (Exodus 28). The early Christians did not gather in a tabernacle or temple but in private homes. They wore what would be considered customary for attending a banquet. There was no differentiation in attire between the ministers and the people.

Once the assembly moved into public basilicas, the clergy undoubtedly kept their "Sunday best" separate from the rest of their wardrobe. Sometimes they were also given robes of more exquisite fabric and design by benefactors of the church to wear for the liturgy.

The modern alb (Greek, *sticharion*) is a long white garment. The newly baptized were instructed to put on a new white tunic after their baptism and wore them during "the week of white robes." The albs worn by ministers with roles in the liturgy are baptismal garments.

The poncho-like chasuble (*casula*, "little house"; Greek, *phelonion*) was the typical outer garment of a Roman gentleman. It fell to the floor bell-shaped and was gathered up over the arms. Later on, material of the chasubles or phelonion was cut away to allow ease of arm movement. By the sixteenth century, chasubles had become sleeveless. In the nineteenth-century romantic revival, the fuller Gothic chasuble was retrieved and is preferred today. Some have tried to revive the older bell-shaped chasubles, but these prove awkward since the material must be gathered over the wearer's arms. An experience of this demonstrates why some of the material was later cut away.

Ornate robes with sleeves called dalmatics were also provided for deacons, which fitted their administrative office. The tunicle is a variation of the dalmatic worn by subdeacons.

In the era of imperial favoritism, bishops were also given insignia of rank and office. Among these insignias were the stole (Greek, *epitrachelion*), a long, narrow strip of cloth draped around the neck. Since it was only worn by the clergy it became a symbol of ordination. Priests and bishops wear it draped around the back of the neck and hanging down in front; deacons wear it draped across the left shoulder diagonally across the body.

There are a number of other pieces of vesture and insignia that belong to the episcopal and pontifical orders. The most common worn today are the crown or mitre. Bishops also carry a crozier or shepherd's crook or staff and wear a pectoral cross. The pallium is a narrow band of lamb's wool decorated with six black crosses, draped about the neck with short pendants front and back, worn by the pope and bestowed by him to metropolitan bishops and archbishops. The cape-like cope, worn in processions or for solemn prayer offices, confirmations, or weddings, etc., is not restricted only to bishops, even though bishops often wear copes.

Once styles of clothing changed (e.g., from the long tunics of the Romans to the short tunics of the Germans) and the clergy kept on wearing the older style of clothing for the liturgies, vestments were born. Clergy wore long dark robes called cassocks when going about their daily work. In the Middle Ages academic clergy also wore a gown over the cassock. In the Reformed tradition cassock and gown were originally anti-vestments because they were the ordinary street clothing of the clergy worn when leading public worship. However, when clergy continued to wear their gowns when leading worship even though they no longer wore them as everyday garb, they became vestments, often with tabs (a sign of professional distinction) added.

The need to don the basic white garment when gathering during the day for the prayer offices led to the development of the surplice in place of the alb because of its wider neckband and billowy sleeves. The rochet is a variation of the surplice with narrower sleeves. Its use came to be reserved to bishops and cathedral canons, who perhaps took more time to get vested. The alb, however, remained the basic undergarment for the Mass or Eucharist, along with stole and chasuble.

The stole and chasuble is now in the color of the day or season, which, by custom in the West, includes purple (Advent and Lent), blue (Advent), white or gold (Christmas, Easter, festivals of Christ), green (ordinary Sundays), and red (Holy Week, martyrs' days, church festivals). A distinction is made between the "passion" or Sarum blood red for Holy Week and the fiery red for Pentecost and church festivals. Black used to be worn for Requiem masses and still is in the extraordinary use. White or the color of the day or season may be worn instead.

For further reading

Eskew, Harry, and Hugh T. McElrath. *Sing with Understanding: An Introduction to Christian Hymnody,* 2d ed. Nashville: Church Street, 1995.

Foley, Edward. *Foundations of Christian Music: The Music of Pre-Constantinian Christianity.* Collegeville: Liturgical, 1994.

Holeton, David R. "Vestments," in *The New Westminster Dictionary of Liturgy and Worship,* ed. Paul Bradshaw, 464–71. Louisville: Westminster John Knox, 2002.

Laurence, John D., S.J. "Vestments, Liturgical," in *The New Dictionary of Sacramental Worship,* ed. Peter E. Fink, S.J., 1305–14. Collegeville: Liturgical, 1990.

Leaver, Robin A., and Joyce Ann Zimmerman, eds. *Liturgy and Music: Lifetime Learning.* Collegeville: Liturgical, 1998.

Mauch, Marchita B. "Architectural Setting (Historical)," and "Architectural Setting" (Modern)," in *The New Westminster Dictionary of Liturgy and Worship,* ed. Paul Bradshaw, 17–25. Louisville: Westminster John Knox, 2002.

Mayo, Janet. *A History of Ecclesiastical Dress.* London: Holmes & Meier, 1984.

Seasoltz, R. Kevin, O.S.B. *A Sense of the Sacred: Theological Foundations of Christian Architecture and Art.* New York: Continuum, 2005.

Westermeyer, Paul. *Te Deum: The Church and Music.* Minneapolis: Fortress Press, 1998.

White, James F. *Protestant Worship and Church Architecture.* New York: Oxford University Press, 1964.

Wren, Brian. *Praying Twice: The Music and Words of Congregational Song.* Louisville: Westminster John Knox, 2000.

11

Participation in Worship

1. How is the body used in worship?
2. What are some standard ceremonies in the Western liturgical tradition?
3. How do processions facilitate popular participation?
4. What should the people have to support their participation?
5. How are children formed into the liturgy?

1. How is the body used in worship?

The Constitution on the Sacred Liturgy promulgated by the Second Vatican Council encouraged "full, conscious, and active participation in liturgical celebrations which is demanded by the very nature of the liturgy" (II, 14). The basic level of such participation is putting one's body into the assembly where the liturgy is being celebrated. Put simply, one must go to church. More specifically, since "church" can be narrowly thought of as a building, one must gather with others to form the church (*ekklesia*), the assembly "called out" of the world.

But once one has put one's body into the liturgical assembly, conscious participation requires the body to be engaged actively in what is happening. Specifically, the body must be engaged in ritual actions.

"Ritual" may still conjure up negative connotations for some, who associate it with vain repetition, meaninglessly going through the motions, deadly dull.[1] The term can also cause confusion among scholars who study ritual as a phenomenon, because it can have different meanings when used in liturgy, in the history of religions, in behavioral sciences such as anthropology, psychology, and sociology, or in biology to describe animal behavior. For liturgists a "rite" is the whole body of texts (e.g., the Roman Rite, the Lutheran Rite, the Anglican Rite). The actions associated with the performance of the texts are called "ceremonies."

The late Catherine Bell studied ritual from all these disciplinary perspectives.[2] She wrote about the roles ritual plays in society, explored the basic genres of ritual action, and analyzed the characteristics of ritual-like activities. It might help those with an antiritual bias to see that ritual is involved in all aspects of personal, family, and social life, from toilet training of toddlers to family reunions to political rallies, and therefore also in the exercise of religion. No groups are without ritual. Even the Quaker gathering in silence and waiting for a revelation and developing a consensus of the community is a ritual. What Quakers lack that some traditions have plenty of are ceremonies.

All ritual activities involve the body. Maurice Merleau-Ponty argued that the human body is fundamental to all experience. I don't just have a body; I *am* a body, and all my relations to the world are bodily relations. He rejects the empiricist view that the body only reacts to external stimuli, although it certainly does. But the body also interacts with the outside world. I don't just stand or sit at an event, I move my head to get a better view. By moving my body I cause my surroundings to exist for me.[3]

If we take seriously this distinction, we can see that there are two ways to engage the body in worship: one is passive and the other is active. One may place one's body in a situation where it can be acted upon or one may place one's body into the action. Some people attend church services only to receive what is being offered. Their involvement in the activities of worship may be minimal. They may stand for the hymns but not sing. Others want to be actively involved. They want to sing the songs and speak the responses and participate in ceremonial actions.

From the viewpoint of liturgical renewal, passive participation is of lesser value than active participation. But there are moments in the liturgy that call for passive rather than active participation. Sometimes we are meant to sit, hear, and inwardly digest the words proclaimed.

We will consider both passive and active uses of the body in worship. Both uses can be considered in a positive way. Under the passive use of the body we will consider how external stimuli appeal to the senses. Under the active use of the body we will consider how the body responds to what is happening in the liturgy through posture and gesture.

Senses

The body has five sense organs: eyes, ears, nose, tongue, and skin. The five senses of sight, hearing, smell, taste, and touch can all be stimulated by what is happening in the liturgy.

Sight. The place of assembly establishes an environment of worship. The body is stimulated by its environment. The worship space can be a symbol of the meeting of heaven and earth and convey meanings through its overall design, material, colors, decorations, furniture, and so forth. The building and its artifacts can affect the worshipers' perception in terms of whether the liturgy expresses primarily the transcendence or the immanence of God, prompts a corresponding attitude of awe or familiarity, and engenders a sense of formality or informality. There has been an interest in liturgical arts and crafts in recent years with the manufacture of vestments and paraments and banners. Statues, altar paintings, and stained glass have been features of Western church buildings. From Eastern Orthodox worship we have received the gift of icons. In Orthodox worship the icons are incensed, as are the altar, the gospel book, other implements of worship, and the people themselves. The clouds of incense can be seen rising to heaven like prayers (Psalm 141).

Hearing. At the heart of Christian worship is speaking and hearing because the Holy Scriptures are read and commented upon and therefore also heard. Up until modern times the Scriptures would have been recited, that is, chanted. This enabled hearing before electronic amplification. Music has had an important role in Christian worship. It has become customary in the West to provide gathering music (i.e., the prelude), traditionally organ music but now praise bands also. Praise music is likely to be loud and engaging. Some detractors of this phenomenon call such amplified music "noise." But noise wakes people up. Awakened people also make noise. Whether the worship is so-called traditional or so-called contemporary, loud gathering music is usually followed by a boisterous opening hymn. Since "faith comes from what is heard" (Rom 10:17), words, whether loud or soft, must be audible.

Smell. Scents immerse us in places and events that we hold in memory. Scents attract or repel us; they warn us of things we cannot see; they make our mouths water and remind us of people and places we love. Many people remember not only the sights but the smells of church buildings from their earliest years.[4] There are many unique odors in the church building. We referred to the sight of clouds of incense, but of course incense has a pungent odor. Fragrant clouds of incense during the liturgy remind us that our earthly celebration is a window onto the heavenly liturgy where the saints worship the lamb amid the "golden bowls full of incense" (Rev. 5:8) that are their prayers. Incense suggests for our noses as well as for our eyes evidence that there is something sacred and extraordinary occurring during the liturgical celebration—Christ is present in the midst of his assembled people, gathering them up into his fragrant self-offering to the Father. Most importantly, we smell the bread and wine of the Eucharist. We smell the bread if it is freshly baked. But wine emits pungent aromas. It is through the aromas of wine that wine is actually tasted. The human tongue is limited to the primary tastes perceived by taste receptors on the tongue, including acidity, bitterness, saltiness, and sweetness. The wide array of fruit, earthy, floral, herbal, mineral, and woodsy flavors perceived in wine are derived from aroma notes interpreted by the olfactory bulb.

Taste. "Taste and see that the LORD is good," writes the psalmist (Ps. 34:8). Human eating has always been more than a way to satisfy hunger. Human meals can be complicated ritual acts, especially as they involve more people in a more formal situation. We have seen that the Eucharist was first celebrated in the context of an actual banquet in a domestic setting. As the assemblies grew larger, they moved into bigger facilities and the amount of food for the eucharistic meal became less. Even so, as late as 200 CE gifts of cheese and olives were presented at the offertory for blessing. Likewise, cups of milk and honey were added to the cups of wine and water in the initiation rite described in the *Apostolic Tradition*, suggesting from Old Testament typology that the newly baptized had come into the promised land of the kingdom of God. Even today other foods have a place in the liturgy. In the Orthodox and Eastern Catholic churches, Easter eggs, dyed red to represent the blood of Christ—whose hard shells symbolize the sealed tomb of Christ and the cracking of which symbolize his resurrection from the dead—are blessed by the priest at the end of the Paschal Vigil and distributed to the faithful. Blessed bread not used in the Eucharist is also distributed at the end of the Divine Liturgy. But the bread and wine of the Eucharist remain the most important food items to be tasted in the Christian liturgy. Since the advent of liturgical renewal there has been a move away from the practical but tasteless individual wafers. Likewise, the use of unfermented grape juice in place of wine does an injustice to the contribution of alcoholic wine to celebration and spiritedness. Wine "gladdens the heart" (Ps. 104:15) in a way that grape juice can't.

Touch. Christians touch other persons and things in the liturgy. Already in New Testament times they greeted each other with a holy kiss (1 Cor. 16:20). There are recent studies on this practice in the ancient church[5] and on the ritual of kissing as a means of bonding in general.[6] The practice passed out of use in the Middle Ages, although kissing the pax board as it was passed through the assembly served as a substitute.[7] In more recent times the greeting of peace has been enacted with a handshake or hug. But there are other forms of touching in Christian liturgy. A prominent ritual act is the laying on of hands, which is used for many purposes, including confirmation, ordination, marriage blessing, and anointing of the sick. The ministry to the sick includes anointing, which is touching the body with oil (see Mark 6:12-13). Also, communicants should be able to touch the bread by receiving it into their cupped hands and drink from the cup placed in their hands by ministers. Touching one another in Christian liturgy invites a serious reconsideration of the use of the human body in worship.

Postures

The postures of worship invite active participation because the worshipers must actually do something with their bodies. Postures are also symbolic uses of the body that express the reality of what the worshipers are experiencing.

Standing. Standing was the normal position for Christian worship in the first thousand years. It symbolized that Christians honored the resurrection of Christ and, by virtue of Holy Baptism, could stand as priests before God. The Council of Nicea agreed that Christians should stand for worship throughout the whole fifty days of Easter in honor of the resurrection. Standing provides a good posture for singing because it expands the diaphragm. One stands for praise and to show respect. We are still ordered to stand when a judge enters the courtroom. So, too, Christians stand during the entrance of the clergy and to sing praise to God.

Sitting. It was perhaps St. Augustine of Hippo who first allowed people to sit during his sermons. There were no chairs, so people sat on the floor or leaned against the walls. Pews did not come into church buildings in the West before the fourteenth century. The Reformation's emphasis on hearing the word of God made benches or pews a great convenience for people. Today we generally sit to listen to the readings, although it is still customary to stand for the Gospel. The congregation may sit during the recitation of psalms but stands for the Gloria Patri.

Kneeling. Kneeling in the ancient church was reserved for penitents. It is a natural posture to show humility. It is the appropriate posture for prayers of confession of sin. It also became customary to kneel or bow during the Nicene Creed at the words "And became man," for petitionary prayers such as the bidding prayer, and during the Great Thanksgiving or Canon of the Mass after the Sanctus to show respect for the sacrament that was consecrated with the words of Christ. The time to kneel during the canon was signaled by the ringing of the "Sanctus bells." Even the presiding minister at the altar genuflected after the words of Christ over the bread and over the cup out of reverence for the real presence of Christ's body and blood.

Bowing and genuflecting. Bowing or genuflecting are other ways of showing respect. These postures are closely related and are sometimes interchangeable. Roman and Anglo Catholics have practiced genuflection (bending the knee—a partial form of kneeling) whenever they pass the reserved sacrament or when the cross passes in procession, and often upon entering their pew from the aisle or the aisle from their pew. They have also genuflected or curtseyed to a bishop, although current Roman practice discourages that during the liturgy. Alternately, one may bow rather than genuflect to the altar, to the cross, to the reserved sacrament, to ministers, or by the ministers to the people. A whole repertoire of bows developed. For example, one bows the head at the mention of the holy name of Jesus, bows from the shoulder during doxologies to the Holy Trinity, but bows from the waist at the Gloria Patri.

Facing. Another posture in worship is facing in a certain direction. Early Christians faced the east for prayer, the direction from which Christ the sun of righteousness was expected to return as judge. In fact, a whole liturgical geography developed: facing the west (darkness) to renounce Satan in the rites of Christian initiation; facing the east not only for prayer but also for the profession of faith in the order for Holy Baptism; facing north (where the heathen lived, if one was in the Mediterranean world) to proclaim the gospel. The rubrics in older worship books directed the minister to face the altar for prayers (sacrificial acts) or face the people for proclamation (sacramental acts). A free-standing altar makes many of these orientations obsolete. However, the congregation may still be directed to face the scene of liturgical action, such as the narthex or font and to follow the movement of the cross at the head of a procession.

Walking. There are times during the liturgy when worshipers must move from one place to another. Sometimes this involves processions of the whole assembly, which we will consider in a separate section. Most typically walking occurs when worshipers go to a communion station to receive the sacrament. The liturgical ministers do a lot of walking during the liturgy as they move from one place to another. When this is necessary it is important to maintain the dignity of a solemn public event. Ministers (presiding, assisting, acolytes, etc.) should walk erect, at a medium pace, without looking around.

If they are walking two abreast they should try to maintain the same speed and go up or down steps at the same time. But they should not march in military precision. Most walking during the liturgy is not ceremonial but to get where one needs to be for the next action. Ministers should walk as naturally as possible and generally avoid diagonal short-cuts. There are often ceremonial paths in the chancel, such as the approach to and around the altar. If ministers are not carrying something, their hands should be folded across their stomachs, not dangling at their sides.

Carrying. Sometimes worshipers have objects to carry, such as candles at vigils. But ministers often are carrying something while they are walking. Acolytes may be carrying a processional cross, torches, banners, or a book. Ushers may be carrying offering basins and sometimes ciboria or baskets of bread and cruets of wine. Deacons or assisting ministers may be carrying books. The presiding minister carries nothing, unless he or she needs a hymnal or worship folder to sing in procession. When books are carried in procession they should be held upright with both hands before the breast with the side of the book that opens to the left facing the carrier so that it can be opened without having to pick it up and turn it around. This applies especially in a gospel procession or when one is holding the book for the presiding minister. Note: ministers serving in the chancel should not carry worship books, bulletins, folders, or other pieces of paper when they move from place to place. Whatever texts the ministers need should be placed where they are needed. The altar book, pulpit Bible, lectionary book, or gospel book will be marked before the liturgy begins. The lessons are read from a pulpit Bible, lectionary book, or gospel book, not from the worship folder or a sheet of paper.

Gestures

We use gestures in worship. Human beings communicate through gestures. In every culture and subculture, gestures are an important means of subjective communication. It is said of some cultures that the people talk with their hands. In liturgy, too, people talk with their hands. For example, the presiding minister extends the hands and arms in a gesture of greeting to the assembly. The assembly should extend their arms in a return greeting. It should go without saying that we look at the persons we are greeting, but, unfortunately, this elementary act of courtesy needs to be mentioned because too many ministers and congregants look in their worship books rather than at one another at greetings.

Gestures are obviously required for the enactment of *the greeting of peace*. In the ancient church this was the kiss of peace. Today in Western churches worshipers typically shake hands or hug one another as they "pass the peace." However this act of reconciliation is enacted, it will be culturally conditioned. But it should be regarded as a solemn time in the liturgy, not a frivolous time for friendly conversation. It has to do with those who will share the Lord's Supper being in a state of reconciliation.

It is also customary for the presiding minister to raise his or her arms in prayer (the *orans* position). This is done for collects and the Great Thanksgiving though usually not during litanies. Worshipers may also raise their hands during prayer or cup the hands in a gesture of receiving. In Pentecostal worship the worshipers raise their hands (or at least one hand) in praise.

An important gesture is *the sign of the cross*. Ministers may make the sign of the cross over things or people as an indication of blessing, although extending hands over things or people is a more ancient gesture. Common uses of the sign of the cross over things would be for blessing water, oils, bread, and wine. Common uses of the sign of the cross over people would be in benedictions. Some ministers regard the apostolic greeting ("The grace of our Lord Jesus Christ, the love of God, and the communion of the Holy Spirit be with you all") as a benediction because it has also been used as such. But if it is intended as a greeting, one does not make the sign of the cross; one extends the arms toward those being greeted.

The people may also cross themselves. Tertullian referred to Christians crossing themselves in all their undertakings—upon entering or leaving one's home, when taking a meal, when arising in the morning and retiring at night, before beginning each task, and so forth. Whenever the name of the Father, Son, and Holy Spirit is invoked, Christians cross themselves, typically at invocations and benedictions. They cross themselves when receiving absolution, when receiving the body and blood of Christ, when receiving a blessing. It has been customary to cross oneself at the words of the Creed that one expects the resurrection of the dead, which is surely the ultimate blessing. They may cross themselves at "Blessed is he who comes in the name of the Lord" during the Sanctus.

2. What are some standard ceremonies in the Western liturgical tradition?

Ceremonies are actions associated with ritual. They are the ways ritual is performed. Many denominations have manuals on the liturgy that provide ritual notes. For example, Roman Catholic ceremony is governed by the *General Instruction of the Roman Missal* (GIRM), which is always updated to accompany the latest typical edition of the Roman Missal. Those who celebrate the pre-Vatican II "traditional" version of the Roman Mass, including some Anglo-Catholics, consult Adrian Fortesque and J. B. O'Connell's *The Ceremonies of the Roman Rite Described*.[8] Ritual manuals have been prepared to accompany versions of the Anglican Prayer Book and various Lutheran worship books. In this section we will not review all these rubrics and notes on the liturgy in detail. But we will offer some general principles for the conduct of the chief liturgies of the church, specifically the Eucharist and prayer offices, that could apply to all performances of the historic catholic liturgies. Those who desire more detail have their manuals to consult.

A. The Holy Communion or Eucharist or Mass

Preparatory office. In the Middle Ages a preparatory office developed for the celebrant and servers in the form of a confession of sins and prayer for forgiveness as an acknowledgment of one's unworthiness to serve at the altar of God and that one does serve only by God's grace. This came to be done on the steps to the altar. In some Reformation liturgies it was turned into a congregational prayer of confession with the minister giving an absolution or declaration of grace. In old Lutheran liturgies this was often done at the chancel entrance. The suggestion of *Lutheran Book of Worship* and now in *Evangelical Lutheran Worship* is to do the Brief Order for Confession and Forgiveness at the baptismal font, thus indicating that the confession of sins is a return to one's baptism. Sometimes the rite at the font involves a blessing of the water and a sprinkling of the people to cause them to remember their baptism.

Entrance procession. The liturgy begins with an entrance song, either the psalmody of the Introit or a hymn. The ministers make their entrance into the chancel during the singing of the song. Sometimes choirs have processed, but the older and more effective arrangement is for the choir to be in place to lead the singing. A simple entrance procession might include the acolyte carrying a cross, assisting ministers, and the presiding minister. More elaborate processions could include a thurifer carrying and swinging incense, the crucifer and torchbearers, a book bearer, assisting ministers, and the presiding minister. The presiding minister is always at the end of the procession, although he or she might give place to a higher pastor such as the bishop. A guest preacher who has no other liturgical role would process ahead of the presiding minister.

Reverencing the altar. When the procession enters the chancel, those who are not carrying an object reverence the altar with a bow or genuflection. The presiding minister may kiss the altar and then also bow toward the people.

Placing objects carried in procession. The processional cross is usually placed behind the altar. The processional candles (torches) are usually placed at the ambo. The altar book, if carried in procession, is placed on the altar. The gospel book, if carried in procession, is placed on the side of the altar toward the people. The Bible or lectionary is placed on the ambo or pulpit.

Incensing the altar. If the altar is incensed during the entrance rite, the thurifer brings the thurible to the presiding minister, who places incense on the coals, receives the thurible from the thurifer, and moves to a position in front of the cross and bows toward it. The cross is incensed three times. Then the presider moves around the altar, swinging the thurible toward the altar, returning to the position in front of the cross, bows again, and hands the thurible to the thurifer.

Place of the presiding minister. During the remaining portion of the gathering rite and during the liturgy of the word, the presiding minister (celebrant) is at the presider's chair, not at the altar. In the basilican style the presider's chair and seats for other ministers are in the apse facing the nave across the altar table. In later styles the presider's (celebrant's) chair and seats for other ministers are at the side of the chancel. The presiding minister (celebrant) does not go to the altar until the offertory.

Gospel procession. The Gospel may be read from the ambo or pulpit or from the midst of the assembly. If it is proclaimed from the midst of the assembly, a procession is formed as follows: reader picks up Bible, lectionary, or gospel book; acolytes retrieve torches and flank the book bearer; the Gospel reader (deacon, preacher) processes last. If incense is used the thurifer, who has stoked up the charcoals, retrieves the thurible and leads the procession. The procession stops at midpoint in the center aisle, the torch bearers flanking the book bearer, who turns and holds the book so that the gospeler can open it. The gospeler announces the reading and then incenses the book. At the end of the reading, the gospeler closes the book, holds it up and declaims, "The gospel of the Lord." The gospeler steps aside to let the others process back to the chancel. Note: the Gospel procession should be accompanied by music of sufficient length, such as an Alleluia verse, a sequence hymn, or organ improvisation to cover the movement.

The greeting of peace. The presiding minister greets the assembly as a whole and then greets the other ministers in the chancel. They extend the greeting to other persons in the assembly, who are also greeting one another. It is inappropriate to say anything at this point other than the specified formula, that is, "The peace of the Lord be with you," or "Peace be with you." This is not a time to socialize with parishioners; it is an act of reconciliation. The form of greeting in Western society is typically a handshake. Some communities are used to hugs.

The offertory. The offertory is the busiest point in the eucharistic liturgy. Ushers are usually gathering monetary offerings from the assembly while the choir is singing, and they may present the offerings to the ministers at the altar with bread and wine in a procession with all of the gifts. While the gifts are being received the veiled chalice and paten are brought from the credence table to the altar and are unveiled and arranged by the deacon or assisting minister. Acolytes or deacons receive the gifts and arrange them on the altar. Monetary offerings may be placed on a horn of the altar or a credence table. The containers with bread and wine are placed on the corporal and are arranged with the bread on a paten or in a basket in front of the chalice and other containers of bread (e.g., ciboria for hosts) and wine (e.g., cruets) behind the chalice.

Incensing at the offertory. The thurifer brings the thurible to the presiding minister, who places incense on the coals and receives the thurible from the thurifer. The presider makes the sign of the cross three times with the thurible over the bread and wine and then makes a circle around them twice in a clockwise direction and once in a counterclockwise direction. The presider hands the thurible back to the thurifer, who incenses the presider three times and then incenses the other ministers at the altar and in the chancel and finally moves to the front of the chancel and incenses the congregation (the priesthood that offers gifts, prayers, and thanksgiving).

Gestures during the Great Thanksgiving. The presiding minister gestures to the assembly in a greeting at "The Lord be with you," lifts his hands at "Lift up your hearts," and

holds her hands up in the *orans* position at "Let us give thanks to the Lord our God."
The presider's hands remain in the *orans* position throughout the prayer, with these
exceptions. The sign of the cross is made over the bread and the cup at the words "gave
thanks" during the institution narrative. The presider extends his or her hands over the
bread and cup during the invocation of the Holy Spirit. During the concluding doxology and great amen, the presiding minister holds up the bread and cup (the elevation).

The Fraction. The bread is not broken during the words of institution but before the
communion. If whole loaves are used, it is not necessary to break the loaves into smaller
pieces at this point. Ministers may continue breaking the bread as it is distributed.

Administration of the sacrament. Every space is different and the method of distribution has to be worked out in every space. Here are some general principles. The presiding minister communes himself/herself first or communes the servers (the assisting
minister, communion ministers, and acolytes) first and then receives communion from
the assisting minister or deacon. If additional baskets or cups are needed for the administration of Holy Communion, they are brought to the altar at this time and the presiding minister places bread and wine in the additional receptacles. The communion of the
people should occur continuously. The presiding minister always distributes the bread.
Acolytes stand in front of the altar holding cruets to replenish the content of the cups
for the communion ministers. Singing accompanies the distribution, but the musicians
should also be invited to receive communion. Silence toward the end of the distribution is appropriate. After all have received communion, the vessels are returned to the
credence table. If bread and wine that remains after communion is to be consumed, this
may be done in the sacristy after the service.

Sending procession. The ministers leave the chancel after the benediction in the order
in which they processed in at the entrance. A sending hymn may be sung during this
procession. The term *sending* implies that there is significance to the departure from the
place of assembly.

B. The Prayer Offices

The ministers of the prayer offices. The prayer offices may be led by bishops, pastors or
priests, deacons, or laypeople. The traditional vestments of leaders of prayer offices are
cassock and surplice. Ordained ministers do not wear a stole when presiding or offici-
ating at a prayer office; stoles are for preaching and sacramental acts. In the Anglican
tradition ordained ministers have worn black scarfs called tippets. At solemn Matins or
Vespers the officiant, whether clergy or lay, may wear a cope. If laypeople are leading the
prayer office the office ends with the Benedicamus: "Let us bless the Lord. R/ Thanks
be to God." If a bishop is present a solemn benediction may be given.

Places of the ministers. Elaborate entrance processions are not required for the prayer
offices. The presiding minister (officiant), other ministers, and choir enter without
singing and go to their places. The entrance procession may be done silently or accompanied by organ or other instrumental music. A choir procession would be preceded by

a processional cross. If there is a chancel with divided choir stalls, the place of the choir and ministers will be in the chancel. There is a tradition of inviting other worshipers to join the choir in the chancel. If the place of the choir is not in a divided chancel, such as a balcony or gallery, the choir does not process. If there is no divided chancel, the officiant might preside in a location outside the chancel at an angle to the congregation. In some situations the seating of the worshipers can be arranged in an antiphonal style in the nave (as in a divided chancel). This arrangement facilitates the antiphonal singing of the psalms and canticles. Ministers remain at their chair, pew, or stall throughout the office except for readings.

Lucernarium. The exception to the above is if Vespers (evening prayer) begins with the service of light. In this case a minister carries in a large candle, singing the versicles in procession. Other ministers follow the candle. If incense is used, it precedes the candle and is placed near the candle. During the singing of the light hymn (e.g., *Phos hilaron*) other candles are lighted.

Incensing. During Psalm 141 in Vespers (evening prayer) the candle, the ministers, and the worshipers are incensed. The candle is incensed three times. The thurifer may walk through the congregation incensing the people. Alternately, incense may burn in a bowl placed before the candle. This use of incense is both an evening offering and a visible absolution.

Incensing the altar. On major festivals the altar might be incensed during the Gospel canticle (Benedictus in Matins [morning prayer]; Magnificat in Vespers [evening prayer]) in anticipation of the prayers that are offered after the canticle. The minister first incenses the cross three times and then circles the altar incensing in its direction while walking.

Litanies and suffrages. The prayer offices usually end with a series of collects: the collect for the day (from the previous Sunday or on that day if one is appointed), the collect for grace in the morning or the collect for peace in the evening, and a morning or evening prayer. Other prayers may be added if desired. Sometimes a litany is sung: either the Great Litany, especially in the morning, or the Litany of Peace at Vespers. The Great Litany is traditionally sung on Wednesdays and Fridays during Lent. The morning or evening suffrages may also be used. It is appropriate to kneel during the prayers, except during the Great Fifty Days of Easter.

The paschal blessing. On Sundays and during the Easter season Matins (morning prayer) may end with the paschal blessing. A hymn may be sung as the ministers and people assemble around the baptismal font. The Easter Gospel is chanted and the Te Deum Laudamus is sung. The people may be sprinkled during the Te Deum. There is a closing collect and a solemn benediction.

Preaching at the prayer offices. The prayer offices are not services of the word in which homilies or sermons are given. However, it would be appropriate for the presiding minister to comment on the readings, perhaps from the chair rather than the ambo. If a longer sermon is desired, this would be given at the end of the office, following the

Benedicamus. The minister goes to the ambo or pulpit while a hymn is sung. After the sermon there is a closing prayer and benediction.

Exiting. Getting ministers out of a service can be as complicated as getting them in. As a rule, ministers and choir exit as they entered. Like the entrance procession, the exit procession should be done silently or to organ or other instrumental music. On major festivals the exit procession might be accompanied by the singing of a hymn.

3. How do processions facilitate popular participation?

Processions are a solemn march and they involve bodily movement. Those who process move from one point to another. Like a parade, processions actively engage both those who march and those who watch.

Once Christian worship became a public event, it also became processional. Much of the liturgy in the period of late antiquity and well into the Middle Ages has been called "stational liturgy" because it began at one gathering station and moved to another, or perhaps to several stations, before arriving at a final destination.

Perhaps the earliest descriptions of stational liturgies are in Egeria's travel diary. She describes the processions of pilgrims from one pilgrimage site to another. Processions were accompanied by the chanting of psalms and litanies. Prayers were offered at stations along the way and at the final station, which sometimes included a full liturgy of word and sacrament. The processions described by Egeria could be of considerable length; for example, from the Mount of Olives into Jerusalem on Palm Sunday or from the Church of the Nativity in Bethlehem all the way back to the Martyrium in Jerusalem on the Epiphany.

Pilgrims to Jerusalem still walk the *via crucis*, following the path Jesus took from Pontius Pilate's judgment seat to the place of execution on Golgotha. The late medieval popular devotion of the Way of the Cross became a way for individuals or groups to undertake a local pilgrimage procession through fourteen stations commemorating the passion of Christ. Stations of the cross were not confined to church buildings; sometimes they could extend for miles down a country road, as in some places in Europe. In Hispanic communities today the whole community joins in a Good Friday *via crucis* through a neighborhood, such as the Pilsen community in Chicago, processing to the fourteen stations of the Way of the Cross, singing hymns along the way and stopping at each station for a reenactment of the passion of Christ and perhaps a meditation on the event. The procession ends at a public place where a reenactment of the crucifixion takes place. After this there is a procession to a church in the community where the Good Friday liturgy is celebrated.

Returning to antiquity, Aidan Kavanagh wrote of the need of the pope and his entourage, beginning in the fourth century, to process through the city of Rome to get from the Lateran Palace where the pope lived to the basilica at which the station liturgy would be celebrated.[9] The great Christian basilicas of Rome ringed the city in what we would today call suburbs. They could not be built in the city center because the forum was filled with government buildings and pagan temples, which were not immediately destroyed because their cults continued to flourish for a century after the Edict of Milan in 312. Chanting psalms and litanies as they processed, with stops for prayer at stations along the way, the entourage of the bishop of Rome gathered participants as it wended its way through the city. There would be several significant stations, such as the basilica where the Eucharist was celebrated, and ending back at St. John's Lateran for Vespers. This day-long procession certainly accomplished an evangelistic purpose: it established the Christian presence in a city whose pagan cults were waning in influence. Christians didn't invent processions; they were common in the ancient world, not least in the city of Rome itself. But, as Kavanagh points out, the time scale of liturgy so conceived was the entire Sunday and the space scale of such a liturgy was the entire city.

Emperor Constantine built a new capital on the site of ancient Byzantium for several strategic military and political purposes. But one of his purposes was to establish a city in which the Christian cult did occupy the city center. Constantinople was laid out with broad boulevards that made possible great processions. Most early Byzantine descriptions of liturgy focus more on these outdoor processions than on what transpired in the equally great church buildings.

Since Constantinople was founded as a Christian city and served as the capital of the later Christian Byzantine Empire, processions did not serve the evangelistic purposes they did in early Roman liturgy. Rather, as John Baldovin documents, most of these processions were a response to natural disasters, like earthquakes and volcanic eruptions, or political upheavals, such as military invasions and sieges, and therefore often had a penitential character.[10] Other occasions for processions were the transfer of relics of the saints and icon processions during and after the iconoclastic struggle. Eyewitness accounts uniformly testify that the crowds participating in such processions were huge and remained huge throughout the Byzantine period.[11]

Stational liturgy and processions were carried into the rest of Europe, East and West, by missionaries from Constantinople and Rome. Throughout the Middle Ages stational liturgy served the same purposes already established in antiquity: processions to pilgrimage sites, episcopal stational liturgy, aversion to plagues and natural disasters, transfer of relics. These processions were occasional, but four annual stational processions connected with days in the church year have more or less survived into our time: Candlemas, Palm Sunday, Rogationtide, and Corpus Christi.

Candlemas. The Feast of the Presentation of Jesus in the Temple and the Purification of Mary on the fortieth day after the Nativity, according to the Gospel of Luke, spread from Jerusalem over the entire church and was later kept on February 2 in the Western calendar (forty days after December 25). It was introduced throughout the entire Byzantine Empire by the Emperor Justinian I (542) in thanksgiving for the cessation of the great pestilence that had depopulated the city of Constantinople. In the Greek Church it was called *Hypapante tou Kyriou*, the Meeting of the Lord and his mother with Simeon and Anna. The Armenians call it "The Coming of the Son of God into the Temple" and still keep it on February 14. Perhaps the decree of Justinian gave occasion also to the Roman Church (to Gregory I?) to introduce this feast, but definite information is lacking on this point. The feast appears in the Gelasian Sacramentary under the new title of Purification of the Blessed Virgin Mary, but the procession characteristic of the medieval feast is not mentioned. Pope Sergius I (687–701) introduced a procession for this day, but since the Gregorian Sacramentary tradition of the eighth century also does not speak of this procession, it is likely that the procession of Sergius was the ordinary stational procession, not the liturgical procession of the Middle Ages and today.

The popular name "Candlemas" comes from the blessing of the church's supply of candles for the year and the candlelight procession. According to the Roman Missal, the celebrant, in purple stole and cope, standing at the epistle side of the altar, blesses the candles (which must be of beeswax). Having sung or recited the five prayers prescribed, he sprinkles and incenses the candles. Then he distributes them to the clergy and laity, while the choir sings the canticle of Simeon, Nunc dimittis. The antiphon, "a light for revelation to the Gentiles and the glory of your people Israel," is repeated after every verse of the canticle, according to the medieval custom of singing antiphons. During the procession which now follows, and at which all the participants carry lighted candles in their hands, the choir sings the antiphon *Adorna thalamum tuum, Sion* ("Let Zion's bridal-room be clothed"), composed by St. John of Damascus, one of the few pieces that, text and music, have been borrowed by the Roman Church from the Greeks. The solemn procession represents the entry of Christ, who is the Light of the World, into the temple of Jerusalem. Today the procession is held inside the church building, especially in northern climes where it is still cold outside on February 2.

Palm Sunday. Again, Egeria gives us the earliest description of the Palm Sunday procession as it took place in late fourth-century Jerusalem. The people assembled in the afternoon of the Sunday at the beginning of the Great Week on the Mount of Olives at the Eleona Church and processed to the Imbomon (where Jesus ascended into heaven) and from there, carrying branches of palm or olive, back to the city repeating, "Blessed is he who comes in the name of the Lord." We also discussed some of the typical medieval Palm Sunday processions in chapter 7, such as the Sarum Use. The Palm Sunday procession provides an opportunity for the whole congregation to gather outside the church building for the reading of the processional Gospel, the blessing of palms, and the procession carrying palms, perhaps through the neighborhood (weather permitting) and into the church. It an opportunity for liturgical evangelism.

Note: the *Easter Vigil* also begins as a kind of stational liturgy. The congregation gathers outside the church building around the new fire for the lighting of the paschal candle, and then processes with handheld lighted candles into the church building proclaiming "the light of Christ." In Orthodox churches, continuing the practice reported by Egeria in Jerusalem, the candles are lighted within the sanctuary, and the bishop or priest emerge, proclaiming, "Christ is risen. Alleluia." But then there is usually a procession around the outside of the church building with lighted candles while Easter hymns are sung with many of the worshipers participating.

Rogationtide. Days of prayer at the time of the spring planting asking for God's blessing of a bountiful harvest probably predate Christianity in Europe. But these days became especially popular in England, where they were known as "Gang Days" and "Cross Week," and in Germany, where they were also called *Bittage, Bittwoche, Kreuz-woche* ("Prayer Days,"Prayer Week," "Cross Week"). The Rogation days were so popular in England that their celebration continued even to the thirteenth year of the reign of the Protestant Queen Elizabeth, 1571, when one of the ministers of the Established Church inveighed against the Rogation processions.

We discussed the origin and spread of the Rogation days in the Western calendar in chapter 8. Here we note that the Rogationtide processions attained great popularity in western Europe. As with all stational processions, psalms and litanies are sung. In the Roman Rite the litany of the saints is chanted. In Anglican use the Great Litany is sung. The purpose of the Rogation processions was to walk and mark out the parish boundaries, often repairing boundary markers as the procession made its way. There are stories of Rogation processions from neighboring parishes bumping into each other. The procession terminates in the parish church where the Mass is celebrated. The color used in the procession and Mass is violet, reflecting the penitential character of the procession.

The popular character of the Rogation procession is evident in all the parochial variations found in local uses. In this day of environmental awareness and renewed concern for the stewardship of the earth, Rogation processions might acquire a new relevance, not only in rural places but in city neighborhoods where the procession could make stational stops at local parks or community gardens, with appropriate prayers for the care of the environment, and concluding with a Mass or Eucharist using propers for the stewardship of creation.

Corpus Christi. If the Rogation processions reflect an agricultural and rural origin, the Corpus Christi procession reflects an urban origin. It has been noted that the feast of Corpus Christi emerged at a time when rural populations were being displaced from the land and moving into the growing cities. In this situation in which social and political structures threatened to disintegrate, Corpus Christi celebrated the sacrament of the body of Christ as the glue that bonded society together and its celebration brought together the whole town.[12]

The promulgation of Corpus Christi as a feast in the Christian calendar is discussed in chapter 8. The main feature of the Corpus Christi celebration became the great procession with the Blessed Sacrament after the Mass.[13] The Blessed Sacrament was held by the bishop or celebrant of the Mass in a monstrance as he walked under a canopy. All the clergy, monks, and nuns of the town processed. The trade guilds of the town provided decorated floats and often jockeyed for a position in the parade close to the canopy of the Blessed Sacrament. There were stations throughout the town at which the procession stopped for readings and prayers.

Like the Rogationtide processions, the Corpus Christi procession attained great popularity because local communities could invest it with what was important to them. There were usually fairs, games, and plays on the feast of Corpus Christi. Full texts of play cycles survive from York, Chester, and Wakefield, and partial texts survive from Covantry, Norwich, and Newcastle.[14] Thus the Corpus Christi festivities gave a great boost to English drama.

In Catholic countries Corpus Christi has retained its great popularity with its outdoor procession. Cognizant of the evangelistic opportunities that outdoor processions provide, Pope John Paul II took the annual Corpus Christi procession from St. Peter's Square to the streets of Rome, with stations along the way, thus replicating the earliest stational processions in Rome.

4. What should the people have to support their participation?

Before the mass production of books made possible by the printing press, people had no materials to facilitate their participation. They simply learned the words by rote. Chanting facilitated memorization and therefore aided participation. Books were expensive and it was a major financial investment even for a parish church to buy a sacramentary, a missal, a gospel book, or a Bible. This may be one reason why liturgy changed so slowly before the mass production of books: books were expensive and people had to commit texts to memory.

By the late Middle Ages, the affluent could have books of the hours written for their use. But with the invention of printing, more books could be placed in the hands of worshipers. In the post-Reformation period, this meant primarily handheld missals for Catholics to follow the Mass, hymnals for Lutherans to sing hymns, and psalters for the Reformed to sing metrical psalms. These resources were not provided by the church; individuals bought them. Not until the nineteenth century did churches begin to buy books and make them available to worshipers.

The next major technological contribution to the mass production of worship materials was the invention of the mimeograph. Actually, Thomas Edison received a patent for "Autographic Printing" in 1876 and a further patent for a "Method of Preparing Autographic Stencils for Printing" in 1880. But the word *mimeograph* was first used by Albert Blake Dick when he licensed Edison's patents in 1887. His company, A. B. Dick, produced these simple printing presses in which a stylus cut through a stencil, which was affixed to a rotating drum into which ink was poured. The mimeograph became popular because it was much cheaper than traditional print. No typesetting or skilled labor was involved. One individual with a typewriter and the necessary equipment essentially became his own printing factory, which allowed for greater circulation of printed material. One begins to see worship bulletins produced by mimeograph already in the early twentieth century. The bulletin typically contained the order of service and parish announcements. The object of this pamphlet was to help worshipers find page and hymn numbers in the worship book or hymnal. But it was also possible to include texts not available in the books the worshipers used. Church publishing houses caught on to this idea and provided bulletin stock with cover designs and back-page information for mimeographing.

As photo duplicators became more affordable for churches, they provided a less messy way of producing worship bulletins. By the 1970s mimeograph machines were being widely displaced in parish offices by photo duplicators. They also made it possible literally to cut and paste pictures, texts, or music into the bulletin and mass produce the bulletin by taking photos.

By the 1980s some pastors were wondering whether worshipers, especially visitors, were having difficulty finding find their way through a big worship book (for Lutherans these were always a combined service book and hymnal) or multiple worship books (Episcopalian worship required use of both the prayer book and a hymnal) and if this discouraged participation in worship. With the use of a photo duplicator, it was possible to cut and paste everything needed for an order of service into the worship bulletin that now became a folder or even a booklet. The development of the Internet and the ability to download and print material simply meant that the cutting and pasting could be done without literally cutting and pasting. Publishing houses like Augsburg and Concordia provided material (*Sundays and Seasons*) that could be downloaded, cut, and pasted into bulletins and worship folders. Publishing houses now made their money not so much by publishing printed material as by licensing downloadable resources.

The advent of Microsoft PowerPoint suggested a new approach to aiding worship participation around the year 2000. It would not be necessary for worshipers to have anything in their hands, including the increasing bulky worship booklets, much less miscellaneous sheets of paper, because everything could be projected on an overhead screen. The evangelical megachurches and their imitators immediately utilized this new technology, along with projecting larger-than-life images of the worship leaders on the large screens.

Liturgical churches have also begun using this technology, although not without considerable debate. Those who promote the use of PowerPoint can answer every objection with almost ideological fanaticism. They even point out that PowerPoint can improve assembly singing because it requires people to lift up their heads rather than bury their heads in a book. However, in view of the emphasis in this chapter on processions as a means of involving people bodily in liturgy, I would note that screens require the assembly to be stationary and face a certain direction in order to see them.

The one objection to PowerPoint that its promoters cannot answer is that it creates disembodied worship. If screens are in a room people will look at them. When a speaker at a meeting is projected as an image on a screen, people will tend to look at the image on the screen rather than the real person at the podium.

This kind of issue raises the question of the quality of participation and even the character of the assembly. The liturgical assembly is a gathering of real people who

interact with one another. And, as we have emphasized, this interaction requires movement. Movement of people requires that worshipers not be dependent on a lot of
material. For example, when processing into a dark church building at the beginning
of the Easter Vigil, it is enough for the people to respond on well-established tones,
"Thanks be to God." In other processions involving litanies it is enough for the people
to respond, "Lord, have mercy." Worshipers in Eastern churches do not have a lot of
printed material, but their liturgies are quite participatory because the people have
learned a repertoire of behaviors and responses.

We have come full circle. Modern Western liturgy has become text dependent. The
ministers of the liturgy certainly have plenty of texts to deliver. But if the assembly
can hear the readings and prayers, and if they are delivered in an intelligible way, a
lot of material in the hands of the people is not required. "Faith comes from what is
heard," wrote Paul. Responsorial psalm singing requires only a brief, repeating refrain,
which the assembly can quickly learn by rote as the cantor or choir sings the verses.
Brief responses can be learned easily and delivered more spontaneously if worshipers
are not looking in their books or folders or at a screen. Perhaps the only texts that are
really needed are of canticles, psalms, and hymns. These could be the only texts (with
musical notes, please) projected on a screen.

5. How are children formed into the liturgy?

There is a special concern about enabling the youngest members of the liturgical
assembly to participate in the liturgy. Liturgy is perceived as a grown-up activity, and
not infrequently children are excused from parts or the whole of the liturgy. They
may even be segregated into "children's church" or sent to a nursery. The ideal is to
include the children in the liturgy since they are baptized members of the church.
Jesus notoriously placed children into the midst of his disciples as models for receiving
the kingdom of God and blessed them (Mark 10:13-16). Isaiah prophesied that in the
last times "a little child shall lead them" (Isa. 11:6). Children, in a sense, set the pace of
worship. What makes it possible for children to participate in the liturgy facilitates the
participation for everyone. Here are some principles that may help make it possible for
children as well as adults to participate.

A. Make sure the liturgy is stable.

People participate in something when they know what to expect, and what is expected
of them. Children are no different. If children are to be formed in worship, the patterns
of worship must be stable. This is because children (and all of us) learn by repetition.
They learn to throw a ball or jump rope or ride a bicycle or spell a word or play the piano
by repetition. It's not mindless repetition. You keep doing something until, suddenly, it
falls into place. You reach a point where your hand-to-eye coordination kicks in, or you
balance on two wheels as the bike takes off, or your fingers go on the keyboard where
the notes tell them to go.

So it is with worship. As Carl Schalk put it, "Worship is best when the actions of worship are second nature, when we don't have to be constantly asking ourselves, 'What do we do now?' As long as we are thinking, 'What comes next?' or "Do we stand or sit or kneel?', we are not worshipping. We are still learning to worship."[15]

We learn through repetition. Repetition is not "mindless," because it frees you to begin thinking about the content or significance of what you are doing. This is why the church wisely uses the same forms and the same responses over and over again. When someone says a prayer that ends, "Let us pray to the Lord," the learned response should be "Lord, have mercy" or "Lord, hear our prayer."

The issue of common and stable texts concerned Martin Luther. Even though he granted that there could be liberty in devising the patterns and words of worship, he thought some forms and expressions should be agreed upon among churches and kept intact so that people would learn them or not be put into bad faith through reckless change. Especially he didn't want the words of the catechism being constantly changed. Otherwise, how would those words be memorized? The same might be said about translations of the Bible used in public worship. There's always another way to interpret and translate something. But if people keep hearing the texts differently, the words of Scripture won't be fixed in their memories.

Liturgies should be stable from week to week, except for the variations that occur in following the church year. Different customs, different music, different orders are used in the different seasons of the church year. But these variations are often what delight and engage children: the Advent wreath, the Christmas creche, the Christmas tree, the veiled crosses of Lent, the paschal candle during Easter, the fiery banners of Pentecost, and so forth.

B. Sing as much as possible.

It's been said that those who sing pray twice. Speaking liturgy is a modern and rationalistic things to do. In Eastern Christian rites almost nothing is spoken. Western liturgy, too, was entirely sung in the forms of the High Mass and the choral office until the age of Enlightenment. Why all this singing? There are several reasons:

Singing injects a sense of ecstasy and eternity in mundane and temporary worship.

Singing heightens the meaning of texts. Various modes are used to bring out the tone of the text. Hymn tunes are often wedded to certain texts.

Singing helped with the projection of texts before electronic amplification. In some buildings singing can still serve that purpose better than amplification.

Singing facilitates memorization. Let's not imagine that all those medieval monks who sang their way through the psalter every week were literate. They learned much of the text, such as the psalms, through rote memorization.

Plato included music in his school curriculum. Singing has been an important part of preschool, kindergarten, and elementary education. Instrumental instruction has been an important part of elementary and secondary education. Educators have studied the positive impact of music education on math skills, reading skills, logical skills, and group interaction skills. But music has a value in itself. The improvement of one's artistic intellect enhances the excellence of life throughout the school years and through the later years. Music is a way of communicating and understanding culture—one's own and the cultures of others. Brain research has demonstrated how music is capable of manipulating the expansion and growth of the superior cognitive procedures of the brain that are usually not possible in other fields.

Children learn music easily and are open to all kinds of musical expressions. The lyrics also ought to sustain the faith. The more liturgy is sung, the faster children will grow into it. It helps to teach them some hymns and responses in Sunday school, but they will also pick up these elements of worship on their own just by being in the midst of a singing people.

C. Involve children in actions

Children's bodies are always in motion. It's hard for them to sit still. The pews are a real prison, and children often try to escape their confinement by crawling under the benches. Children also like to see what's going on. Many parents make a major mistake by sitting in the back of the nave out of concern that their children will disturb others. My experience is that children are more engaged when they sit in the front of the assembly and can see what's going on. Let's grant that provision might have to be made to handle the "terrible twos." Most churches provide nurseries. But some parents just take their kids into the narthex and let them crawl around out there so they can bring them back into the assembly when it seems safe. Boxed pews provided a natural playpen for children, regardless of their other limitations.

Worship should be action oriented and children should be placed where they can see what is going on. If there are processions, they should be on aisles so they can watch the acolytes and ministers process. Children can participate in some processions, such as the palm procession on Palm Sunday or the candlelight procession at the beginning of the Easter Vigil.

Children can be invited to gather where the action is, such as around the baptismal font or pool. They can be encouraged to remember their baptism by dipping their hand in the font and making the sign of the cross as they pass by it.

And children can be invited to participate in the sacramental meal. Some churches are struggling over the issue of communing all the baptized, including infants.[16] The Orthodox commune children at their baptism. Roman Catholics typically observe first communion at age seven. Children are being admitted to Holy Communion at an earlier age in Protestant churches. Children can receive instruction appropriate to their level of comprehension and continue to discern meanings in the Eucharist throughout a lifetime of participation.

D. Provide children's time.

Children's homilies are becoming a standard feature in Protestant worship and Roman Catholic parish masses. I almost hesitate to recommend this practice, because it is so often done poorly. Children are invited to the front of the church and are often seated on chancel steps facing the congregation so those in the assembly can see them. The children are put on display. The minister often presents some object lesson and the point gets lost in the object. The children are asked questions and, of course, as Art Linkletter demonstrated years ago on TV, "Children say the darndest things." This becomes great entertainment for the adults.

The better use of children's time is to draw them into the mysteries of faith being celebrated in the liturgy. Children's homilies can be edifying and instructional for everyone. This should be a time of catechesis that communicates basic information about worship.

Invite the children to come forward and sit in the front rows so that the children are not put on display and so that the pastor can speak to the whole assembly. Giving the children's homily before the readings makes it possible to alert children and adults alike to what they are going to hear. If the reading is a story, simply retell it for the children and then tell them to listen to it when it is read. If it a special day in the church year and something special is going on, talk about that. This also clues in the adults, especially visitors.

The whole point of focusing especially on the children is to show them that they are noticed and valued. Actually, all worshipers want to be noticed and valued by their shepherd. That's why they are greeted individually after the service.

The presiding minister stands in the role of Christ not only in preaching and serving the sacrament, but throughout the whole liturgy, which includes the rituals enacted after the final blessing is given.

For further reading

Brugh, Lorraine S., and Gordon W. Lathrop. *Using Evangelical Lutheran Worship: The Sunday Assembly*. Minneapolis: Augsburg Fortress, 2008.

Fortesque, Adrian, J. B. O'Connell, and Alcuin Reid, osb. *The Ceremonies of the Roman Rite Described*, 15th rev. ed. London: Burns and Oates/Continuum, 2009. "Fortesque and O'Connell" has been the standard ceremonial manual for the celebration of the Roman Rite for decades. Successive editions have reflected changes in the general instructions. The 15th edition has been updated in the light of Pope Benedict XVI's Summorum Pontificum.

Galley, Howard E. *The Ceremonies of the Eucharist: A Guide to Celebration*. Cambridge: Cowley, 1989.

Hovda, Robert W. *Strong, Loving, and Wise: Presiding in Liturgy*. Washington, DC: The Liturgical Conference, 1982; subsequent printings Collegeville: Liturgical, with a foreword by Godfrey Diekmann, OSB. With an eye for detailed planning of the liturgy, Hovda does not fail to develop the spirituality of the presiding minister.

Kavanagh, Aidan. *Elements of Rite: A Handbook of Liturgical Style*. New York: Pueblo, 1982. A how-to guide for worship leaders (especially the clergy, but also laypeople) that is less concerned with explaining rubrics than inculcating a deeper understand of the nature of ritual and its theological basis.

Micks, Marianne H. *The Future Present: The Phenomenon of Christian Worship*. New York: Seabury, 1970.

Pfatteicher, Philip H., and Carlos Messerli. *Manual on the Liturgy: Lutheran Book of Worship*. Minneapolis: Augsburg, 1978.

Schalk, Carl. *First Person Singular: Reflections on Worship, Liturgy, and Children*. St. Louis: Morning Star Music, 1998.

Senn, Frank C. *The Pastor as Worship Leader: A Manual for Corporate Worship*. Minneapolis: Augsburg, 1977. Long out-of-print, but still available with some searching.

Afterword
In Lieu of a Bibliography
of Current Denominational Worship Books

had intended to include in this introduction to Christian liturgy a bibliography of current denominational worship books but concluded that it would be an impossible job.

What denominations should be included? Some traditions, like Orthodox and Pentecostal, don't provide books "in the pews" as the Reformation traditions have done. It's not that the Orthodox don't use books; indeed, it takes about twenty books to get through the whole round of liturgies—and that's for every Eastern Orthodox tradition! On the other end of the liturgical spectrum, those who offer contemporary services buy music for the worship team but words are projected on screens for the worshipers.

What languages should be included? Even in American denominations one finds official denominational resources in, for instance, Spanish or Mandarin Chinese as well as English, like the *Chinese Lutheran Book of Worship* (2005) and *Libro de Liturgia y Cántico* (1998). But churches from other parts of the world are also producing significant worship resources in their own language, and in the context of global Christianity these should not be ignored.

What books should be included within denominational traditions? Some book-centered traditions, like the Anglican and Lutheran, are producing an ongoing series of resources to supplement their principal worship books. A case in point would be *Common Worship*, the series of services authorized by the General Synod of the Church of England and launched on the first Sunday of Advent in 2000, which is up to seven books and still counting. Also, in these traditions parishes and congregations are free to continue using books authorized prior to the current official ones. Thus parishes in the Church of England may still use the 1662 *Book of Common Prayer*, and many still do. In the Evangelical Lutheran Church in America, one can still find congregations using the *Service Book and Hymnal* (1958) as well as *Lutheran Book of Worship* (1979), *Evangelical Lutheran Worship* (2006), and the supplemental *With One Voice* (1995). In the Lutheran Church–Missouri Synod, one can still find congregations using *The Lutheran Hymnal* (1941) as well as *Lutheran Worship* (1982) and *Lutheran Service Book* (2006).

In the Roman Catholic Church, the new English-language Sacramentary and Missal is being implemented just as this book goes to press. But parishes may also receive permission to celebrate the 1962 *Ordo Missae* in Latin (the final version of the so-called Tridentine Rite).

And then there is the situation that some resources regarded as excellent by professional liturgists, such as *The United Methodist Book of Worship* (1992) and the *Book of Common Worship* (1993), are not used by many United Methodist and Presbyterian congregations, which also have their previous books and the influence of revivalism.

This brief survey provides an opportunity to reinforce a view I have long espoused, namely, that the liturgy is not the book. The liturgy is the public work of the people. It is what the people of God do when they assemble for word and sacrament and prayer. That includes everything that is done in this assembly, from the rituals of gathering to the rituals of sending. This doesn't mean that there won't be a script. The script may be exactly what's in the prescribed worship books or it may be cobbled together from several sources. But the liturgy will include things that are in the books and things that are not in the books. Some of the nonscripted practices or uses will be determined by local conditions in terms of space and leadership personnel available and the cultural heritage of the assembly. This public work is all done in the presence of God, who also works through these means of grace to communicate his saving grace to his people, thus making the people's Spirit-inspired work his own. The liturgy is finally the work of God, the divine liturgy: offered in the Spirit to the Father through the Son.

Chronology
of Events and Documents

c. 30 CE	Crucifixion, death, resurrection, and ascension of Jesus the Christ; the outpouring of the Holy Spirit on the Day of Pentecost. The birth of the Christian church.
50–100	New Testament writings
70	Destruction of the Jerusalem temple
90	Rabbinic Council of Jamnia finalizes the canonization of the Tanak (Old Testament).
c. 100	*Didache.* The earliest church order.
c. 110–115	Letters of Ignatius of Antioch discuss the relationship of the bishop and the Eucharist.
c. 150	*First Apology* of Justin Martyr. Chapters 65–67 describe Christian sacramental liturgies.
c. 150	*The Shepherd of Hermas.* An early witness to the practice of penance.
c. 165	The Paschal Homily of Melito of Sardis. A witness to the Quartodeciman Pascha (Easter) in Asia Minor.
c. 190	Conflict over the date of Easter between Asia Minor and Rome
c. 200–220	Writings of Tertullian of Carthage on baptism, penance, prayer, etc.
c. 200	*Mishnah.* The compilation of cases that reflect debates between 70–200 CE by the group of rabbinic sages known as the Tannaim.
c. 215	*The Apostolic Tradition* attributed to Hippolytus of Rome (date and author now questioned).
249–251	Reign of Emperor Decius. Empire-wide persecution of Christians. Dispute between Bishops Cyprian of Carthage and Stephen of Rome over the reconciliation of lapsed Christians.
c. 250	*Didascalia Apostolorum* (Doctrine of the Twelve Apostles). A Syrian church order that incorporates parts of the *Didache.* Originally written in Greek, it survives in Syriac.

c. 300	*Apostolic Church Order*. A church order that served the Egyptian, Ethiopian, and Arabian churches, and rivaled in authority and esteem the *Didache*, under which name it sometimes went.
284–305	Reign of Emperor Diocletian. He reorganized the Roman Empire, attempted to restore old values, initiated an empire-wide persecution of Christians, then abdicated.
306–337	Reign of Emperor Constantine; co-emperor, 306–323; sole emperor 323–337.
313	Edict of Milan. A letter signed by emperors Constantine I and Licinius that proclaimed religious toleration in the Roman Empire, including Christianity. Property the Roman government confiscated during persecution was returned to the churches.
c. 313ff.	The Lateran Palace was given to the bishop of Rome by Emperor Constantine. The palace basilica was converted and extended, eventually becoming the cathedral of Rome, the seat of the popes as bishops of Rome.
321	Emperor Constantine proclaims Sunday a day of rest.
325	Council of Nicea. The first ecumenical council, which promulgated an ecumenical creed and established the date of Easter (Pascha).
325ff.	Emperor Constantine orders a pilgrimage church to be built on the site of Christ's death and resurrection in Jerusalem (The Church of the Holy Selpulchre) and on the site of his birth in Bethlehem (The Church of the Nativity), under the direction of his mother, Helena. In the excavations for the Selpuchre church it was believed that the true cross of Christ was discovered.
c. 350	Prayer Book (*Euchologion*) of Sarapion of Thumis in the Nile Delta, a strong supporter of Athanasius in his battle against Arianism. Contains a eucharistic prayer similar in structure to the Anaphora of St. Mark, which quotes the *Didache*.
367	Thirty-Ninth Festal Letter (Easter Letter) of Athanasius of Alexandria. In it, he listed the same twenty-seven books of the New Testament that are in use today as well as a twenty-two-book Old Testament (several combined that are separate in the English Bible).
c. 313–387	Cyril, bishop of Jerusalem (350–387). His catechetical and mystagogical homilies describe the process of Christian initiation and the liturgy in late fourth-century Jerusalem.
c. 380	*Apostolic Constitutions*. A West Syrian church order. The first six books are based on the *Didascalia Apostolorum*. The seventh book is based on the *Didache*. The eighth book is a mixed compilation that includes the *Apostolic Tradition* attributed to Hippolytus, a forty-six-book Old Testament canon which essentially corresponds to that of the Septuagint, a twenty-six-book

New Testament canon (excludes Revelation). The liturgy in Book 8 has been erroneously called the Clementine Liturgy.

381–384   Pilgrimage of the Spanish nun Egeria to the Holy Land. She describes the liturgies she witnessed in her travel diary.

340–397   Ambrose, bishop of Milan (374–397). His treatises *On the Mysteries* and *On the Sacraments* describe Christian initiation in northern Italy and express his sacramental theology. He is the author of several Latin office hymns.

347–407   John Chrysostom, presbyter in Antioch (386–398), bishop of Constantinople (398–407). Known for his forceful preaching, with clues both to liturgical practices and to the deportment of worshipers.

350–428   Theodore, bishop of Mopsuestia (392–430). Known for his mystagogical catecheses.

354–430   Augustine, bishop of Hippo in North Africa (396–430). Greatest teacher in the Latin Church of antiquity. His sermons and letters give clues to worship in his small church in a North African port city.

379–395   Reign of Emperor Theodosius I. Nicene Christianity is made the state religion.

410   Conquest of the city of Rome by Alaric the Visigoth.

416   Letter 25 of Pope Innocent I to Bishop Decentius of Gubbio in which he asks for unity in worship on the basis of the liturgy in Rome.

431   Council of Ephesus. Defined Mary as Theotokos (God-bearer or Mother of God) to protect the divinity of Christ and condemned Nestorius, bishop of Constantinople, for making a sharp distinction between the humanity and divinity of Christ.

440–461   Pontificate of Pope Leo I the Great.

451   Council of Chalcedon. Defined Christ as one person in two natures with the help of Pope Leo's *Tome*. Followers of Cyril of Alexandria in Alexandria and Antioch stressed the union of the two natures and were called "monophysites."

476   Fall of Rome to Attila the Hun. The last Roman emperor in the West.

492–496   Pontificate of Pope Gelasius I, to whom liturgical texts are attributed that are included in the Verona Sacramentary.

c. 530   The Rule of Benedict composed in Italy, based on earlier compilations. It defined the cenobitic- (community) type monastic life that came to be the norm in the West.

532–537   Construction of the Church of the Holy Wisdom (Hagia Sophia) in Constantinople on the order of Emperor Justinian. It was the largest cathedral in the world for nearly a thousand years and served as the patriarchal church of Constantinople and the religious focal point of the Eastern Orthodox Church. When Constantinople was conquered by the

	Ottoman Turks in 1483, Sultan Mehmed II ordered the building to be converted into a mosque. Mosaics were whitewashed and minarets added. In 1935 it was converted into a museum by the Republic of Turkey. The mosaics have been uncovered.
590–604	Pontificate of Pope Gregory I (the Great). Reforms of the Roman liturgy; mission to England of Augustine of Canterbury and forty Benedictine monks.
622	The birth of Islam.
633	The Fourth Council of Toledo. Presided over by Bishop Isidore of Seville (d. 636). Gave the Hispanic or Mozarabic Rite its final form.
638	Muslim conquest of Jerusalem.
c. 700	*Ordo Romanus Primus.* The order of the papal liturgy in the station churches of Rome. It describes the Easter Day liturgy.
c. 750	*Ordo Romanus XI.* This baptismal ordo compiled in Gaul attests to Roman usage transplanted north of the Alps. It provides for seven scrutinies of the elect between the third week of Lent and the morning of Holy Saturday.
c. 750	Gelasian Sacramentary (Codex Reginensis 316) copied near Paris. A Roman presbyteral liturgical book. It provides prayers for Christian initiation that relate to Ordo XI and the oldest extant version of the Roman Canon (eucharistic prayer).
785	Pope Hadrian sends a "Gregorian" Sacramentary, a pontifical liturgical book, to Charlemagne. It was copied with a supplement (*Hucusque*, "Up to this point") to provide texts for Frankish feasts.
787	The Seventh Ecumenical Council (Nicea II) resolves the iconoclastic controversy that began in 711, although the struggle continued until 843.
799	Theodore becomes abbot of the Stoudion monastery in Constantinople and begins working on blending of Palestinian monastic traditions with Constantinopolitan cathedral tradition, providing the so-called Byzantine liturgical synthesis.
c. 800	First textual evidence of the Byzantine liturgies of St. John Chrysostom and St. Basil (although the latter is not named) in *Codex Barberini gr.* 336.
800	Pope Leo III crowns Charlemagne Holy Roman Emperor on Christmas Day.
825	Controversy over the Eucharist between two monks of Corbie, Paschasius Radbertus and Ratramnus that lays out the eucharistic debates in the West leading to the doctrine of transubstantiation.
875	Death of Rabbi Amram Goan or Amram bar Sheshna, a famous Gaon or head of the Jewish Talmud Academy of Sura in the ninth century. He was the first to arrange a complete liturgy for the synagogue. His Prayer Book (*Siddur Rab Amram* or *Seder Rav Amram*), which took the form of

	a long *responsum* to the Jews of Spain, is still extant and was an important influence on most of the current rites in use among the Jews.
909	Founding of the monastery of Cluny. By the close of the eleventh century there were about six hundred Cluniac monasteries in western Europe that promoted common liturgical customs.
c. 950	Romano-Germanic Pontifical. A set of Latin documents of liturgical practice compiled in St. Alban's Abbey, Mainz, under the reign of William, Archbishop of Mainz.
988	Conversion of Russia to Byzantine Orthodoxy. During the ninth century the Greek missionary brothers Cyril and Methodius invented a Slavic alphabet using Greek characters and translated the Bible and the liturgy into Slavonic.
1054	Mutual excommunications of the bishops of Rome and Constantinople and the East-West schism.
1073–1085	Pontificate of Pope Gregory VII (Hildebrand). This "second Gregorian reform" undertook the restoration of the Roman ordo and insisted that episcopal sees of the Latin Church follow it.
1137–1144	Building of the great abbey church of Saint-Denis near Paris by Abbot Suger that displayed the first characteristics of Gothic architecture.
1215	The Fourth Lateran Council convened by Pope Innocent III. It promulgated the doctrine of transubstantiation; reaffirmed in the requirement that every Christian who has reached the age of reason (seven to eight years old) confess their sins and receive Holy Communion at least once a year at Easter (Canon 21); forbade noncelibate living among the clergy; regulated Jewish-Christian relationships and placed restrictions on the Jewish communities (Canons 67–70).
1225–1274	Thomas Aquinas, greatest scholastic theologian. Author of texts for the Mass and Office of Corpus Christi as well as the *Summa Theologia*.
1264	The bull *Transiturus de hoc mundo* of Pope Urban IV extends the Feast of Corpus Christi to the universal Church.
1300s	Rise of the mendicant religious orders (Dominicans, Franciscans, Augustinians). The invention of missals and breviaries to include all necessary materials for the celebration of Mass and praying the liturgy of the hours in one portable book.
1400s	Rise of paraliturgical popular devotions such as the rosary and stations of the cross.
1453	The conquest of Constantinople by the Muslim Ottoman Turks.
1517	Martin Luther's Ninety-Five Theses concerning the sale of indulgences.
1520	Luther's reformatory writings. *The Babylonian Captivity of the Church* attacks the medieval sacramental system.
1523	Luther's *Form of the Mass and Communion for the Church of Wittenberg*.

1523	Ulrich Zwingli's *An Attack on the Canon of the Mass*.
1524	First German liturgies appear.
1525	Zwingli's Service of the Word and *Action or Use of the Lord's Supper*.
1526	Luther's *German Mass and Order of Service*.
1529	Luther's Small and Large Catechisms.
1529	The *Church Manual* of Olavus Petri (first vernacular occasional services book).
1531	Olavus Petri's *Swedish Mass* for use in Stockholm.
1533	Brandenburg-Nuremberg Church Order.
1536	First edition of the reformed Breviary of Cardinal Quinonez.
1537	Martin Bucer's German Service at Strassburg.
1540	John Calvin's French Service at Strasbourg.
1540	The Mark Brandenburg Church Order.
1542	John Calvin's *Form of Prayers* at Geneva.
1543	The Cologne Church Order of Archbishop Hermann von Wied prepared by Martin Bucer and Philip Melanchthon.
1544	The English Litany published.
1545	Valentin Babst *Geystliche Lieder*. Complete Lutheran hymnal with the preface by Martin Luther.
1545–1563	The Council of Trent meets intermittently.
1548	Order for Communion in English inserted into the Latin Mass.
1549	The First Prayer Book of King Edward VI authorized by an Act of Uniformity.
1552	The Second Prayer Book of King Edward VI authorized by an Act of Uniformity.
1556	John Knox, *The Forme of Prayers*.
1559	*The Book of Common Prayer* under Elizabeth I authorized by an Act of Uniformity.
1560	The Latin Edition of *The Book of Common Prayer* for use in universities.
1562	Genevan (French) Psalter—complete versification of psalms set to tunes by Louis Bourgeois (1510–1561).
1562	Sternhold and Hopkins (English) Psalter.
1562	*The Book of Common Order* of the Church of Scotland, based on Knox's *Forme of Prayers*
1563	The Council of Trent adjourns and authorizes the Roman Curia to reform the liturgy.
1568	The Roman Breviary of Pope Pius V.
1570	The Roman Missal of Pope Pius V.
1571	The Swedish Church Order of Archbishop Laurentius Petri.
1576	The controversial "Red Book" Liturgy of King Johan III of Sweden.
1593	The Uppsala Synod adopts the Augsburg Confession and restores the Church Order of Archbishop Laurentius Petri.

1594	The Roman Pontifical. The book of services requiring a bishop such as confirmation and ordination.
1604	Hampton Court Conference. Fourth Book of Common Prayer.
1611	English Bible authorized under King James I (King James Version).
1614	The Roman Ritual. The book of occasional services.
1618–1648	Thirty Years' War. Ravages of war destroy liturgical books in Germany.
1630–1715	The Chinese Rites controversy. A dispute within the Roman Catholic Church between the Vatican and the Society of Jesus about whether certain elements of Chinese folk religion (including ancestor veneration, devotional practices at Confucian academies and the various rites and ceremonies of the Imperial cult) should be considered idolatrous. These practices were condemned in a papal bull of Clement XI in 1715.
1637	Scottish *Book of Common Prayer* ("Archbishop Lauds' liturgy").
1641	John Cotton's *The True Constitution of a Particular Visible Church Proved by Scripture*. The order of service used by Puritans in New England.
1642	Beginning of English Civil War.
1644	The Westminster Directory authorized by Parliament for the Church of England during the Puritan Commonwealth.
1661	Savoy Conference on Prayer Book revision.
1662	Fifth Book of Common Prayer and fourth Act of Uniformity.
1685–1750	Johann Sebastian Bach, cantor of St. Thomas School and Church in Leipzig 1723–1750.
1689	William III and Mary II jointly reign in England and Scotland. Abortive "Liturgy of Comprehension." Establishment of Presbyterianism in the Church of Scotland. Non-jurors' schism in England and Scotland.
1721	Czar Peter the Great convenes a Holy Synod, a council of ten clergymen, to take the place of the Patriarch and reform the Russian Orthodox Church.
1740s	First Great Awakening in North America.
1748	Henry Melchior Muhlenberg organizes the first Lutheran church structure in North America, the Ministerium of Pennsylvania, which adopts Muhlenberg's Liturgy.
1741–1790	Joseph II, Holy Roman Emperor (1765–1790) and ruler of the Habsburg lands from 1780 to 1790. He promoted religious toleration and Enlightenment Catholicism.
1784	John Wesley's Sunday Service for the Methodists in North America.
1786	Synod of Pistoia. A diocesan synod held under the presidency of Scipione de' Ricci (1741–1810), bishop of Pistoia, and the patronage of Leopold, grand-duke of Tuscany, with a view to preparing the ground for a national council and a reform of the Tuscan Church to make church rites more intelligible to lay worshipers.
1789	First *Book of Common Prayer* of the Protestant Episcopal Church in the U.S.A.

1801	Cane Ridge Camp Meeting. The beginning of the Second Great Awakening in America.
1833	John Keble's Sermon on "National Apostasy" in St. Mary's Church in Oxford. This sermon marks the beginning of the Anglo-Catholic movement, which was also known as the Tractarian Movement after its series of publications Tracts for the Times (1833–1841).
1833	Reestablishment of the Solesmes Abbey or St. Peter's Abbey, Solesmes (Abbaye Saint-Pierre de Solesmes). This Benedictine monastery in Solesmes (Sarthe) became famous as the source of the restoration of Benedictine monastic life in France and liturgical research under Dom Prosper Guéranger.
1835	Charles Grandison Finney's *Lectures On The Revival of Religion*. A uniquely American approach to worship.
1844	Wilhelm Loehe's *Agende für christliche Gemeinden des lutherischen Bekenntnisses*. A liturgy for Lutheran emigrant congregations in the American Midwest that reflects the confessional and liturgical revival in Germany.
1868	The *Church Book* of the General Council of the Evangelical Lutheran Church.
1888	The Common Service of the Evangelical Lutheran Church. An English language liturgy based on the sixteenth-century church orders adopted by Lutheran synods.
1903	*Tra le Sollecitudini. Motu Proprio* of Pope Pius X on Sacred Music, which encourages the use of Gregorian chant and congregational singing.
1906	Azusa Street revival in Los Angeles. The birth of Pentecostalism.
1917	*The Common Service Book of the Lutheran Church.*
1922	*Book of Common Prayer* for the Anglican Church of Canada.
1928	Proposed revision of the 1662 *Book of Common Prayer* defeated. Revised American *Book of Common Prayer*.
1941	*The Lutheran Hymnal* authorized by the Synodical Conference of North America.
1940s	The first National Liturgical Weeks in America promoted by the Benedictines of St. John's Abbey, Collegeville, Minnesota. The Liturgical Conference is organized.
1940s	Protestant ecumenical monastery founded in Taizé, France, which develops new forms of chant and prayer.
1950s	Billy Graham crusades exemplify post–World War II religious revival.
1951, 1956	The Liturgies of Holy Week restored by Pope Pius XII.
1958	The *Service Book and Hymnal* of the Lutheran Church in America.
1958	*The Agenda* of The United Lutheran Church in Germany.
1962	The Roman Missal of Pope John XXIII incorporates calendrical changes.

1962–1965   The Second Vatican Ecumenical Council. *Sancrosanctam Concilium*, the Constitution on the Sacred Liturgy, is promulgated on December 4, 1963.

1969   The Roman Missal of Pope Paul VI, based on principles of the Second Vatican Council.

1970s   Liturgical renewal in Protestant Churches inspired by the reformed Roman Mass.

1970s   The Zairean Rite of the Eucharist. An inculturated variation of the Ordinary Form of the Roman Rite of the Roman Catholic Church used to a very limited extent in some African countries since the late 1970s.

1975   Willow Creek Community Church in Barrington, Illinois, popularizes seeker services.

1976   *The Book of Common Prayer* of the Episcopal Church in the U.S.A.; trial use in 1976, authorized in 1979.

1978   *Lutheran Book of Worship* prepared by churches participating in the Inter-Lutheran Commission on Worship.

1980   *Alternative Services* of the Church of England.

1982   *Baptism, Eucharist, Ministry.* Statement of ecumenical convergence approved by the Faith and Order Commission of the World Council of Churches meeting in Lima, Peru (and hence called the "Lima" Statement). A eucharistic liturgy based on the principles of the Lima statement was prepared for use at the Sixth Assembly of the World Council of Churches in Vancouver, B.C. in 1983 (called the Lima Liturgy).

1983   Consultation on Common Texts issues the Common Lectionary.

1985   *Alternative Services* of the Anglican Church in Canada.

1989   The United Methodist *Book of Worship*.
       A New Zealand Prayer Book (Anglican). Noted for its inculturation in the Maori culture.

1992   Revised Common Lectionary.

1993   *The Book of Common Worship* of the Presbyterian Church (USA).

1995   *A Prayer Book for Australia* (Anglican).

1996   The Nairobi Statement on Worship and Culture. The report from the third international consultation of the Lutheran World Federation's Study Team on Worship and Culture, held in Nairobi, Kenya, in January, 1996.

1998   *Libro de Liturgia y Cántico.* A Spanish-language worship resource prepared by the Evangelical Lutheran Church in America.

1998   *Worship and Praise Songbook.* A contemporary song resource prepared by the Evangelical Lutheran Church in America.

1999   *This Far By Faith: An African American Resource for Worship.* Prepared by the Evangelical Lutheran Church in America and the Lutheran Church–Missouri Synod.

1999   *Evangelische Gottesdienstbuch.* Used in the United Lutheran Church in Germany and the Evangelical Church in Germany, a union of Lutheran and Reformed territorial Churches.

2000   *Common Worship* (Church of England). Not one book, but several. Available as downloadable material.

2005   *Chinese Lutheran Book of Worship.*

2006   *Evangelical Lutheran Worship* commended for use in the Evangelical Lutheran Church in America and the Evangelical Lutheran Church in Canada

2006   *Lutheran Service Book.* Authorized in the Lutheran Church–Missouri Synod.

Glossary
of Liturgical Terms

ablutions
Washings, such as washing one's hands before touching holy things (*lavabo*) at the offertory or rinsing out the chalice after communion.

absolution
Pronouncement of forgiveness.

advent
Four-week season before Christmas in the Western church.

agape (love) feast
A fellowship meal that is not the Eucharist/Lord's Supper.

alb
Long white robe. May be worn alone or under other vestments.

altar
Table on which the bread and wine of the Eucharist are placed.

altar cloths
The linens cloths that cover the altar (e.g., fair linen).

alleluia
Latinization of the Hebrew *hallel*, meaning "praise the Lord."

Alleluia Verse
What *Lutheran Book of Worship* calls the Gradual in the older orders of service.

ambo
The podium to which one "walks" to read and proclaim the word.

anamnesis
Memorial. In eucharistic prayers it usually begins, "Remembering therefore."

anaphora
A name for the eucharistic prayer, from the invitation that precedes it: "Lift up your hearts."

anthem
A piece of choir music; derives from "antiphon."

antiphon
A brief text sung before and after, and sometimes repeated throughout, a psalm or canticle.

Ash Wednesday
The first day of Lent, on which ashes are customarily imposed on the heads of penitents in the form of a cross.

baptistery
Space within the church building that houses the pool or font used for baptism.

benediction
Solemn blessing, usually given by the presiding minister at the end of a service.

bema
Platform from which the word is proclaimed and from which the choir sings
In Byzantine churches (e.g., Hagia Sophia) it used to be in the middle of the church.

Benediction of the Blessed Sacrament, Solemn
A popular devotion in which, after Sunday Vespers, the reserved communion host is exposed to the people and adored.

breviary
Book or set of books that includes all the material needed for the daily prayer services.

burse
A liturgical purse that is placed on the veiled chalice and contains purificators for wiping the rim of the chalice during the administration of Holy Communion.

canticle
A prose hymn, some of which are biblical.

cassock
The gown worn by clergy, usually but not necessarily black.

catechumenate
The process of preparing catechumens for Holy Baptism.

catechumens
The group of candidates being prepared for Holy Baptism.

chalice and paten
The cup and plate used for Holy Communion.

chancel
Portion of the worship space occupied by the ministers.

chasuble
The poncho-like outer vestment worn by the presiding minister at the Eucharist.

chrism
Oil used to anoint the baptized and the sick.

Christmas season
The twelve days between December 25 and January 6.

Compline
Prayer office at the end of the day (before retiring) that "completes" the day, from the Latin *Completorium.*

cope
An ornate cloak worn by the officiant at solemn services other than the Eucharist.

communion in both kinds
Receiving both bread and wine in Holy Communion.

corporal
Square cloth placed on top of the fair linen on which the corpus (body of Christ) is laid.

cross, sign of the
Tracing the outline of the cross on one's body (head, stomach, shoulder, shoulder).

crucifix
A cross with the body of Christ affixed to it.

devotions
Prayers and readings that are not part of the official liturgy, sometimes called "paraliturgical."

doxology
An expression of praise, usually of the Trinity, often at the end of canticles and hymns.

Easter season
The fifty days between Easter Day and the Day of Pentecost.

Easter Vigil
Night service on Easter Eve that includes a service of light, many readings, baptism, and the Eucharist.

epiclesis
An invocation, usually of the Holy Spirit.

Epiphany, the
January 6. Celebrates the visit of the wise men to the infant Jesus or the baptism of Christ.

Eucharist
Another name for Holy Communion, from the Greek word for "thanksgiving."

eucharistic prayer
The Great Thanksgiving over the bread and wine or over the font.

euchology
A collection of prayers of blessing.

exorcism in baptism
A command to the devil to depart from the candidate being claimed for Christ.

fasting
Abstaining from eating and drinking for a period of time. It was common to fast before receiving communion. Lent is a season of fasting. Penitential days are days of fasting.

fair linen
The white linen cloth placed on the altar mensa.

Gloria in excelsis
A canticle known as the greater doxology, "Glory to God in the highest." sung in the Mass/Holy Eucharist/Service of Holy Communion on Sundays and festivals except during Advent and Lent.

Gloria Patri
The lesser doxology, "Glory (be) to the Father, and to the Son, and to the Holy Spirit; as it was in the beginning, is now, and will be forever Amen." It is usually sung at the end of psalms and canticles.

Good Friday
The day on which Christ's death on the cross, his atoning sacrifice, is commemorated.

Gospel acclamations
"Glory to you, O Lord" at the announcement of the reading of the Gospel; "Praise to you, O Christ" at the conclusion of the reading. *Evangelical Lutheran Worship* calls the Alleluia Verse the Gospel acclamation.

Gradual
The psalmody between the Epistle and Gospel in the Mass. "Alleluia" was sung before and after the psalm verses except during Lent.

Holy Week
The week between Palm Sunday and Easter Day.

homily
A commentary on and application of the biblical texts read at liturgies.

hours, liturgy of the
The daily prayer offices that mark of times of the day.

hymn
A song addressed to the deity.

icons
Images of Christ and the saints, used especially in the Orthodox churches as "windows into heaven."

Introit
Psalmody sung at the beginning of the Mass as an entrance song. In the Middle Ages it acquired this form: antiphon, verse, Gloria Patri, antiphon.

laity
The people of God. They have an indispensable role in the liturgy.

Lauds
Morning praise at sunrise.

lectionary
A system of biblical readings.

Lent
The forty-day penitential season between Ash Wednesday and Easter Day, not including Sundays.

litany
A prayer with a repeating refrain sung or said by the people.

liturgy
1. "The people's work," from the Greek *leitourgia* 2. Official orders of worship.

Lord's Prayer
The prayer taught by Jesus to his disciples ("Our Father in heaven").

Matins
An early morning prayer office before lauds, sometimes called the vigil office.

Maundy Thursday
The day on which the anniversary of the institution of the Lord's Supper is observed Receives its name from the "mandate" or "new commandment" of Christ to love one another, as demonstrated in the washing of feet.

minister
Generic name for anyone with a liturgical leadership role. May be lay or ordained.

missal
Book that contains all the material needed for the celebration of the Mass, both the ordinary and the propers.

music, liturgical
Music used for the liturgy, including chants, hymns, and music for choir.

mystagogy
Teaching about the sacraments, called "mysteries" in Greek.

nave
The central portion of the worship space occupied by the assembly.

Offertory
1. The gathering of the gifts of the people while the table is set for Holy Communion.
2. The psalmody sung during this action.

officiant
The minister who officiates at a service, especially an occasional service (e.g., wedding, funeral) or the prayer offices.

ordinary
The portions of the Mass that do not change.

ordination
Rite of setting aside by prayer and the laying on of hands to exercise a public office in the church.

Ordinary Time
The seasons after the Epiphany and after Pentecost. The color green is used.

ordo
The sequence of parts or order of a service.

paraments
Clothes in the color of the liturgical day or season that hang from the altar and ambo.

penance
1. The sacrament of absolution or reconciliation. 2. An act of satisfaction for sin imposed on the penitent by the confessor.

penitential days
Days of fasting on which the Great Litany may be sung. Includes the seasons of Advent and Lent (never Sundays) and the Ember Days in the Roman tradition.

Pentecost
The fiftieth day after Passover/Easter. Commemorates the outpouring of the Holy Spirit on the disciples in Acts 2.

pontifical
Book that contains all the rites used by a bishop, including confirmation and ordination.

presiding minister
The minister who presides over the liturgy. The term has been used in liturgical renewal in place of "officiant." A shortened form is "presider."

propers
Texts that change in an order of service according to the day or season.

pulpit
A preaching platform. In medieval churches often attached to a pillar in the nave.

purificator
Cloth used to wipe the rim of the chalice after people drink from it.

reredos
A screen or decoration behind the altar in a church, usually depicting religious iconography or images. In French and sometimes in English, this is called a retable.

reservation of the Eucharist
Setting aside bread (and sometimes wine) from the eucharistic celebration for later distribution or Solemn Benediction. Places of reservation include a sacrament house (free-standing miniature house on a pedestal), an ambry (a box in a side wall), or a tabernacle (a box placed above the altar mensa or table top).

responsive reading
A text read by a leader and the people in alternation.

responsory
Words of psalmody or other Scripture sung after the reading in Matins, Vespers, or Compline.

rubrics
Directions for performing a liturgy, printed in red.

sanctuary
The portion of the worship space around the altar. Sometimes it refers to the entire worship space.

sacramentals
Material objects, things or actions (*sacramentalia*) set apart or blessed. Examples: crosses, statues, icons, ashes, bells (especially church bells), blessed salt, candles, chalk, the nativity scene, the Advent wreath, crucifixes, holy oil, holy water, incense, liturgical vessels (e.g., chalices), medals (e.g., the Miraculous Medal or the Saint Benedict Medal), palm branches, graves, funeral palls, religious habits, vestments, rosaries, wedding rings. The use of holy water as a sacramental for protection against evil is almost exclusive to Roman Catholics.

sacraments
Definitions vary among Christian traditions. Broadly understood as ordinances instituted by God or Christ that use a material element (e.g., water, oil, bread, wine) and promise blessings (e.g., forgiveness of sins). St. Augustine of Hippo defined sacraments as outward signs of an inward grace. The number of sacraments varies: Catholics and Orthodox count seven, most Protestants count two (Holy Baptism and Holy Communion). Augustine counted at least twelve.

sermon
An address on a biblical text, doctrinal loci, or ethical topic.

sponsors
Those who present the candidates for baptism and make promises on their behalf. Also called "godparents."

stole
The long narrow band of cloth in the color of the day or season given to ministers at their ordination. Worn around the neck and hanging down in the front.

thurible
Vessel used for burning incense on coals, usually with a chain for swinging.

torches
Candles carried on poles in processions.

triduum
Three days. Historically there were three days of the passion (Thursday, Friday, Saturday in Holy Week) and three days of the resurrection (Sunday, Monday, Tuesday in Easter Week).

validity, concept of
As applied to the sacraments, it concerns the conditions under which a sacrament is considered valid. Concern for validity often looks for minimal conditions under which a sacrament "works."

Vespers
The late afternoon prayer office. Usually prayed at sundown.

vestments
Garments worn by liturgical ministers only for the liturgy.

voluntary
Piece of music played on the organ or other instruments during the offering or communion.

For further reading

Bradshaw, Paul F., ed. *The New Westminster Dictionary of Liturgy and Worship*. Louisville: Westminster John Knox, 2002.

Fink, Peter, ed. *The New Dictionary of Sacramental Worship*. Collegeville: Liturgical/Michael Glazier, 1990.

Patte, Daniel, ed. *The Cambridge Dictionary of Christianity*. Cambridge: Cambridge University Press, 2010

Notes

1. Liturgy: A Practical Science

1. Hans-Joachim Schulz, *The Byzantine Liturgy: Symbolic Structure and Faith Exposition*, trans. Matthew J. O'Connell (New York: Pueblo, 1986), 17–20.

2. See Jean Daniélou, *The Bible and the Liturgy* (Notre Dame: University of Notre Dame Press, 1956; repr. 1966), 70–113.

3. Robert Taft, "The Liturgy of the Great Church," *Dumbarton Oaks Papers* 34/35 (1980–81): 62.

4. See Daniélou, *Bible and the Liturgy*, 262–86.

5. Gordon Lathrop, *Holy Things: A Liturgical Theology* (Minneapolis: Fortress Press, 1993), even sees theological meaning in the juxtaposition of parts of the ordo.

6. Leonel L. Mitchell, *Praying Shapes Believing: A Theological Commentary on The Book of Common Prayer* (Harrisburg: Morehouse, 1985) is a fine example of a pastoral exercise in liturgical theology.

7. Aidan Kavanagh, *On Liturgical Theology* (New York: Pueblo, 1984), 73ff.

8. See Margaret Barker, *Temple Themes in Christian Worship* (London: T & T Clark, 2007).

9. Martin Luther, *Luther's Works*, vol. 5: *Lectures on Genesis, Chapters 26–30*, ed. Jaroslav Pelikan (St. Louis: Concordia, 1968), 141.

10. See David N. Power, *Sacrament: The Language of God's Giving* (New York: Crossroad/Herder and Herder, 1999).

2. History and Culture

1. Kurt Niederwimmer, *The Didache: A Commentary*, trans. Linda M. Maloney, ed. Harold W. Attridge, Hermeneia (Minneapolis: Fortress Press, 1998).

2. See Paul F. Bradshaw, Maxwell E. Johnson, and L. Edward Phillips, *The Apostolic Tradition: A Commentary*, ed. Harold W. Attridge, Hermeneia (Minneapolis: Fortress Press, 2002).

3. See John Julius Norwich, *A Short History of Byzantium* (New York: Knopf, 1997).

4. Robert Taft, S.J., *The Liturgy of the Hours in the East and West* (Collegeville: Liturgical, 1986), 277.

5. See Eric Palazzo, *A History of Liturgical Books from the Beginning to the Thirteenth Century*, trans. Madeleine Beaumont (Collegeville: Liturgical, 1998), 19–82, 173–86.

6. Ibid., 107–10, 169–74.

7. Ibid., 229–32.

8. Ibid., 233–35.

9. See Theodore Klauser, *A Short History of the Western Liturgy*, trans. John Halliburton (New York: Oxford University Press, 1969), 117–35.

10. See R. Po-Chia Hsia, *The World of Catholic Renewal 1540–1770: New Approaches to European History* (Cambridge: Cambridge University Press, 1998), 165–93.

11. See Bryan D. Spinks, *Liturgy in the Age of Reason: Worship and Sacraments in England and Scotland, 1662–c. 1800* (Farnham, UK: Ashgate, 2008).

12. See Luther D. Reed, *The Lutheran Liturgy* (Philadelphia: Fortress Press, 1959), 148–49.

13. See Ernest B. Koenker, *The Liturgical Renaissance in the Roman Catholic Church* (St. Louis: Concordia, 1954).

14. See Dennis E. Smith, *From Symposium to Eucharist: The Banquet in the Early Christian World* (Minneapolis: Fortress Press, 2003).

15. James F. White, *Protestant Worship: Traditions in Transition* (Louisville: Westminster John Knox, 1989), 171–91.

16. Ibid., 192–208.

17. See Blake Leyerle, "Meal Customs in the Greco-Roman World," in Paul F. Bradshaw and Lawrence A. Hoffman, eds., *Passover and Easter: Origin and History to Modern Times*, Two Liturgical Traditions, vol. 5 (Notre Dame: University of Notre Dame Press, 1999), 29–61.

18. See Frank C. Senn, *The People's Work: A Social History of the Liturgy* (Minneapolis: Fortress Press, 2006), 32–34.

19. See Klauser, *A Short History of the Western Liturgy*, 32–37.

20. Robert M. Royalty, *The Streets of Heaven: The Ideology of Wealth in the Apocalypse of John* (Macon: Mercer University Press, 1998), 101.

21. See Yitzhak Hen, *The Royal Patronage of Liturgy in Frankish Gaul* (London: Henry Bradshaw Society, 2001).

22. See Jean Bony, *French Gothic Architecture of the 12th and 13th Centuries* (Berkeley: University of California Press, 1983).

23. H. Richard Niebuhr, *Christ and Culture* (New York: Harper & Row, 1951).

24. See Geofrey Wainwright, *Doxology: The Praise of God in Worship, Doctrine, and Life* (New York: Oxford University Press, 1980), 382–87, who adds a "pluralist" attitude to Niebuhr's five types.

25. *Christian Worship: Unity in Cultural Diversity*, ed. S. Anita Stauffer (Geneva: Lutheran World Federation, 1996), 14ff.

26. See Anscar J. Chupungco, *Liturgies of the Future: The Process and Methods of Inculturation* (New York: Pueblo, 1989).

3. The Principal Order of Service

1. See Dennis Smith, *From Symposium to Eucharist: The Banquet in the Early Christian World* (Minneapolis: Fortress Press, 2003).

2. See Robert Taft, S.J., "How Liturgies Grow: The Evolution of the Byzantine Divine Liturgy," in *Beyond East and West: Problems in Liturgical Understanding* (Washington, DC: Pastoral, 1984), 167–92.

3. See Louis Duchesne, *Christian Worship: Its Origin and Evolution: A Study of the Latin Liturgy Up To the Time of Charlemagne*, Eng. trans., 5th ed. (London: SPCK, 1923), 189–227.

4. For a description see G. G. Willis, *Further Essays in Early Roman Liturgy* (London: SPCK, 1968), 16–20.

5. Duchesne, *Christian Worship*, 185.

6. Martin Luther, "An Order of Mass and Communion for the Church at Wittenberg," in *Luther's Works, vol. 53: Liturgy and Hymns*, ed. Ulrich S. Leupold (Philadelphia: Fortress Press, 1965), 20.

7. Ibid., 61.

8. See Luther D. Reed, *The Lutheran Liturgy*, 2d ed. (Philadelphia: Muhlenberg, 1959), 96.

9. Bard Thompson, *Liturgies of the Western Church* (Minneapolis: Fortress Press, 1980), 147–48; for the Communion Service, see 149–55.

10. H. Wayne Pipkin and John H. Yoder, eds., *Bathasar Hubmaier, Theologian of Anabaptism* (Scottdale: Herald, 1992), 395–96.

11. William D. Maxwell, *An Outline of Christian Worship: Its Development and Forms* (London: Oxford University Press, 1937), 87–111; see also Thompson, *Liturgies of the Western Church*, 159–81.

12. Maxwell, *An Outline of Christian Worship*, 112–19; Thompson, *Liturgies of the Western Church*, 185–210.

13. *The First and Second Prayer Books of King Edward VI*, Everyman Library 448 (London: Dent/New York: Dutton, 1968).

14. Thompson, *Liturgies of the Western Church*, 345–53.

15. Reed, *The Lutheran Liturgy*, 183.

16. *Lutheran Book of Worship* (Minneapolis: Augsburg /Philadelphia: Board of Publication, Lutheran Church in America, 1978). *LBW* was published in Pew and Minister's Editions. The Minister's Edition, used on the altar, contains additional eucharistic prayers.

17. *The Book of Common Prayer and Administration of the Sacraments and Other Rites and Ceremonies of the Church Together with the Psalms of David According to the Use of The Episcopal Church* (New York: Oxford University Press, 1979), 351–82.

18. *The United Methodist Book of Worship* (Nashville: United Methodist Publishing, 1992).

19. *Book of Common Worship* (Louisville: Westminster John Knox Press, 1993).

20. See James F. White, *Protestant Worship: Traditions in Transition* (Louisville: Westminster John Knox, 1989), 192–208.

21. Heather Josselyn-Cranson, "Local and Authentic: Music in Emerging Congregations," *Worship* 83 (2009): 415–30.

22. See Nathan Nettleton, "'Free-Church Bapto-Catholic': A Story of Possibilities Embraced," *Liturgy: The Journal of The Liturgical Conference* 19, no. 4 (2004): 57–67, for a truly unique example of an emergent liturgy.

23. See Horace T. Allen Jr., "*Common Lectionary*: Origins, Assumptions, Issues," *Studia Liturgica* 21 (1991): 14–30.

24. See Donald Gray, "The Contribution of the Joint Liturgical Group to the Search for an Ecumenical Lectionary," *Studia Liturgica* 21 (1991): 31–36.

25. See Karl-Heinrich Bieritz, "The Order of Readings and Sermon Texts for the German Lutheran Church," *Studia Liturgica* 21 (1991): 37–51.

26. See Paul F. Bradshaw, *The Search for the Origins of Christian Worship*, rev. ed. (New York: Oxford University Press, 2002), 118–43, for a synopsis of the current state of scholarship.

27. See Ralph Keifer, "Oblation in the First Part of the Roman Canon: An Examination of a Primitive Eucharistic Structure and Theology in Early Italian and Egyptian Sources," PhD diss., University of Notre Dame, 1972.

28. See Carl F. Wisløff, *The Gift of Communion: Luther's Controversy With Rome on Eucharistic Sacrifice*, trans. Joseph M. Shaw (Minneapolis: Augsburg, 1964).

29. See Martin Luther, "The Babylonian Captivity of the Church," in *Luther's Works, vol. 36: Word and Sacrament II*, trans. Frank C. Ahrens, ed. Helmut T. Lehmann and Abdel Ross Wentz (Philadelphia: Fortress Press, 1959), 35–57.

30. See Frank C. Senn, ed., *New Eucharistic Prayers: An Ecumenical Study of Their Development and Structure* (Mahwah: Paulist, 1987).

31. Yngve Brilioth, *Eucharistic Faith and Practice, Evangelical and Catholic*, trans. A. G. Hebert (London: SPCK, 1965; orig. Swedish pub., 1927).

32. Geoffrey Wainwright, *Eucharist and Eschatology* (London: Epworth, 1971).

33. On the differences in ceremonies between a High Mass and a Low Mass, see A. Fortescue and J. O'Connell, *The Ceremonies of the Roman Rite Described*, new ed. by Alcuin Reid, (London: Burns & Oates, 2009).

4. The Liturgy of Time

1. See Philip H. Pfatteicher, *Liturgical Spirituality* (Valley Forge: Trinity Press International, 1997), 32–39.

2. Robert Taft, S.J., *The Liturgy of the Hours in East and West: The Origins of the Divine Office and Its Meaning for Today* (Collegeville: Liturgical, 1986), 5–11.

3. Ibid., 15.

4. The first scholar to notice the difference between "monastic" and "cathedral" offices was the Philippine Benedictine Juan Mateos, O.S.B., in *Lelya-Sapra. Essai d'interpretation des matines chaldéennes*, in *Orientalia Christiana Analecta* 156 (Rome, 1959) and *Le Typicon de la Grande Eglise* (Hagia Sophia), in *Orientalia Christiana Periodica* 165–166 (Rome, 1962–63). His most accessible articles in English are "The Origin of the Divine Office," *Worship* 41 (1967): 477–85, and "The Morning and Evening Office," *Worship* 42 (1968): 31–47. Mateos's work was utilized by William G. Storey in his work on the Divine Office in the liturgical studies program at the University of Notre Dame. This distinction between types of prayer offices has been taken up by other liturgiologists such as Paul Bradshaw, *Daily Prayer in the Early Church*, Alcuin Club Collections 63 (London: SPCK, 1981/New York: Oxford University Press, 1982), and Taft, *Liturgy of the Hours in East and West*; Taft had been a student of Mateos.

5. James W. McKinnon, "Desert Monasticism and the Late Fourth Century Psalmodic Movement," *Music and Letters* 75 (1994): 505–21.

6. I participated with other students of William G. Storey in experiments with a cathedral-style office of evening prayer at the University of Notre Dame in the early 1970s that was published in *Morning Praise and Evensong*, ed. William G. Storey (Notre Dame: Fides, 1973).

7. Taft, *The Liturgy of the Hours in East and West*, 225ff. See Juan Mateos, "L'office divin chez les chaldéens," in *La prière des heures*, ed. Msgr. Cassien and B. Botte, *Les orandi* 35 (Paris: Cerf, 1963), 253–81.

8. See *East Syrian Daily Offices*, trans. from the Syriac with Introduction, Notes, and Indices and an Appendix Containing the Lectionary and Glossary by Arthur John Maclean (London: Rivington, Percival and Co., 1894).

9. See W. F. Macomber, "A Theory on the Origins of the Syrian, Maranite and Chaldean Rites," *Orientalia Christiana Periodica* 39 (1979): 235–42.

10. See Juan Mateos, "La synaxe monastique des vêpres byzantines," *Orientalia Christiana Periodica* 36 (1970): 248–72.

11. Pierre Salmon, O.S.B., *The Breviary through the Centuries*, trans. Sister David Mary, S.N.J.M. (Collegeville: Liturgical, 1962), 9.

12. *Breviarium Romanum a Francisco Cardinali Quignonio*, ed. Johanne Wickham Legg (Cambridge, 1888; repub. Westmead, Farnborough, Hants: Gregg International, 1970).

13. See J. Neal Alexander, "Luther's Reform of the Daily Office," *Worship* 57 (1983): 348–60.

14. See Frank C. Senn, *Christian Worship: Catholic and Evangelical* (Minneapolis: Fortress Press, 1997), 338–42.

15. See E. C. Ratcliff, "The Choir Offices," in *Liturgy and Worship: A Companion to the Prayer Books in the Anglican Communion*, ed. W. K. Lowther Clarke and C. Harris (London: SPCK, 1932), 257–95.

16. *Service Book and Hymnal of the Lutheran Church in America* (Minneapolis: Augsburg, 1958), 129–56.

17. See *The Liturgy of the Hours: The General Instruction with Commentary*, commentary by A.-M. Roguet (Collegeville: Liturgical, 1971).

18. See William G. Storey, "The Liturgy of the Hours: Cathedral versus Monastery," in John Gallen, ed., *Christians At Prayer* (Notre Dame: University of Notre Dame Press, 1977), 61–82.

19. See n. 6 above.

20. *The Daily Prayer of the Church*, ed. Philip Pfatteicher (Delhi: American Lutheran Publicity Bureau, 2005).

21. See Judith Maltby, "The Prayer Book and the Parish Church: From the Elizabethan Settlement to the Restoration," and William L. Sachs, "Plantations, Missions, and Colonies," in *The Oxford Guide to The Book of Common Prayer: A Worldwide Survey*, ed. Charles Hefling and Cynthia Shattuck (New York: Oxford University Press, 2006), 91, 157.

22. *Lutheran Service Book* (St. Louis: Concordia, 2006), 294–98.

23. *For All the Saints: A Prayer Book for and by the Church*, 4 vols., ed. Frederick J. Schumacher (Delhi: American Lutheran Publicity Bureau, 1995).

24. *Benedictine Daily Prayer: A Short Breviary*, ed. Maxwell E. Johnson, Oblate of St. John's Abbey, and the Monks of St. John Abbey (Collegeville: Liturgical, 2005).

5. The Church-Year Calendar

1. The decree concerning Sunday as a day of rest was "Given the 7th day of March, Crispus and Constantine being consuls, each of them for the second time." *Codex Justinianus*, lib. 3, tit. 12, 3; trans. Philip Schaff, *History of the Christian Church*, vol. 3 (1902), 380, note.

2. In 1 Cor. 16:8 Paul declares his intention of staying in Ephesus until Pentecost. This statement, in turn, is clearly reminiscent of Paul's second missionary journey, when he traveled from Corinth to Ephesus, before going to Jerusalem for Pentecost (cf. Acts 18:22).

3. See Robert Taft, S.J., *Beyond East and West: Problems in Liturgical Understanding* (Washington, D.C.: Pastoral, 1984), 66–68.

4. Thomas Talley, *The Origins of the Liturgical Year* (Collegeville: Liturgical, 1986), 148.

6. The Church Year: Advent through Lent

1. See Terrance W. Klein, "Advent and the Evangelical Struggle for Cultural Symbols," *Worship* 60 (1995): 538–55.

2. Leo the Great, Sermon XVII, in *Nicene and Post-Nicene Fathers*, ed. and trans. Alexander Roberts, James Donaldson, and Philip Schaff (Edinburgh: T & T Clark, 1885), 12:126.

3. See Patrick Regan, "Two Advents Compared: Ordinary and Extraordinary," *Worship* 84 (2010): 527–49.

4. See Maxwell E. Johnson, "The Feast of the Virgin of Guadalupe and the Season of Advent," *Worship* 78 (2004): 482–99.

5. Josef Pieper, *In Tune with the World: A Theory of Festivity*, trans. Richard and Clara Winston (Chicago: Franciscan Herald, 1973), 32.

6. Scholars of liturgical history in the English-speaking world are particularly skeptical of the "solstice" origin of Christmas. See Susan K. Roll, "The Origins of Christmas: The State of the Question," in Maxwell Johnson, ed., *Between Memory and Hope: Readings on the Liturgical Year* (Collegeville: Liturgical, 2000), 273–90.

7. Clement, *Stromateis* 1.21.145. In addition, Christians in Clement's native Egypt seem to have known a commemoration of Jesus' baptism—sometimes understood as the moment of his divine choice, and hence as an alternate "incarnation" story—on the same date (*Stromateis* 1.21.146). See further on this point Thomas J. Talley, *Origins of the Liturgical Year*, 2d ed. (Collegeville: Liturgical, 1991), 118–20, drawing on Roland H. Bainton, "Basilidian Chronology and New Testament Interpretation," *Journal of Biblical Literature* 42 (1923): 81–134; and now especially Gabriele Winkler, "The Appearance of the Light at the Baptism of Jesus and the Origins of the Feast of the Epiphany," in Johnson, ed., *Between Memory and Hope*, 291–347.

8. See Talley, *Origins of the Liturgical Year*, 91–99. The calendrical calculation of the date of the birth of Jesus was first proposed by Louis Duchesne, *Christian Worship: Its Origin and Evolution*, 5th ed., trans. M. L. McClure (London: SPCK, 1923), 261–65.

9. See Michele Renee Salzman, *On Roman Time: The Codex-Calendar of 354 and the Rhythms of Urban Life in Late Antiquity* (Berkeley: University of California Press, 1990).

10. Quoted in Talley, *Origins of the Liturgical Year*, 100.

11. Francis X. Weiser, *Handbook of Christian Feasts and Customs* (New York: Harcourt, Brace, and World, 1952), 86.

12. See Carl Halter and Carl Schalk, eds., *A Handbook of Church Music* (St. Louis: Concordia, 1976), 66–68.

13. See Talley, *Origins of the Liturgical Year*, 129ff.

14. Ibid., 194ff.

15. Ibid., 137f.

16. English text © United States Catholic Bishops' Conference, 1989.

17. Luther R. Reed, *The Lutheran Liturgy*, rev. ed. (Philadelphia: Fortress Press, 1959), 485–86.

18. In the United States Lenten fasting among Roman Catholics is pretty much restricted to Ash Wednesday and Fridays. Bishops have also abrogated the Friday fast during Lent if one of the following days falls on a Friday: St. Patrick's Day (March 17), St. Joseph's Day (March 19), and the Annunciation (March 25).

19. Martin Luther's *Large Catechism* is based on a series of sermons on the five main parts of the catechism: Ten Commandments, Apostles' Creed, Lord's Prayer, Baptism, and Holy Communion, with an exhortation to individual Confession and Absolution. This material would provide appropriate sermons for the Wednesdays in Lent, ending on the Wednesday in Holy Week.

20. *Rationale Divinorum Officiorum* I, 3, n. 34. The *Rationale Divinorum Officiorum* of William Durandus is arguably the most important medieval treatise on the symbolism of church architecture and rituals of worship. The treatise is ranked with the Bible as one of the most frequently copied and disseminated texts in all of medieval Christianity. It served as an

encyclopedic compendium and textbook for liturgists and remains an indispensable guide for understanding the significance of medieval ecclesiastical art and worship ceremonies.

7. The Church Year: Holy Week

1. See John Wilkinson, *Egeria's Travels* (London: SPCK, 1971; 2d ed.: Warminster, 1981; 3d ed.: 1999).

2. *Egeria: Diary of a Pilgrimage*, Ancient Christian Writers, trans. George E. Gingass (New York: Newman, 1970), 103–104.

3. Athanasius, "Letter 1: Of Fasting, and Trumpets, and Feasts," in *Nicene and Post-Nicene Fathers*, Second Series, vol. 4, ed. Philip Schaff and Henry Wace, trans. R. Payne-Smith (Buffalo: Christian Literature Pub. Co., 1892). Rev. and ed, for New Advent by Kevin Knight, http://www.newadvent.org/fathers/2806001.htm.

4. For a description of the Paschal Vigil at the time of its restoration see Alfred Shands, *The Liturgical Movement and the Local Church*, rev. and enl. ed. (New York: Morehouse-Barlow, 1959, 1965), 121–26.

5. Liturgies of Holy Week are also in the *Book of Common Prayer* of The Episcopal Church (1979), *The United Methodist Book of Worship* (1989), and *The Book of Common Worship* of The Presbyterian Church (U.S.A.) (1993).

6. See Dennis E. Smith, *From Symposium to Eucharist: The Banquet in the Early Christian World* (Minneapolis: Fortress Press, 2003).

7. See Frank C. Senn, "Should Christians Celebrate the Passover?," in *Passover and Easter: The Symbolic Structuring of Sacred Seasons*, Two Liturgical Traditions, vol. 6, ed. Paul F. Bradshaw and Lawrence A. Hoffman (Notre Dame: University of Notre Dame Press, 1999), 183–205.

8. The Church Year: Easter and Beyond

1. Daniel T. Reff, *Plagues, Priests, and Demons: Sacred Narratives and the Rise of Christianity in the Old World and the New* (Cambridge: Cambridge University Press, 2005), 100.

2. Francis X. Weiser, *Handbook of Christian Feasts and Customs* (New York: Harcourt, Brace, and World, 1952), 254ff.

3. Miri Rubin, *Corpus Christi: The Eucharist in Late Medieval Culture* (Cambridge: Cambridge University Press, 1991), 169ff.

4. See Nathan Mitchell, *Cult and Controversy: The Worship of the Eucharist Outside Mass* (New York: Pueblo, 1982), 176–81.

5. Philip H. Pfatteicher, *New Book of Festivals and Commemorations: A Proposed Common Calendar of Saints* (Minneapolis: Fortress Press, 2008), 530f.

6. See Cody C. Unterseher, "The Holy Cross in the Liturgy of Jerusalem: The Happening at the Center of the Earth," *Worship* 85 (2011): 329–50.

7. John Baldovin, S.J., "All Saints in Byzantine Tradition," in *Worship: City, Church, and Renewal* (Washington, D.C.: Pastoral, 1991), 51.

8. Glanville Downey, "The Church of All Saints (Church of St. Theophano) near the Church of the Holy Apostles at Constantinople," *Dumbarton Oaks Papers* 9/10 (1956): 301–305.

9. See John Bossy, *Christianity in the West 1400–1700* (New York: Oxford University Press, 1985), 28–34.

10. See Jacques Le Goff, *The Medieval Imagination*, trans. Arthur Goldhammer (Chicago: University of Chicago Press, 1988), 67–77.

11. See 2 Macc. 12:41-46; Matt. 12:31-32; 1 Cor. 3:11-15; Luke 16:19-31 (the parable of the rich man and Lazarus).

9. Life Passages

1. See Paul F. Bradshaw, *The Search for the Origins of Christian Worship*, 2d ed. (New York: Oxford University Press, 2002), 144–70.

2. Everett Ferguson, *Baptism in the Early Church: History, Theology, and Liturgy in the First Five Centuries* (Grand Rapids: Eerdmans, 2009), 850.

3. Ibid., 363.

4. Ibid., 378–79.

5. Cited in ibid., 807.

6. See E. C. Whitaker, *Documents of the Baptismal Liturgy* (London: SPCK, 1970), 166–204.

7. See J. D. C. Fisher, *Christian Initiation: Baptism in the Medieval West* (London: SPCK, 1965), 101–40.

8. See J. D. C. Fisher, *Christian Initiation: The Reformation Period* (London: SPCK, 1970), 9–16, 23–25.

9. See ibid., 17–22.

10. See Aidan Kavanagh, *The Shape of Baptism* (New York: Pueblo, 1978).

11. For the Episcopal Church's material see *The Catechumenal Process: Adult Initiation and Formation for Christian Life and Ministry*, ed. Ann E. P. McElligott (New York: Church Hymnal Corp., 1990). For Lutheran material see *Living Witnesses: The Adult Catechumenate* (Division for Parish Life, Evangelical Lutheran Church in Canada, n.d.) and *Welcome to Christ: Lutheran Rites for the Catechumenate* (Minneapolis: Augsburg Fortress, 1997). See also Frank C. Senn, *The Witness of the Worshiping Community: Liturgy and the Practice of Evangelism* (Mahwah: Paulist, 1993), 134–64.

12. Cited in A. Winkler, "Confirmation or Chrismation? A Study in Comparative Liturgy," *Worship* 58 (1984): 16.

13. Martin Luther, *Luther's Works, vol. 36: Word and Sacrament II*, trans. Frederick C. Ahrens, ed. Helmut T. Lehmann and Abdel Ross Wentz (Philadelphia: Fortress Press, 1959), 91–92.

14. Arthur C. Repp, *Confirmation in the Lutheran Church* (St. Louis: Concordia, 1964), 29–32, 34–39.

15. See Jeffrey A. Truscott, *The Reform of Baptism and Confirmation in American Lutheranism* (Lanham: Scarecrow, 2003), 149ff.

16. See Frank C. Quinn, O.P., "Confirmation, Does It Make Sense?," *Ecclesia Orans* 5 (1988): 312–40.

17. Martin Luther, *The Small Catechism*, in *The Book of Concord*, ed. and trans. Theodore G. Tappert (Philadelphia: Fortress Press, 1959), 349.

18. This is a hotly debated issue in Anglican/Episcopal churches. See articles pro and con by James Farwell (opposed to open communion) and Kathryn Turner (in favor of open communion) in the *Anglican Theological Review* (*ATS*): James Farwell, "Baptism, Eucharist, and the Hospitality of Jesus: On the Practice of 'Open Communion,'" *ATS* 86 (2004): 215–38; Kathryn Turner, "In Praise of Open Communion: A Rejoinder to James Farwell," *ATS* 86 (2004): 473–85; James Farwell, "A Brief Reflection on Kathryn Turner's Response to 'Baptism, Eucharist, and the Hospitality of Jesus,'" *ATS* 87 (2005): 303–10. Also in favor: Stephen Edmondson, "Opening the Table: The Body of Christ and God's Prodigal Grace," *ATS* 91 (2009): 213–34.

19. Lawrence A. Hoffman, "Jewish Ordination on the Eve of Christianity," *Studia Liturgica* 13, nos. 2, 3, 4 (1979): 11–41.

20. See Alan F. Detscher, "Ordination Rites," in *The New Dictionary of Sacramental Worship*, ed. Peter E. Fink, S.J. (Collegeville: Glazier, 1990), 915–21; Jan Michael Joncas, "Ordination. 3 Medieval and Roman Catholic," in *The New Westminster Dictionary of Liturgy and Worship*, ed. Paul F. Bradshaw (Louisville: Westminster John Knox, 2002), 345–47.

21. Paul F. Bradshaw, "The Reformers and the Ordination Rites," *Studia Liturgica* 13, nos. 2, 3, 4 (1979): 95–107.

22. See Ralph W. Quere, "The Spirit and the Gifts Are Ours: Imparting or Imploring the Spirit in Ordination Rites?," *Lutheran Quarterly* 27 (1975): 322–46.

23. See Philip H. Pfatteicher, *Commentary on the Occasional Services* (Philadelphia: Fortress Press, 1983), 200–201.

24. Martin Luther, *Luther's Works, vol. 53: Liturgy and Hymns*, ed. and trans. Ulrich S. Leupold (Philadelphia: Fortress Press, 1959), 111.

25. Kenneth Stevenson, *Nuptial Blessing: A Study of Christian Marriage Rites* (New York: Oxford University Press, 1983), 13.

26. K. Ritzer, *Le marriage dans les Eglises chrétiennees du Ier au Xie siècle*, Lex orandi 45 (Paris: Les Éditions du Cerf, 1970).

27. On the social history of marriage in the Middle Ages, see John Bossy, *Christianity in the West 1400–1700* (New York: Oxford University Press, 1985), 19–26; Edward Muir, *Ritual in Early Modern Europe*, New Approaches to European History (Cambridge: Cambridge University Press, 1997), 31–44.

28. See Frank C. Senn, *The People's Work: A Social History of the Liturgy* (Minneapolis: Fortress Press, 2006), 214–23.

29. Alexander Schmemann, *For the Life of the World: Sacraments and Orthodoxy* (Crestwood: St. Vladimir's Seminary Press, 1973), 91.

30. See Peter Brown, *The Cult of the Saints: Its Rise and Function in Latin Christianity* (Chicago: University of Chicago Press, 1981), 4–5, 7–8, 42–43.

31. Bossy, *Christianity in the West 1400–1700*, 28–29.

32. See William D. Maxwell, *The Liturgical Portions of the Genevan Service Book* (Edinburgh: Oliver and Boyd, 1931), 58–59, 160–64.

33. *The Book of Common Prayer…According to the Use of the Protestant Episcopal Church in the United States of America* (Oxford: University Press/New York: Henry Frowde, 1892), 298.

34. *Common Service Book of the Lutheran Church* (Philadelphia: The Board of Publication of the United Lutheran Church in America, 1917), 245–64.

35. See Julia Upton, "Burial, Christian," in *The New Dictionary of Sacramental Worship*, ed. Fink, 140–49.

10. The Liturgical Arts

1. *Documents of the Christian Church*, trans. Henry Bettenson (New York: Oxford University Press, 1947), 6–7.

2. Robin A. Leaver, "Liturgical Music As Homily and Hermeneutic," in *Liturgy and Music: Lifetime Learning*, ed. Robin A. Leaver and Joyce Ann Zimmerman (Collegeville: Liturgical, 1998), 340–59.

3. See Jeffrey A. Truscott, *Worship: A Practical Guide* (Singapore: Genesis, 2011), 84–88.

4. See Steve Miller, *The Contemporary Christian Music Debate: Worldly Compromise or Agent of Renewal?* (Waynesboro: OM Literature, 1993).

5. Frank C. Senn, "The Pastor and the Church Musician," in *Thine the Amen: Essays on Lutheran Church Music in Honor of Carl Schalk*, ed. Carlos R. Messerli (Minneapolis: Lutheran University Press, 2005), 241–58.

6. See Robb Redman, *The Great Worship Awakening: Singing a New Song in the Postmodern Church* (San Francisco: Jossey-Bass, 2002), 36–37.

11. Participation in Worship

1. See Mary Douglas, *Natural Symbols: Explorations in Cosmology* (New York: Vintage, 1973), chap. 1.

2. See Catherine Bell, *Ritual: Perspectives and Dimensions* (New York: Oxford University Press, 1997).

3. Maurice Merleau-Ponty, *Phenomenology of Perception*, trans. Colin Smith (London: Routledge and Kegan Paul, 1962).

4. See Nathan D. Mitchell, "The Mute Sense," *Worship* 85 (2011): 75–85.

5. Edward Phillips, *The Ritual Kiss in Early Christian Worship* (Cambridge: Grove, 1996).

6. Michael Philip Penn, *Kissing Christians: Ritual and Community in the Late Ancient Church* (Philadelphia: University of Pennsylvania Press, 2005).

7. See John Bossy, *Christianity in the West 1400–1700* (New York: Oxford University Press, 1985), 70.

8. Adrian Fortescue and J. B. O'Connell, *The Ceremonies of the Roman Rite Described*, rev. Alcuin Reid, OSB, 15th rev. ed. (London: Burns and Oates/Continuum, 2009).

9. Aidan Kavanagh, *On Liturgical Theology* (New York: Pueblo, 1984), 57–69.

10. John Baldovin, S.J., *The Urban Character of Christian Worship. The Origins, Development, and Meaning of Stational Liturgy* (OCA 228, Rome, 1987), 186–89.

11. See Robert J. Taft, S.J., *Through Their Own Eyes: Liturgy as the Byzantines Saw It* (Berkeley: InterOrthodox Press, 2006), 30–47.

12. See John Bossy, "The Mass As a Social Institution 1200–1700," *Past and Present* 100 (1983): 59.

13. See Miri Rubin, *Corpus Christi: The Eucharist in Late Medieval Culture* (Cambridge: Cambridge University Press, 1991), 243–71.

14. Ibid., 271–87.

15. Carl Schalk, *First Person Singular: Reflections on Worship, Liturgy, and Children* (St. Louis: Morning Star Music, 1998), 13.

16. See Frank C. Senn, *A Stewardship of the Mysteries* (Mahwah: Paulist, 1999), 155–70.

Index

absolution, 14
Acts 2, 8, 77
Addai and Mari, anaphora of, 68
Advent, 107–13
  hymnody, 110–11
  wreath, 111–12
altar, 184–85
All Saints' Day, 151–52, 154
All Souls' Day, 152–54
allegory, 11
Amalarius of Metz, 12
ambo, 185
antiphons, 80
Apostolic Tradition, 17, 68
Ascension Day, 143–44
Ash Wednesday, 124
assembly, 6
Assumption/Dormition of Mary, 149–50
Augustine of Hippo, 15, 159–60

Baptism, 157–64
  Affirmation of, 165
  Anglican Prayer Books, 162
  believer's, 163
  font, 157–58, 185
  infant, 158–61
  original sin, 159
  Reformed, 162
baroque architecture and music, 35
basilicas, 24
bells, 183–84

Benedictine Office, 83–85
Benedictine Daily Prayer, 95–96
bishops, 9
blessing, 14–15
Book of Common Prayer (English), 54–56
  Morning Prayer, 89
  Evening Prayer, 89–90
Book of Common Prayer 1979, 61–62, 94
Book of Common Worship, Presbyterian, 62–63
Book of Worship, Methodist, 62–63
books, worship, 204–5, 211–12
Brandenburg-Nuremberg Church Order, 50–51
breviary, 85–86
Brilioth, Yngve, 71
Bucer's Communion Service, 53
bulletins, worship, 205
Byzantine Divine Liturgy, 45–46
Byzantine Office, 82–83
Byzantium, 18–19, 24–25

calendar, civil, 29
calendar, liturgical, 97–106
  Eastern, 101–2
  Jewish, 99
  Western, 100–101
Calvin, Jean, 53
Calvin's communion service, 53–54
canticles, 178
Cassian, John, 78–79
catechumenate, 125, 160, 164

241